CELIA IMRIE

The Happy Hoofer

HODDER

First published in Great Britain in 2011 by Hodder & Stoughton
An Hachette UK company

First published in paperback in 2011

3

A CIP catalogue record for this title is available from the British Library.

ISBN 978 1 444 70929 2
eBook ISBN 978 1 444 70930 8

Typeset in Bembo Book by Palimpsest Book Production Limited,
Falkirk, Stirlingshire

Printed and bound by CPI Group (UK) Ltd, Croydon, CR0 4YY

Hodder & Stoughton policy is to use papers that are natural, renewable
and recyclable products and made from wood grown in sustainable forests.
The logging and manufacturing processes are expected to conform to
the environmental regulations of the country of origin.

Hodder & Stoughton Ltd
338 Euston Road
London NW1 3BH

www.hodder.co.uk

The
Happy
Hoofer

Celia Imrie is an Olivier Award-winning actress. In a career starting in the early 1970s, Imrie has played Marianne Bellshade in *Bergerac*, Philippa Moorcroft in *Dinnerladies*, Celia in *Calendar Girls* and most famously Miss Babs in *Acorn Antiques*, among many others. She has been described as 'one of the greatest British actresses of recent decades' and now lives in London and the Isle of Wight.

To everyone who has helped, supported and
encouraged me in my life and career

CONTENTS

The Prologue   1

Act I
Chapter 1   9
Chapter 2   13
Chapter 3   23
Chapter 4   29
Chapter 5   41
Chapter 6   49
Chapter 7   61
Chapter 8   67
Chapter 9   75
Chapter 10   95
Chapter 11   107
Chapter 12   119
Chapter 13   127
Chapter 14   133
Chapter 15   143
Chapter 16   147
Chapter 17   157

Interval   161

Act II
Chapter 18   169
Chapter 19   179
Chapter 20   191

Contents

Chapter 21   197
Chapter 22   203
Chapter 23   207
Chapter 24   213
Chapter 25   231
Chapter 26   237
Chapter 27   243
Chapter 28   257
Chapter 29   271
Chapter 30   281
Chapter 31   285
Chapter 32   293
Chapter 33   301

The End   309
Curtain Call   311

THE PROLOGUE

It is usual in theatrical autobiographies for the reader to have to wade through certain phrases: the ladder of success, turning point in my career, resting, making it, the big break, a stepping stone, got there, my career path . . .

You won't find them in mine – not only because they are clichés, and I don't like them, but also because they are not true.

Before my story begins I'd like to explain what it's really like on the inside of an actor's life.

If you're not interested please shuffle-tap-step straight on to Chapter 1.

In talking about my career I don't want to add to the mound of literature which gives the false impression that most successful lives in acting go in one direction – up. Even the most famous stars spend periods treading water, or even sliding backwards. Most of us will find ourselves living in a board game of snakes and ladders.

Unknown to you, even when we are 'successful' we spend weeks waiting for the phone to ring.

Bette Davis, for instance, had great dips in her career, and a year after completing *Whatever Happened to Baby Jane?*, went so far as to put an ad in *Variety* under the column 'Situations Wanted – Women Artists'. The rest of us don't have such chutzpah.

My pal Rupert Everett called his novel *Hello Darling, Are You Working?* Because that is how most actors, even the famous ones, greet each other. People outside the business think they are awfully understanding when they archly ask if you are 'Resting?' But believe me when you haven't got a job there is no rest. You spend every waking moment searching for your next chance.

Like girls at a Victorian ball, we all have to wait to be asked to dance. And that is the same for everyone, from movie stars, knights and dames, down to beginners just out of drama school. It's no good playing *Hedda Gabler* alone in your bedroom in the middle of the night. We cannot decide: next I ought to play a great tragic role, like Anna Karenina, and after that I will have a bash at the rough and tumble of a farce. Other people: directors, producers, casting directors decide that for us.

As for career paths, I am not going to pull the wool over your eyes by talking about repertory theatre as 'a training ground' because it isn't. Some of my favourite jobs (and the best shows I have ever seen) were in rep. If the part and director were tempting, I would work again in rep. I would not think of it as 'going back'.

Nor is there a route from those perceived Early Learning Stages – of regional theatre – to bits parts on TV, to West End, and onto Hollywood.

It has never been a question of good actors starting at the bottom and working their way up, and bad actors staying at the bottom. We're all in it together, shambling along like Moll Flanders, grasping one mad thing after another, not only to advance ourselves, but to survive.

When Glenda Jackson was at the top of the tree, interviewed in the papers every day, picking up enough Oscars, Golden Globes, BAFTAs and Emmies to furnish a couple of chess boards, she was asked what it felt like to be the greatest actress alive. She replied that she wasn't, there were many actresses just as good, some better than her, who hadn't had her luck, hadn't been in the right place at the right time, and who, sadly, no one had heard of. At the time I thought this was a piece of false modesty. But Glenda's remark has haunted me. Even now I see how right she was.

Let's say we get the job. The best bit is the moment we receive the news. But when we are given the start date, we are also told the date the job will finish.

More often than not, the next thing we do is pack our bags and prepare to leave home and stay away for weeks on end. Theatres aren't all in London, and TV and films are frequently shot elsewhere.

Next, we go to work. Our day-to-day schedules – the time we are wanted on set or in the rehearsal room in the morning, what time we should finish, whether we are called at all – are rarely predictable more than 24 hours in advance. So it is that, as an actor, your presence at relatives' weddings or christenings, and attending other celebrations or one-off events can never be guaranteed. On more than one occasion, I have had to explain to family members or friends that there is no understudy in a film (and rarely in theatre, these days either) and even if there was, you cannot expect the rest of the cast and crew to work around your own private life.

If you are very lucky, as one job comes towards an end, an offer to do something else will come in. If you are very, very lucky a *couple* of offers will come in and then you will have a choice to make.

When deciding, other less obvious factors come into play. A certain acting job might give you the opportunity to be seen in a different light, or you might want to work with that particular director or cast. For most actors, except a handful of stars, money always matters. But some jobs pay, literally, nothing. You work for the joy of doing it (like I did in *The Way of the World* and *Performing Ceals*). Other jobs (think Julia Roberts' films) might bring in millions. You could earn a few thousand pounds on a TV job and then have to spread it out over two years of sporadic, fulfilling, but often ill-paid theatre work.

Not only that – we are financially penalised in our profession. We were once, not so long ago, classified by English law as 'rogues and vagabonds'. In many ways, legally speaking, we still are. For instance, actors have to pay more for their household and car insurance. Many insurance companies won't cover you at all once you declare you earn your living as an actor. During my stint at Derby Rep (Chapter 7), desperately trying to get home for Christmas, I tried to rent a car. I was brusquely told no cars could be hired to 'blacks, jockeys or actors'.

So, after you've worked out that you and your dependants can survive on the money you already have, then you might be in a position to decide *not* to take a job, and, instead, wait at home, sitting it out, hoping something better will come along. You might not be able to face eight weeks or longer living out of suitcase in the back of beyond, other times personal commitments would make going away impractical. For instance, when my son was doing his GCSEs I could not think of doing a tour which would have kept me away from home for months.

And truth be told, the real reason I take any job is often simply a case of 'Why not?'

Our lives are divided up into three very unequal thirds. The smallest part is the time where you are working: rehearsing, playing, filming. The next part is the dealing with being unemployed, how you occupy your days while trying to keep yourself feeling worthwhile and positive. The last, largest and most tricky part is the social side. That would include sitting in the waiting room outside a casting director's office, going to first nights and premières, and presenting yourself in interviews and at parties. How you handle this last third will either help or hinder you get the work – the first part.

Whenever an aspiring child asks me for my advice on whether they should become a professional actor I always say the same thing. 'You have to want to do it or die'. There is no point drifting into this uncertain business with dreams of fame or fortune. The truth is – you have to be unable to live without performing – because our life is less about the actual acting than the time between.

If you want your life to have a ladder best become a decorator. If you want oodles of money, work in high finance. If you want fame and your name in the papers, sleep with a politician or a footballer.

In a discussion with the director Philip Prowse, he talked about a life in the theatre being like balancing on a speeding automatic walkway. It was hard, he said, to stay on, almost impossible to keep your balance and all the while it was so tempting to step off the speeding track, and slip back into 'normal' life.

But we, who have chosen to spend our lives pursuing this mad job, resist the easy choice. We prefer to cling on, juddering from day to day, on this hair-raising ride to who knows where. Every day is like a day at the roulette tables of Monte Carlo. Because of this uncertainty many of us are superstitious. Sometimes you win, next roll you may lose your shirt. But, gripping your lucky charm, you carry on because you never stop believing that next time your number might come up.

I hope this introduction explains the 'why', and 'how' and the haphazardness of all the work I talk about in this book, and makes clear why I believe that there truly is no such thing as having 'made it' (made what?), 'got there' (got where?).

Living as an actor is rather like living life on the trapezes in a circus. Every time you jump on, you have to pray that when the time comes for you to jump off there is another trapeze swinging your way.

I have been very lucky. So far they have kept swinging by.

Touch wood.

ACT I

CHAPTER 1

'So when am I going to see you on the goggle-box?' my father said to me when I left drama school. Sadly he never did.

When he said this, he was 78, I was 17. My first TV appearance came three years later in *Upstairs, Downstairs*. I played a First World War nurse complete with head hanky and cape, rushing about a busy ward, nursing the shell-shocked Simon Williams. My father had died a few months before it aired.

Biographies generally start with the subject's old age and death, the days of decrepitude and decay. Autobiographies, on the other hand, as Maria Von Trapp commands in the song 'Do-Re-Mi', must 'start at the very beginning, a very good place to start'. So here we go.

I was born in Mount Alvernia Nursing Home in Guildford, Surrey in 1952. It was run by nuns. And, to tell the truth, I don't remember a thing about it.

After my birth, my mother was given another little porcelain statuette for her mantelpiece. There were three Royal Worcester figurines already there, representing my brother and two sisters. Each one bore a verse about the day the child had been born. Rosa's 'Monday's child is fair of face' was represented by a pretty little blonde girl in a white dress with blue sash. Andrew's 'Thursday's child has far to go' statuette was a boy striding out with a hiking stick. Five years after I arrived, a similar female Thursday came along to represent my younger sister, Katie. Juliet's figure, 'The child who is born on the Sabbath day is bonny and blithe and good and gay' depicted a girl sitting on a rock, throwing both arms up while looking as though butter wouldn't melt in her sweet little bone china mouth.

As I had been born on a Tuesday and 'Tuesday's child is full of grace', my statuette took the form of a ballet dancer.

From the nursing home, I was taken to my parents' house, Crubie (Gaelic for 'house on the hill'), a rambling and ramshackle place, full of dark rooms and corridors piled high with dusty objects, to join a nursery comprising my two older sisters and brother. There I was immediately put under the strict care of our nanny, Miss Thelma Baker.

In upper-class families it is usual to aim for an heir and a spare, in other words at least two boys. I was due to be the spare (another boy to carry on the family name) and in fact during the pregnancy, so certain were they that I would be a boy, my parents had decided I was to be called Charlie.

My arrival therefore was a total disappointment and another try was sought, with the result that another sister arrived five years later. So there I was, fourth of five, not the oldest, not the boy, not Nanny's favourite (that was Juliet, the third), and not the youngest. I was just another. Or as my mother put it, in racing terms, 'an also ran'.

Perhaps I have given the impression that my family was typically upper class, but the truth is that although my mother, Diana, was a true-blue *Burke's Peerage* listed aristocrat, my father, David, was from a poor, hardworking Scottish family.

He was born in Glasgow, and, according to the 1901 census, when he was 8, his large family (three brothers, two sisters, and father, a steam ship agent – his mother by now dead) was living in a small tenement flat in Shields Road, Glasgow. My father, very Scottish in looks with his tuft of red hair and long upper lip, went on to qualify as a doctor, dentist and radiologist and did military service with the Royal Navy in both world wars. For many years he was known as the 'Galloping Doctor' as he provided a medical service on the hoof to injured jockeys on Epsom Downs to check for broken bones.

However, my mother, Diana, had not come from such humble beginnings. In fact she descended directly from royalty on both sides. Her family tree goes back to God, by way of all kinds of thrilling people, like Herod, Helen of Troy, and more recently William the Conqueror. Her maiden name was Cator, as in Cator Park, Beckenham, south London, once owned by her family, along with Beckenham Hall, and many other castles, stately homes plus large swathes of Norfolk, Suffolk, Yorkshire and Ireland. And that was only on her father's side. On her mother's side, she was a Blois (the family name of King Stephen I, William the Conqueror's grandson, and various conniving London bishops who specialised in running 'Stews', or strings of brothels, in Southwark). On both sides, my mother's parents, uncles, cousins, grandparents and all, were earls and dukes, with names like Baron Blois of Grundisburgh and Cockfield, George Augusta Lumley, Earl of Scarborough, and Peregrine Albemarle Bertie, Duke of Ancaster. She was related to the Queen Mother, and, more excitingly, John of Gaunt, and Old King Cole.

Obviously, with a background like this, it was designed that Diana would herself marry into the nobility and accordingly she became engaged to Sir George Porter (Bart). The wedding date was announced in *The Times*, reported in papers across the country from the *Daily Mirror* to the *Aberdeen Press and Journal*, and invitations sent out. Presents and congratulations came pouring in. Then, a few nights before the marriage was due to take place, my mother realised she did not love the noble baronet, knew that she was only joining in with the dastardly plan in order to please her parents, and recognised that the only things which prevented her from cancelling were sheer fear and embarrassment.

She confided in her mother, Adeline Cator (née Blois, daughter of Sir John Ralph Blois, 8th Baronet), expecting an earful. But the practical Adeline ordered her daughter immediately to pack her bags. The gifts were returned to sender. Another advertisement, this time cancelling the wedding, was put in *The Times*, and my mother was whisked off to Monte Carlo to enjoy herself until the shameful brouhaha had died down. Incidentally, to the end of her days, one of my mother's favourite phrases was, 'rien ne vas plus' or 'no more bets', maybe picked up during her little anti-nuptial mini-break at the gaming tables of Monaco.

But once back in London, my mother started up her compulsory husband search once more and attended all the usual society bashes. And it was at one of these that she fell in love.

However, her beau was not an invited guest. Indeed, so bored of all the braying toffs on the dance floor, my mother went out to take some air and ended up chatting with the much livelier men in attendance outside in the car park, the drivers.

My father was a chauffeur that night, bringing a couple to and fro in his car (one of the few around at the time) and while the bright young titled things partied inside, his place was to wait by his car in the drive until the time came to take the guests home. But when he saw my mother come out, he took a fancy to her and offered her an apple.

And as in the earlier case of Adam and Eve (also on my mother's family tree) that apple caused a whole lot of trouble, and led eventually to my existence.

David, the doctor/part-time chauffeur, and Diana, the *Debrett*-listed socialite, made secret liaisons. She bicycled from Hartley Wintney to Guildford for clandestine assignations. But as soon as she openly confessed her love to her family, both her father and brother told her that marrying a commoner like my father was absolutely out of the question.

But in spite of their protestations, she went ahead and became engaged. The family beseeched her to stop the whole silly nonsense. Right up to the eve of the wedding, her father was heard, in the middle of the night, howling up from the newel post at the foot of the great staircase, 'Diana, *must* you marry this man?'

Flying in the face of their disapproval, and despite the huge drop in social class and a 20-year age difference, this time my mother went ahead with the wedding. My father wore a kilt, my mother traditional white and, because my mother was Hartley Wintney's 'Brown Owl', the guard of honour was provided by a posse of local Brownies. The happy couple danced the Highland fling.

Now, enough genealogy and back to me!

CHAPTER 2

I was always stubborn. I was always secretive. I was always wilful. I was always determined. Some things never change.

But Nanny ran a strict house. We had routines. We brushed our (long and unruly) hair a hundred times and kept very quiet during the day, 'mustn't disturb your father's patients', because the surgery was downstairs. The children ate with Nanny, at prescribed times. We went on walks and did arts and crafts.

Our family given names were all those of Shakespearean characters, Rosalind – *As You Like It*, Andrew – *Twelfth Night*, Juliet – *Romeo and . . .*, Katherine – *Taming of the Shrew* and me. Can you believe it? Celia! Mine was only a support role, the sidekick rather than the lead, in *As You Like It*. Why could I have not been a main part too? There were plenty more Shakespearean heroines to go around. How about the names Cressida, Portia, Cleopatra or Tamara, Queen of the Goths?

Not content with her own Shakespearean leading name, my oldest sister, Rosa, gave us all flower inspired nick-names, which stuck. Nanny became Pop, short for Poppy. I was an unlikely Snowdrop.

We didn't see that much of our parents, except on Christmas Day. I remember my father sitting in an armchair, with his upright tuft of (now white) hair, frequently in a temper and growling in his lilting Glasgow accent, 'God's truth', while complaining about our noise. Or, when we demurred about settling down to some activity, the reprimand, 'Always *going to*, always going to . . .' It must have been hard for him. Remember, when I was 10, he was 70.

I was once asked by a journalist if my mother went out to work, and naturally I said no. In the ensuing article, that single syllable was translated as 'her Mum was a stay-at-home-housewife', which couldn't have been further from the truth. For my mother could never have been described as a housewife and she did not believe for an instant that staying at home was even a tiny part of the equation of motherhood. I do remember vividly the odd moments when, as a young child, I saw just the glint of her jewels or smelt her perfume as she crept into the dark bedroom of an evening to say hello having just come home from the races, and before going out to a ball.

On Pop's weekly day off and on her annual fortnight's holiday, we saw much more of Mums. We looked forward to those more relaxed times. It was fun. In fact absolute mayhem broke loose.

One day, my sister Juliet and I raided Mums's make-up chest. Using her lovely Chanel lipstick, we smeared our faces with every shade of red, leaving out only our noses. She came upstairs and found us *in flagrante*. Her friend, a local doctor who we all called Beetle on account of his shiny black sports car, seeing my mother collapse in shock, roundly told us off.

On another occasion, while Mums was busy doing something else downstairs, Beetle was left in charge of us while we took a bath. He brought his camera and posed Juliet and me standing nude astride the bath with our hands thrown up above our heads. Even as I stood there, damp and naked and seven years old, forcing a smile for the camera, I thought, 'I'm sure this isn't quite right.' It was an early taste of some of the episodes which were to come.

But it was without the help of her camera-toting friend that, in Nanny's absence, Mums was left in charge of taking us out en masse into Guildford.

On these days, when the shopkeepers in Biddles, the stationery shop, saw us approach without Nanny, they would hide under the counters. Once inside, we would disperse, tumbling into display cases, trying out the pens on the lovely clean paper, playing catch round the counters, while my mother wailed, 'Gaahhhd HELP me with the chooldren'. Then in a stage whisper, directed straight at us, 'How I loathe you all. I *absolutely* loathe you.' It was marvellous fun.

Whenever we came up to a main road, Mums would grab onto our long hair, and, shouting, 'Over!' steer us across the highway, as though we were wild ponies and she the proud driver of a quadriga.

I think her attitude (like our upbringing) was similar to Nancy Mitford's, 'I love children. Especially when they cry, for then someone takes them away.'

Now school was something I really enjoyed, but I did have a tendency to do sudden things just for devilment's sake. The first of these moments came upon me when I was in kindergarten.

Whenever a class took art, the room was set up specially. Ten wooden A-frame easels were each hooked together by a small square, acting as a table, and were placed in two neat rows. Upon every square stood a jam-jar filled with water, a selection of paintbrushes and a little metal fairy-cake tin. Each cake 'dip' was filled with a portion of powder paints, rising in eight gloriously coloured peaks.

One day, as I entered the room at the back of a crocodile of younger children passing through on our way to lunch, the devil entered my soul. I stuck out a foot and pushed. It was a movement so slight and effortless that no one noticed me do it. But the mayhem it caused was absolute.

The easel which I touched with my foot toppled. The water splashed to the floor in a spray of cracking glass. Meanwhile the powder paint flew in rainbow arcs till it blended with the water creating Jackson Pollock puddles all over the floor. But it wasn't just the one easel, for of course they were linked together, and as one went it landed domino-like upon the next, nudging it into action, till all ten crashed to the floor in a heavenly multi-coloured mess.

No one realised it was my furtive and intentional action which had started it. Even if they had done I'm sure they would all have thought it must have been an accident, that my skirt had got caught or something. But, no, I really did do it on purpose. I did it because I wanted to see what would happen. And the deep secret feeling that followed was wonderful. My heart beat so fast I felt as though I might pop with joy.

In my first year at junior school, I was again smitten by a bout of roguery, this time during an arithmetic lesson. It came upon me after the junior headmistress, Miss Hamilton, gave us a lecture on plugs.

'The lavatories are in a dreadful state,' she told us. 'The sinks are left messy, there is water all over the floor, and there is an extraordinary lack of plugs. I don't know what you children are doing with the plugs, but please stop it.'

Instantly I put up my hand and asked to be excused. The Spirit of Mischief had again entered my soul. I went straight to the lavatories, walked along the row of sinks and carefully picked up each and every plug and posted it down into the gaping hole of every single overflow. Having now left the entire washroom totally devoid of *all* plugs, I calmly returned to the arithmetic class, and sat down at my desk, hugging the secret of my naughtiness to my bosom. Again my heart brimmed with joy, almost to the point of ecstasy.

Though I was never the most intellectual pupil in the class, I did love biology and Greek mythology. I was also rather good at sport. I loved playing rounders and all kinds of athletics, especially the ones where you threw things.

In fact my great sporting achievement, which I know impresses most people far more than any amount of acting, is that once I threw the javelin for Surrey. I am very proud to have been Guildford's own mini-Amazon.

Music was another favourite occupation. I started to learn the piano at school and, having passed various elementary grades, was entered to appear at the Woking Piano Festival when I was 7 years old. It was there that something happened which I think subconsciously spurred me into a life of performance.

I was to play a little set piece. I knew it so well I decided that I would show off, putting the other contestants to shame by playing it without the sheet music.

Very excited by the thought of how much I was going to impress the judges, the audience and my schoolmates, I climbed up onto the stage. I took a smug look at the audience and spread my hands out over the ebony and ivory keys, ready to start. Then something weird happened to me. I was hit by a kind of blindness. My mind went blank. Suddenly I didn't have a clue of either the tune or where to put my fingers. If I'd been asked I couldn't have even *hummed* the blessed tune, let alone play it.

So I just sat there.

And sat there.

I stared at the keys and went into something like a trance.

After a little while I was aware of the audience rustling and people whispering to one another, but all I did was swallow and stay in my place. My music teacher, Mrs Dines, had to rush up onto the stage with the sheet music, which she hastily spread out on the stand and stood nodding alternately at me and it.

I looked at her. I looked at the music. But it might as well have been written in Arabic. How could all those black lines and blobs relate to anything to do with this keyboard in front of me? I blinked and swallowed again, pinching myself to make sure I was not in the middle of a dream, until eventually, not having played a note, I was led gently from the platform.

It was a disaster.

I seriously think that my absolute failure that day inclined me forever to attempt to make it good in front of an audience. I wanted to show the world that I *was* able to get up onto a stage and prove to them I COULD do it, so there.

Most female children of my era loved either ponies or ballet. For me there was no choice. Dance was always my first love and I adored the ballet. I was that thing called a balletomane. I collected ballet books and magazines and pored over them for hours on end. I still can tell you the story of *Coppélia* or *Swan Lake*, *Spectre de la Rose* or *Les Sylphides*. As I grew older the love of ballet did not diminish. While others around me swooned over the Beatles, the Who and the Rolling Stones, I worshipped Rudolf Nureyev and Lynn Seymour, and my other pin-ups included Ninette de Valois, Isadora Duncan and Antoinette Sibley.

While my friends were learning the Twist, the Madison and the Mashed Potato, I was practising pliés, pirouettes and grands battements and generally prancing around in the steps of Balanchine and Ruby Ginner.

My favourite was the Greek dance and, throwing my arms in the air and my legs out before me, I flung myself around the garden, to the dismay of Nanny, who cried out on more than one occasion, 'How many times do I have to tell you? You must NOT do handstands in the garden when there are men in the house.'

I was going to be a dancer and that was that. I practised whenever I could, and yearned for the day when I would have a tutu of my own. I pressed my parents to let me go to Elmhurst Ballet School, like Hayley Mills. After all, it was in Camberley, just a few miles down the road. But my pleas fell on deaf ears. Instead, every Saturday morning I marched myself down the cobbled stones of Guildford High Street to ballet class. It was my treasured time of the week. I was by myself too, as my brother and sisters did not share my enthusiasm and preferred to stay at home and play, so the Saturday dance class became my private, personal, secret joy. I adored it.

When I was 10, I begged my mother for a tutu. When my birthday came around she handed me a rather scrunched parcel. I could feel that it was something made of fabric. She beamed at me, 'Well, darling, you said you wanted a tutu.' My heart pounded with joy and expectation. How I longed to put it on and pirouette in front of the mirror in the hall.

I tore open the paper and pulled out the garment. It was not actually a tutu. In fact it bore no resemblance at all to a tutu. I stood gaping at a white gypsy-style broderie anglaise blouse with puffed sleeves and a strange gathered knee-length see-through beribboned petticoat with elasticised waist. It was floppily frilly and lacy and neither looked nor felt anything like a tutu. But from the look on my Mother's face, she obviously believed it did. If I had wanted to enter a fancy dress competition as a Spanish-dancing Christmas fairy I might have come fifth. But I am afraid this was not, by any stretch of the imagination, what I had asked for.

I had tried to describe one to her in detail a few weeks before as I knew Mums always tried to do her very best for us. Nonetheless, as far as making my birthday wish come true, she had not quite managed it this time.

My disappointment was totally crushing, as huge and unstoppable as a sudden blush. But I knew I couldn't let her down. Crumpled inside, I put on the brightest smile I could muster and held out the bizarre and horrible garment as though it really was the tutu I had always yearned to wear. It is in moments like this when you truly learn the art of acting.

Tutu or not, I had my dancing career planned. I would go to White Lodge, the junior branch of the Royal Ballet School, serve my time in the chorus before being discovered and given the prima roles, finally dancing in the arms of Rudolph Nureyev, who would worship and probably marry me.

I practised and practised and went in for every exam I could enrol for as an external student for the Royal Academy of Dance. I bounded through the grades* until I was good enough for my teachers to send me off, aged 11, to audition for a place at the Royal Ballet School.

I waited anxiously at home for the results to arrive. I snuggled up at night, smug with my little escape plan, yearning for the day when I would be whisked away to start my new life as a ballet student. Secretly, I started dressing up in a turquoise tweed suit which I imagined would be the kind of thing girls at dancing-boarding school would wear, and stood admiring myself in a mirror.

One week. Two weeks. A month. But the letter never came. I knew something was up and went on the search. I broke into my mother's bureau and found the letter. There it was, with its royal coat of arms, in the private corner of the desk, lying beside a photograph of my mother's ex-boyfriend, Dougie. Trembling, I slid the already opened letter from its envelope and read the fatal words, 'Celia is very good and advanced for her age, but sadly she is going to be too big ever to become a dancer.'

Too big? I was shattered. Surely this could not possibly be true. All right, so I might be too large *at this moment*, but I had seen the diet adverts in the papers, and TV commercials for Nimble bread, where women got so thin they simply floated away holding a balloon.

---

* I looked out my certificates recently and was horrified to find the examiner's remark for my Prepared Enchaînement, Dance and Mime in Grade II: 'Pleasing Mime; Curtsey needs care: well danced, but hornpipe needed more character.' More character – I am mortified!

Surely I could do that, and if I worked hard enough at not eating, I would get small enough for the whole judging panel at the Royal Ballet School to get fat themselves, eating their own words.

Over eighteen months I lost weight in astonishing amounts. It was noticed first at six months by Nanny's eagle eye when we had to try on (and hand down from sister to sister) the summer clothes for our annual family holiday in Middleton, near Bognor Regis. After that I realised I was being watched at the dreaded mealtimes. Every day I would look at myself in the mirror and, even though I couldn't see how I was something near a skeleton, I didn't think I had gone far enough. In despair, and I am sure, now, looking back, with some embarrassment (my father being an eminent doctor) my parents brought in a child psychologist.

I was 5 foot 2 inches tall and weighed 4 stone. What was the problem? Why couldn't they make me eat? In those days there was not the excess of food that is now everywhere. People at home ate three pretty meagre meals a day, if they were lucky, with no snacking in between. There really was no opportunity to snack. Many people in those days were malnourished, but not through personal choice. So it was a mystery to the psychiatrist to find someone who had decided not to eat, just as it might have been then to find someone who was obese.

I was sent for a brief spell in St Luke's, the local hospital, where, bewildered by a condition they had not seen before, the staff simply offered me three meals a day, which I politely refused. After a few weeks the hospital gave up and released me to spend Christmas with my family.

I was happy to come home, but, far from being cured, I now knew that in future I must find even better ways of avoiding eating. The regulation meals were set before me but I would not eat them. Frequently I was left at the table with the same meal for hours on end. I became sly. I worked out every way to dispose of food. In fact, I was so successful at it, that soon I was little more than a carcass with skin.

Desperate now, my parents decided to send me away to St Thomas's Hospital on Waterloo Bridge in London, to enter one of the special wards belonging to the Department of Psychological Medicine. And once there I was placed under the special care of the world-famous psychiatrist, William Sargant.

I was 14.

CHAPTER 3

Now, more than twenty years after his death, William Sargant is notorious. Famed for his work for the CIA, MKULTRA and MI5, Mr Sargant was, even then, the world's expert on brain-washing and mind control. Today his books are said to be studied by Al Qaeda, and his work has links to the mysterious death of a CIA biochemist, Frank Olson, the Jonestown massacre and to the mind-bending and occasionally lethal drug experiments performed on unwitting human guinea-pigs at Porton Down.

Sargant's methods were simple: electro-convulsive therapy (electric shock treatment to you and me), and insulin-induced comas leading to continuous narcosis (or deep-sleep therapy) complete with tape-recorded 'brain-washing' orders being played at the patients from beneath their pillows. And to think, all this came free on the NHS!

The hospital building is actually still there and even today sends a chill through me when I pass it on my way to Waterloo Station, the Imax or the National Theatre. It is a gloomy dark red brick edifice, the green and white ceramic tile lettering still proudly declaring it to be the Royal Waterloo Hospital for Children and Women, although today it actually houses the Schiller International University.

From the Imax roundabout, you can see the window where I would sit waiting for my mother to emerge from Waterloo station, hurrying across the road, looking frantic. She was the only one who ever came to see me and I often wonder whether anyone else in the family even knew about her rushed, desperate visits. After all, I was the black sheep of the family.

At 14, I was the youngest in the ward. Most of the other inmates were middle-aged women suffering from depression. From my bed, I watched them howling, moaning and screaming, fighting with the nurses, and thought, 'I don't want to be mad. I must get out of here.'

The doctors and nurses did their daily rounds. Sometimes, twice a week or so, we were treated to a bedside visit from the Great Man himself. William Sargant still features in my nightmares, resembling a ghoulish version of Raymond Massey, the senior doctor in TV's *Doctor Kildare*. He was brusque and cold, and he never talked directly to you, just issued orders over your head, talking about 'this one' and 'that one'. But, truly, that was preferable to making eye contact with this proud, incorrigible man with his dark, hard, evil eyes. I have only seen eyes like that on a couple of other people in my life, and one was President Zia of Pakistan – but he comes later in my story.

After Mr Sargant left the ward, the nurses would start preparing the horrors he had prescribed for the day, the electro-convulsive therapy.

Friends have asked what it was like to have electrodes put either side of your skull, and huge surges of voltage fired through your brain, while you squirmed and wrestled and shrieked and moaned and dribbled into the pillow, but the truth is I don't remember.

I do however vividly remember watching the woman in the next bed when it was her turn to be assaulted in the name of health. I remember every sight, every sound and every smell. The huge rubber plug jammed between the woman's teeth; the strange almost silent cry, like a sigh of pain; the shuddering contortions and jerky gyrations of the tormented body; the scent of burning hair and flesh.

I remember also the famous Sleep Room, a ward where patients were forced into a drug-induced sleep for days on end while tapes played instructions to them from under the pillow.

Whenever I have been asked about William Sargant's Narcotic Room, I can describe it perfectly. I used to sneak out of the ward to peer through the portholes in the swing doors, and gaze at the dead-looking women lying on the floor on grey mattresses, silent in a kind of electrically-induced twilight. When people ask if ever

I spent any time inside, being treated to a Sargant-induced coma, I used to reply, 'No' for I do not remember that ever happening.

However it has recently occurred to me that everyone, in order to be put into the Sleep Room, would first be drugged, and that although I saw many women come back to the ward from there, I never saw any patient emerge from the place awake. You went in asleep, you came out asleep. I don't think anyone who was treated by Sargant's Sleep Therapy was at any time aware of going in or coming out of that room, and of course, while inside, the whole point was that you were totally unconscious. So maybe I was in the Sleep Room. I could not possibly know.

It is probable, I realise now, that I did go in. Like the electric shocks: I presume it definitely happened to me, though I can only recall it happening to the others. I was certainly injected with huge doses of insulin, morning and night, and these insulin injections are now understood to be one of the methods Sargant used to kick-start his Sleep Therapy process. I cannot know whether Mr Sargant's mind control methods worked on me as I do not know what the tape-recordings under my pillow were telling me to do.

Some years back I did a search, trying to find the hospital records of my teenage spell inside St Thomas's, to see whether I could find out the limits of my treatment and if I had been in the Sleep Room, what had been the exact instructions which would have been on the tape constantly playing under my pillow, Sargant's wishes, drummed relentlessly into my young unconscious brain.

But it is well-known in the medical profession that when Sargant left St Thomas's, he not only (illegally) took away with him all his patients' records, but also by the time of his death in 1988, every one of those files, every single piece of paperwork about his inhumane treatment of us, the human guinea-pigs, had been destroyed.

So I will never know the absolute truth. None of us will.

I remember also being given massive doses of largactil, (an anti-psychotic drug) three tumblers a day.

The effects of these drugs on my frail teenage body were startling. My hands started shaking uncontrollably for most of the day, like an aged drunk. I'd wake in the morning to find clumps of my own hair lying on the pillow. Meanwhile I started growing hair down my spine, as an animal does. But the worst consequence of these drug cocktails was that everything I saw was multiplied by four, like looking through some weird kaleidoscope. When Sargant came into the room I saw four of him. It was horrific and terrifying.

Having quadruple vision puts you totally out of control of yourself and all your actions. Simple things like picking up a glass of water or walking unaided become impossible. I fought.

I overheard the nurse saying to her senior, as even then she increased the dosage of largactil, that I was exhibiting a 'dangerous resistance' to the drugs. Dangerous for whom, I wonder? Who could tell in that terrible place where, as far as I can see, the truly insane were the workers rather than the patients. Sargant used to say that every dog has his breaking point. The eccentrics, he added, just took longer. I suppose my 'dangerous resistance' was what he was talking about. I certainly hope I am being as disobedient as is humanly possible. I like to think that I am one of those eccentric dogs he did not manage to break.

Many years later, I went with my pals Fidelis Morgan and Pam St Clement to see a film called *Coma*. It was a second rate thriller starring Michael Douglas and Geneviève Bujold, in which Bujold discovers a strange ward full of patients suspended in hammocks in drug-induced comas. When we came out into the swallow-shrieking evening of Leicester Square, Fidelis and Pam were laughing at the silliness of the plot, but I had the shakes and it took me some days to recover. I think that they both thought I was coming down with something and simply had poor taste in films. In fact it wasn't till years later, that I myself saw the link and realised why that film had upset me so deeply.

I'd like everyone to know that, whatever Sargant might have thought, my eventual cure was nothing to do with him, his methods or his bizarre techniques of mental care. The events which saved me from my self-induced anorexia came about in a very simple and human way.

Two things happened in short succession.

One of the nurses, quite improperly I am sure, said to me one morning as she made up the bed, 'You do realise that your selfish act of starving yourself means you are stealing the bed of a truly sick, possibly dying, child?' She described to me the fates of other stricken children she had treated: children with polio; cancer; bone diseases and brain malformations.

She had no idea, I'm sure, but what she said was more powerful than any of Mr Sargant's insulin injections and tape recordings. What she said pierced my heart, and my conscience was well and truly pricked.

Then a few days later, my dance teacher came to visit me. I didn't know the true reason at first, but when I did, it was to send a chill through my barely-there flesh. She had been told that medical opinion was agreed that my weight was way below that which could possibly sustain life for any length of time, and that I would not survive the few weeks till Christmas.

Miss Hawkesworth had come to say goodbye.

Unlike tactful, do-gooding people, who tiptoe around the painful subject of illness and death, Miss Hawkesworth simply came out with it. 'I came to visit you, Celia, because they told me you would die in two weeks and I thought I ought to say goodbye before you left us forever.'

Well!

I had spent three whole years with everybody around me telling me one thing, over and over and over. 'You must eat. You will eat. If you don't eat you will fade away. Please eat. Eat. Eat. Eat.' And so I didn't.

Now here was a new order – 'You will die!' Die! Die? How DARE anyone tell me what to do! I wasn't going to die just to please them.

My instinct whenever I am issued with an absolute order has always been the same. Do the opposite. And thanks to Miss Hawkesworth, I decided there and then I would not oblige these horrible self-appointed gods of psychiatry and die just to satisfy their theories, and so slowly, I started to eat.

I reversed the action that had been my secret weapon against them, and in twisting it round, it became my new secret weapon against them. I decided I would show them that they knew nothing about me. Plus, I was not going to let anyone think that my selfishness was responsible for depriving a sick child of treatment.

It was as simple as that.

CHAPTER 4

I returned to school, somewhat changed in appearance. I had not started menstruating, and during a consultation with my psychiatrist (when I often couldn't think of a thing to say and lurched around to any subject I thought might interest them) I had said I very much would like to have a baby one day, and hoped that would still be possible since I had upset the usual order of puberty. The specialists at St Thomas's then decided to give me a massive dose of oestrogen, to kick-start the process. The trouble was that practically overnight, it sent me from being flat-chested to a 38 inch, double D cup.

So, resembling a teenage brunette version of Jayne Mansfield in a fright wig, I took my O levels and got the same number as Princess Diana (you can look it up if you're so interested).

I left school the day I hit 16, the earliest day I legally could. Determined to follow a life on stage, preferably with some dance connection, I applied for and won a place at the local drama school in Guildford, known to its pupils as 'Tap & Tickle'. I took the dance teacher's course, to please my family by having that famously useless thing, 'Something to fall back on'.

Personally speaking, if I ever had any intention of falling back, I would choose a sofa.

The headmistress at the time was a wonderful inspiration, an Italian named Bice Bellairs. She wore her greying hair back in a style exactly like Dame Ninette de Valois, and was always decked out in long flowing blouses and skirts in various shades of grey. Rumour had it that she never wore any knickers, but I was never in a position to verify that for myself.

At the end of a show, while audience and performers mingled, she would lean over you, stroking your shoulder and say, 'You were absolutely marvellous'.

Surprised, you would turn and respond, 'But I wasn't in it, Miss Bellairs!'

Then, spinning about, she would laugh, 'I know!' before swooping off. It was very disconcerting.

I heard later from her beautiful sculptress daughter, Lorna, that every single morning, at 8am, even when she was 80 years old, she always did twenty minutes of Greek dancing in her bedroom, to start her day.

It wasn't all barefoot arabesques, in flowing silk gowns and scarves, we did have time off. One weekend I spent with my friend Debbie at her parents' place in Windsor. We went out that evening to the local pub and there was a competition going on, some charity thing. Naturally I had a go. You had to guess the number of pennies in a huge bottle on the counter so I filled in my form and thought nothing about it. Towards the end of the evening, the landlord spilled the pennies out on the counter, and they were all arranged in piles. Eventually the number was announced and it seemed that I had been spot on, and had therefore won the Grand Prize, a date with a famous footballer called Rodney Marsh.

Not being much interested in football, I did not know who he was, let alone that he was at the time a footballing hot ticket, second in importance only to George Best. But I was certainly going to claim the prize. After all I was a 16-year-old student and students will do almost anything for a free dinner.

So along I went to the assignation. But, as the saying goes, 'there is no such thing as a free lunch' and naturally the date started with a photo call. A handful of photographers from local newspapers gathered around Mr Marsh's lime green Lamborghini, popping flash bulbs at the car. (In those days, flash photography really did involve popping bulbs which made a sizzling noise and had to be replaced after each flash!) While I lingered behind them, the footballer himself, all tan and long dyed blonde hair, sprawled out across the front seat.

I was then told to get into the passenger seat beside him and the blind date would begin. A few more photos then 'Rodders' would fire up the motor and speed me off to spend a luxury evening with him. So as I opened the car door, I carefully lowered myself into place and said 'hello'.

By reply, Mr Marsh hiccuped.

It was only once I was squashed down in the sunken leather seat beside him that I realised 'Rodders' was totally, utterly, blind drunk. He reeked of booze and could barely sit up. He leered at me through heavily lidded eyes. A shimmer of sweat hung on his top lip.

'Let's have a kiss, now,' called a journalist. I shut my eyes, puckered up and thought of England. We had to hold the pose, and kiss over and over again while the photographers changed their sizzling bulbs. Then, content with their work, the journalists all went and left us to it. Rodney Marsh looked me up and down, let out a huge sigh and fell asleep on the steering wheel. And that was the end of the date.

Some prize!

After such excitement, the rest of my drama school days sped along. Once I had my diploma and any number of certificates as a teacher of Greek dance, I launched myself into the world of professional theatre.

I had my photo taken by a very keen man, who thought it would be nice if I took my top off. He scraped my hair back into a knot, which pleased me immensely as it was very Nadia Nerina, and, in a strange prescience of *Calendar Girls,* he gave me a book to hold to cover my naked bosoms. (We're going to need a bigger book . . . anyone got an atlas?)

Not really perceiving that the resulting photo was a weird kind of kiddy porn, I proudly used it for my entry in *The Spotlight*, putting myself into the category 'Musical and Straight'.

I became popular with photographers and was chosen by Donald Silverstein, famous for his *Vogue* covers and portraits of the Beatles and Jimi Hendrix, to model for a poster for the poverty action group, Shelter. The brief was 'A Modern-day Madonna and Child'.

Mr Silverstein told me to dress scruffily, so I raided my mother's wardrobe (most of her clothes were the same things she had been wearing since the 1940s) and flung on a motley collection of her garments. When I arrived at the shoot I was told I looked perfect.

The set-up was in a derelict damp house in Byfleet where I portrayed a young mother holding a crying baby. It was a very harrowing photo, most powerful. So powerful in fact that it caused quite an uproar. The poster was eventually banned when people discovered I was not a 'real' person, but only a model. Apparently money-donating people only want to be disturbed by the real thing, not by art!

My first actual acting job was playing a rat in the pantomime *Dick Whittington* at Colchester Rep. On unearthing the ancient programme the other day, I was amazed to read in the long list of chorus parts next to my name, that, apart from being 'A Citizen' and 'A Turkish Handmaiden', I was also 'A Sausage'. Although I had completely forgotten that credit and strangely hadn't included it on future CVs, let's hope I gave a sizzling performance in the sausage role.

I had heard from another girl at my drama school, who was already cast, that they needed a third chorus girl at Colchester. I made a nuisance of myself and found out the telephone number of the choreographer and was told by her brother (a mere two weeks later to become my boyfriend) 'We're not sure yet' (a euphemism for, 'we're waiting to see if someone else turns down the offer'). 'Please call back in a few days.'

I must have phoned at least nine times and got the same reply, until finally I was offered the job. My wages were £12 a week, and my digs, a tiny room with an electricity meter which took an enormous supply of coins to keep me warm and lit, cost £6 a week. There was no kitchen and I boiled eggs in the kettle. I remember that it was a marvellous day when, towards the end of the run, the Equity minimum wage (and therefore my own pay) was raised to £18. An extra 30 per cent, as you might imagine, made all the difference. For instance I no longer had to choose between heating and food.

At the end of the show, I moved into Theatre in Education (T.I.E), otherwise known as frightening children. The company was based in Edinburgh. My director was Sue Birtwistle, later to become Lady

Richard Eyre, and the producer of *Cranford*. I got up early and schlepped round schools telling stories to Scottish kids who thought I talked like the Queen. So I tried to loosen up. I wore smocked Laura Ashley dresses which went down to my ankles, and let my hair down. I looked like a regency, floral, smiling version of Janis Joplin on a bad day, only with quite the wrong voice.

While in Edinburgh, I shared a flat with a nurse and a school teacher, and through them met John Tangeuy, an army officer with the Argyll and Southern Highlanders. It was the early 1970s, the height of the Troubles, and John was just back from serving in Northern Ireland. I remember walking along the streets with him when every time someone slammed a door or screeched at their kids he would jump in the air which was quite alarming. We discovered various things we had in common, one of which was that he lived in nearby Godalming, and he very kindly offered to drive me to my next job, which was to start at the end of the T.I.E. engagement, all the way from Edinburgh to Worcester.

When Mums (or as we all called her, Mrs Bennett) took one look at him, an officer and a gentleman, she brought me in for questioning.

'Has he kissed you yet?'

'Yes, Mums.'

'Wet or dry?'

'Never mind.'

'Has he asked you to marry him?'

'Yes, Mums.'

'Good. An autumn wedding with apricot bridesmaids. Oh how lovely, Ceek.'

'No.'

'You must.'

'But I don't love him, Mums.'

'Don't worry, darling,' she said, patting me on the arm. 'That will come.'

But sweet as John was, I had no intention of becoming a wife, let alone an army wife. The nearest I ever got was when I played an army wife, along with Alexandra Pigg, in *The Last Waltz* at the Soho Poly.

But I did accept that lift from him and arrived in Worcester to play chorus again, this time in *Stop The World I Want To Get Off*. One night I got the phone call telling me that my father had suffered a series of strokes, and the hospital had decided to stop feeding him. My father was much older than the fathers of my peers. I was 19, he was 80. So although it was not a surprise, it was still awful.

I went on stage that night and had to stand in line and sing the Bricusse/Newley song 'Gonna Build a Mountain'. When we came to the words, 'If I build my mountain with a lot of care, I'll take my daydream up the mountain, Heaven will be waiting there. When I've built that heaven, as I will some day, and the Lord sends Gabriel to take me away . . .' I burst into tears and could not sing. Lally Percy, the actress next to me in the line, grabbed my hand and sang my lines for me. To this day, she is still one of my greatest friends.

At the end of the show, I came off stage and knew come hell or high mountain I had to get back home. But the last train had left Worcester station at 8.15pm, in the middle of the show. In a blind panic, somehow I got myself to Birmingham, then jumped on the very last 'milk' train to Euston. Arriving at what felt like, and probably was, three o'clock in the morning, without thinking straight, I hailed a taxi to take me through the night to Guildford. I remember the alarming numbers lit up on the little black box beside the driver but unbeknown to me my brother had kindly waited in London that night to collect me.

I wanted very much to get to my father, I suppose to say goodbye. I wasn't really at all prepared for how the sight of someone you love in a coma is so completely unreal. In some ways, I wish I hadn't seen him like that, as it was so hard, and took forever to erase that last memory.

Thankfully now when I think of him, it is on the dance floor in his swinging Gordon tartan green and blue kilt, whizzing a nearby unsuspecting lady partner off her feet.

I took a performance off to attend my father's funeral in Guildford. To this day (touch wood) it is the only time I have ever missed a show. But my efforts in the chorus at Worcester were well appreciated by the theatre's director, John Hole. So much so that I was asked back. But sometimes you are not asked back so much for your talent as the convenience.

For my next appearance . . . I was now a puppeteer! (Well, I can't really call it an appearance for I spent the whole run under a table eating Angel Delight with one hand while the other hand was stuck up a rabbit.) Job satisfaction was definitely not coming my way. I was lucky enough to get a tiny part in a movie called *The House of Whipcord*. The film's tagline might give you an idea: 'Many young girls have entered these gates – none have yet come out!'

It was strange to be back on a set which resembled the Royal Waterloo Hospital, and acting in a film with a plot which reminded me of those grim days. I played a girl imprisoned by mad people in a phoney lunatic asylum. If there hadn't been cameras and booms all over the place, I really might have freaked out. But luckily we all had to freak out as part of the story anyway! For instance, I had a scene in which I fought with another girl while trying to throw a Bible from a high window to attract attention to us. In the story, Anne-Marie, the main character, played by Penny Irving (later of *Are You Being Served?* and *Hi-de-Hi!* fame), escapes, goes through dreadful trials to get out in one piece, staggers through brambles in pouring rain, is chased by dogs and eventually lurches half-dead onto a road where she flags down a passing lorry driver. Once safely in his cab she is so relieved that she collapses, and therefore does not see him turn into the hospital gates, taking her back to the place she just left.

Whenever I am in one of those awful out-of-the-frying-pan situations where you escape only to end up back where you started I still use the phrase, 'How *House of Whipcord*!'

Many years after these, my first footsteps into acting, I was playing in Edward Bond's *The Sea* at the National Theatre. A certain Dame Judi Dench read my programme notes, pointed accusingly at my early film credit and asked, 'What's this?' I calmed her down by reassuring her it was just a soft porn film I had done when I was 17.

A few days later, onstage, while poor Sam West acted his heart out near the footlights, the other actors were all gathered round a table at the back of the scene, apparently having a serious lecture from Judi's character. Judi pointed again, this time at a mysterious white parcel on an upstage table laid out with white paper costume designs. She thrust the package in my direction then, silently mouthing an emphatic instruction to 'Open it', I slowly unwrapped the paper, revealing the lurid jacket on the video-tape of *The House of Whipcord*.

I moved to London, as all actors who want to work have to, and found a dingy room in Terrapin Road, Tooting, and in order to pay my way took any jobs going, all of which were domestic jobs.

First I waited at dinner parties at the house of the critic and scourge of old-fashioned theatre, Kenneth Tynan. He wasn't actually there himself, sadly, but was letting out his sought-after residence to some rich Americans.

'Celia, come here,' said the American lady to me one day. 'You gotta see this.'

She took my hand and led me through dark corridors to a bedroom, Mr Tynan's own, I was told.

'Look up,' she said.

Suspended from the ceiling was a smoky mirror, dangling uneasily over the bed. How horrible, I thought, thanking the gods that I was in no danger of ever falling in love with the dreaded Mr Tynan.

One day while the Yanks were dining, I was summoned into the dining room to remove the dirty plates. I arrived with a tray. The hostess jerked me by the hand and snapped, 'This is not the way to do it, Miss. Lose the tray!'

All this was performed quite loudly and in full view of her guests. It was very embarrassing. Speaking as someone who had come from the kind of family where the rules of table were drilled into me from birth, I thought to myself, 'Here is a woman who thinks she knows all the social rules, but actually hasn't a clue. You don't shout at your servants, and if you really must, you shout at them privately.'

I was lucky next time to get a job charring for the film producer and composer, Arthur Schwartz, who penned such wonderful songs as 'Dancing in the Dark', 'A Gal in Calico' and 'That's Entertainment'. When I told him that I was really an actress, working to pay the rent, he gave me these fabulous words of wisdom: 'My advice to you, Celia, is to make a nuisance of yourself.' I have to admit that I have followed his instruction to the letter.

On alternating days, I briefly cleaned for a famous English actor and scriptwriter. One day I needed to find the hoover, so naturally I headed for the understairs cupboard. I was transfixed by what I found there: scores of gold-framed photos.

They were all 10-by-8-inch black-and-white mugshots of famous women, glamorous actresses, models, sexy film and TV stars. The exceedingly well-known pretty faces all looked straight to camera, with pouting lips and sultry eyes. *Each and every* photo was personally signed: 'To darling [the name of the actor/scriptwriter], with everlasting love from your very own . . . Tiger.'

While charring by day, I also managed to get an evening engagement, selling programmes at something which may have been the Lord's Taverner's ball. I lined up with the other gals, wearing my poshest gown and high heels, to shake hands with Prince Charles. I was so mesmerised by how titchy he was, I forgot to curtsey until he'd gone way past down the line, at which point I bobbed down and up like a jack-in-the-box, to thin air.

(My next meeting with the Prince of Wales was at Stratford-upon-Avon, in 1998 when lined up in my rather too low-cut Mrs Candour costume. The heir to the British throne came along the line and this time stopped before me, eye to cleavage. He lingered, I thought, rather too long in front of me, and did not look up much.)*

Knowing I wasn't cut out for domestic work, I jumped at the next job offer, especially because it finally gave me the opportunity to move into legitimate theatre. I was to appear in a series of plays including *How the Other Half Loves*, *A Man for All Seasons* and

---

* I hope I don't end up in the Tower for that observation.

Dry Rot on a number four tour, with Rampart Productions.* We played such glamorous venues as Skegness, Grimsby, Kendal and Mablethorpe and the actors had to drive themselves in a huge unwieldy lorry through the night between venues and put up and take down the scenery.

The highlight of the season for me was that I was to play Olivia in *Twelfth Night*. One night, sitting freezing in my dressing room, on the end of the Mablethorpe pier wearing Olivia's compulsory black lace Elizabethan dress, I felt cold. I put on a rather ghastly fluorescent pink cardigan which was covered all over with woollen excrescences, not unlike huge puce nipples. Mmm, how lovely and warm it was. That felt better.

I chatted gaily to the other actors until I heard my call over the tannoy. Then I went to the wings and diligently waited for my cue. I was not aware that I was still wearing the puce cardigan until I walked onto the stage and the woollen nipples somehow got caught up in the gigantic twig which represented shady bower or whatever symbolised Olivia's garden in this cheap touring show. I plunged relentlessly onwards into the scene, spouting my Shakespearean verse, pink cardigan glowing in the footlights, and did the whole scene dragging round a tree on my back.

After the last night of the tour, at Boston, Lincs, I asked the landlady at my digs to wake me early, for I had a most important train to catch. I was moving up in the world. I had an early call next morning in London to start filming two episodes of the prestigious TV series *Upstairs, Downstairs*.

She woke me an hour before I was due to leave for the station, so I turned over for a little doze. An hour and a half later I re-awoke. I had missed the train! I had to persuade a taxi to take me the whole long trip to London. Luckily, the driver knew all about car chases and sped down the motorway like Stirling Moss with hair. Torn between the dangers of the road and the imperative of arriving on

---

* Tours are generally rated number one, and number two, although I have never heard any actor admitting to be on anything but a number one. If ours had really been rated it would surely have fallen short of the usual requirements.

the set on time, I told him I hoped he would not be stopped by the police.

'Don't worry,' he said. 'I can always say you're having a baby.'

It was almost enough to turn a girl anorexic again.

Upstairs, Downstairs was at this time probably the most popular drama series on TV and my episodes were in the fourth series. I might have had a tiny part, but at last I was doing something people had heard of.

For my scenes, it was back to hospital. It seemed there was no escaping this medical motif in my career. I played a nurse accompanying Lesley-Anne Down on the wards during the First World War. I only had a few lines, but I had to nurse Simon Williams, who saw that I was totally inexperienced and he was very sweet to me. 'Bend down a little lower in that shot,' he advised. 'And then your face will be in both your shot and mine.'

Well! Who knew that there were such tricks? They never taught you that one at 'Tap & Tickle'. But I made good use of it, notably a few years later when I appeared in a line-up of servants (again playing a maid) outside a stately home very early on in the film *Death on the Nile*. Although I played a character of no importance whatsoever (you couldn't even call it a cameo) whichever direction the camera is pointing, there I am. I'm not quite sure how, but in that scene I managed to get myself into practically every shot.

Simon and I worked together many years later. But the next time we were 'married'.

CHAPTER 5

From the heady heights of my introductory role on TV, I waited for the offers to pour in but there was only one. The local theatre asked me to appear in the pantomime. It was to be *Sinbad the Sailor* and I was offered a part in the chorus. Once rehearsals began, I learned it would include the testing role of 'a pebble', hired to jeté around and create a few waves on the sea bed I suppose. Could things get any worse?

Then, as always, I was yearning for new beginnings, and in the New Year of 1975 an offer came in which I could easily have refused. My dear friend Jane had been offered a job she didn't really want to do. Would I like it?

It was for the Royal Shakespeare Company. The actual job was to be an assistant stage manager, otherwise known as a gofer, tea-girl and general dogsbody, on a tour of Ibsen's *Hedda Gabler*. Every instinct told me not to do it. After all I was meant to be an actress not a servant. But needs must. I had no money and my career was hardly blooming. I was working my guts out, appearing nightly as a pebble in the sea (little knowing that the next time I could tell people I was appearing in *The Sea* it would be a play going by that name at the National Theatre), but for some reason the plaudits were still not coming my way.

OK. So the RSC job did not involve any acting, but on the plus side, up till then I had never been abroad and this tour was to go right round the world in a clockwise direction. On top of this, the show was to be directed by Trevor Nunn, and boasted a cast of possibly the most famous actors in the world. Firstly there was Glenda Jackson, straight from the glory of winning her second Oscar, playing Hedda. Jennie Linden, her co-star in *Women in Love*, would play Thea Elvsted. Timothy West, who was at that time all over the TV, particularly as King Edward VII, was to play Judge Brack. Patrick Stewart, handsome RSC heart-throb, was Eilert Loevborg and Peter Eyre, the lugubrious typically English actor who is in fact American, played George Tesman. Auntie Julie was to be played by Constance Chapman, a character actress famed for her roles in films and TV written and directed by such prestigious auteurs as Lindsay Anderson, Peter Nichols and David Storey, and the company was completed by the wonderful Pam St Clement, an actress whom I had not heard of. Pam, later to become a household name playing Pat in *EastEnders*, took the role of the maid, Berta. On top of my duties as tea-girl, I would be understudying her.

Rehearsals at the YWCA in Great Russell Street started at 10am and went through till 4pm with no break for lunch, so that by the time, early one February morning in 1975, when we assembled at Heathrow to climb on the first of so many planes, I hadn't really spoken to anyone except my boss, the stage manager, Barbara Penney. A few days before we flew out, the company was completed by the addition of a pair of understudies called Fidelis Morgan (now an actress, novelist and playwright), who was to understudy Glenda and Jennie, and Oz Clarke (now the wine expert), who was to cover all the men.

The first, endless flight bounced down onto the tarmac for refuelling in Athens, Bahrain, Sri Lanka and Singapore before arriving finally, two days later, in Melbourne. It was the first time in my life I had set foot outside England! So it really should have felt very different. But it was rather like arriving in Cheltenham, except that this town was more than 10,000 miles from anyone you knew. The phones were useless – you had to ring an operator and book any phone call to the UK. If you phoned at 9am, the operator might say, 'I have a slot for 7.30 tonight or maybe you'd prefer tomorrow morning at 3.15am.' And anyway the cost of international phone calls was at that time prohibitive, especially on our wages. So there was to be no moral support from family and friends at home. We were on our own, on the other side of the world, and for encouragement, companionship, laughter and anything else necessary for human intercourse, we only had each other.

Tim West, as Equity deputy, sat us all down and gave us a talk on Australia and how the isolation from friends and family had driven a handful of British actors to commit suicide while on tour there. We were instructed to keep our eyes on one another and make sure everyone was all right. If anyone hid away or seemed depressed or unhappy, we were to report it to him. Tim did not want our tour to be famous for all the wrong reasons, as a few previous ones had been.

I started regretting having taken this job. Not only were we in this far-flung country where English thespians ran round topping themselves, I was really only the tea girl and it was going to tie me up till September, lurking behind the scenes rather than staying at home and trying to get a real part, onstage.

Our first venue was the Princess Theatre, a Second Empire-inspired Victorian pile. We were all surprised to see that Australian audiences arrived very smartly dressed to attend the theatre. The men wore black evening suits, bow ties, complete with waistcoats, colourful cummerbunds and glossy patent leather pumps, while the women were decked out in floor length gowns and dangling jewellery, with over-the-shoulder fur wraps. The audience in turn were very shocked by the sight of us exiting the stage door each night wearing our t-shirts and jeans. Or should I say the rest of the company wearing *their* t-shirts and jeans. One of the knock-on effects of my anorexia was that I now dressed like a moving Bedouin tent, topped with a fluff of what a nearsighted person might describe as Pre-Raphaelite hair, but which a more sane person might compare to dilapidated thatch.

Backstage I faithfully did my job, and brought round the interval tea, making it all a bit special by going out and buying a daily selection of tasty biscuits to accompany it.

It was usual when on tour for the major artists to eat in posh restaurants, while the underlings like me, the stage crew and the understudies, would find any cheap dive which was open and served food that late at night.

But Glenda did not let this happen. She led the company with the finest principles of socialism, and insisted from the start that we, the paupers, stay with the main part of the company. Where she was invited, we were invited. More often than not we would gather at the end of the meal to work out our share of the bill only to find she had already paid for us. She always made sure it was possible for us to be part of anything that the main players were doing. Regularly we would meet in her hotel suite after the shows and order room service, or, whenever there was a stove in sight, Fidelis, a keen cook, would create a dinner for us all, while we enjoyed Glenda's private pools and bars and lounged about in her sitting room. As a result this tour was unique in its unity. We made friendships which still endure to this day. Glenda set an amazing example of what it means to be a star.

After having played (on matinée days, twice) one of the longest and most intense roles on the world stage, in theatres as big as sports arenas, every night Glenda Jackson sat in her dressing room while a queue of fans filed in to get her autograph. The signing would frequently last for an hour or more. When we, the stage management team, had finished clearing up and resetting everything for the next day, Glenda was usually still at it, signing and posing for photographs, always with a smile. I was in awe of her immense professionalism.

By the end of the month-long run in Melbourne, we roared round the place in little gangs. Oz Clarke rambled off into the countryside with Tim West and discovered that Australia made rather scrumptious wine. In fact, Oz built his career from the findings he made on that tour. Connie developed a habit of stripping off and jumping stark naked into anyone's pool, wherever we were. You'd be sitting on a sofa in the living room of some Australian grandee and suddenly outside the French windows a ghostly figure would dart past, totally starkers. Then you'd hear a small plop. Connie would re-emerge into the room some time later, slightly damp and smiling like a Cheshire cat. We all started to live life as we never had before.

There was a party in Glenda's magnificent suite, which overlooked the bright lights of Melbourne. Diane Cilento was there, sitting on a tall bar-stool, talking about her 10-year-old son, Jason Connery. Andy Phillips, the ebullient lighting director, known to all as the Prince of Darkness for more than one reason, was drunkenly joshing Glenda. He was due to leave on a 6am flight to London. But by the time we all left the suite Andy was spark-out, flopped over Glenda's bed.

Next morning we asked if Andy had woken in time to get his flight. 'I slept on the sofa,' said Glenda. 'He was out for the count, unconscious, impossible to wake. So, as I said, he slept on the bed and I was on the sofa, all night. Till the early hours when he came tiptoeing in before he left, to say goodbye to me, there, on the sofa, presenting me with freshly squeezed orange juice.'

We all realised that they had started an affair. The clue which clinched it was the unnecessary detail of the orange juice. But Andy was gone now and for us it was next-stop Sydney.

Most of the actors took the train. I was rather jealous. Jennie Linden and her husband decided to drive it. But Ba Penney, the stage manager, and I had to fly on ahead to prepare the get-in at the next theatre.

The tattered but huge Elizabethan Theatre in Sydney was actually somewhat outside the city in a run-down suburb, and entailed a long car ride each evening to get us there and back.

Jennie arrived late, only a few minutes before the show, as she and her husband had got lost in a typhoon somewhere between Melbourne and Sydney. The weather, according to the papers, was driving huge herds of gigantic spiders into the city. I didn't see those, but we did experience the tail-end of the storm. During the show the sky went deep purple and the wind started to howl. The theatre was ancient and the roof over the stage was made up of rusty corrugated iron strips. With hailstones the size of golf balls pounding down on it, the noise on set was incredible. No one back-stage could hear anyone else. The actors were doing the whole show by lip-reading their cues and so were we. Working in the wings was also impossible with the sound of ten thousand drummers echoing round the fly-tower. Strangely, according to the understudies who went out front to check, in the insulated auditorium it wasn't at all bad and the actors could be heard quite clearly. If anything they seemed to be shouting.

Great gusts of wind sucked round the prop tables. Pieces of paper, important prop letters which I was meant to hand to the actors, flew up into the fly-tower. Ba was trying to screech lighting cues above the din from a prompt copy which would not stay open at the right page. It was mayhem. Finally, with an enormous tearing sound, a section of the roof flew quite away.

Glenda and Tim were sitting on sofas onstage, yelling the scene at one another, when suddenly enormous ice balls started falling into John Napier's sunlit set and rolling downstage on the Persian carpet like frozen ping pong balls. Tim rose and said the line, 'I must be getting back.'

Dodging a shower of thundering hailstones in Hedda's living room, Glenda glanced towards the safety of the set's sunlit garden and replied 'Do you really want to go out through the garden?'

It brought the house down.

I should point out that during the 1970s, Australia was still in the 1840s. Women were only permitted to drink in hotel bars or with a meal in a restaurant. If you wanted to go into a pub you couldn't. You had to stand outside on the pavement with the dogs, while the men brought drinks out to you, for the inner world of the pub was strictly a male domain. We were all rather shocked at this and other strangely macho customs dictated by those the locals laughably called the 'menfolk'.

The only men we encountered seemed to fall into two groups: leather-faced men so butch they could only spend time with other leather-faced men (and possibly sheep) and effete girlish kind of men, who also seemed to prefer male company.

We girls had started to wonder in fact whether all Australian men were gay. Certainly every single one we had encountered in the theatre over the six weeks we'd been there had been as camp as a jamboree. Perhaps the world of theatre was Australia's answer to Gays Anonymous, or something. So we started a bet. Whichever of us found the first guaranteed straight Australian man around the theatre would win £10 from the others.

One day I crashed into Fidelis in a dressing room corridor. She was running.

'Quick, quick,' she said. 'I've won.'

'No,' I said. 'I was coming to find you to tell you that I've won.'

We dragged one another down to the stage, where the crew were flying pieces of scenery in and out. We both pointed up at the same man. Dangling from a rope about 20 feet above the ground, was a swarthy hunk, with a look of Clark Gable about him. As he hitched himself from one rope to another he gave us a little demonstration of his muscles and then did a little mock fall to make us gasp. Set against the swathes of red velvet curtain, he looked very dashing, most piratical. He gave us a wink. We felt assured that we had both won (and therefore both lost).

''Ello, there gerls,' the hunk shouted down to us. 'What you two laffin' at?'

He had an unmistakably Liverpool accent. Neither of us had won.

We were all put up in a swanky new hotel in the lively Kings Cross area. I don't know that I have ever stayed in a hotel so crammed with famous people. I travelled up in a lift with Don McLean, of 'American Pie' fame, who gave me a piece of cinnamon chewing gum. (It was disgusting. He was lovely.) Rolf Harris seemed to be sitting in the corridor playing a didgeridoo at all hours of the day and night. Margaret Powell, a briefly famous author who wrote of her life as a domestic servant 'below stairs', could be heard cackling in the bar. Roberta Flack was flitting in and out on her way to concerts, and Bette Davis was often in the foyer, sitting in a wheelchair and yelling. Being forever star-struck, the first time I saw her, I knew that this was a chance in a million. I ran forward, still wearing my blue school overall that I wore for the prop-setting. I leaned over the electrifying presence that was Miss Davis and was stunned to take in how tiny she was, so I shook her hand quickly and said how much I adored her. She smiled fleetingly with the slightest nod of acceptance. The second my back was turned I heard her shrieking impatiently for 'Gloria', her poor assistant, humiliating her quite publicly as they went out through the electric doors. John Wayne was knocking about somewhere too.

One night we sat in the hotel restaurant (kept open so late especially for us) and in walked David Frost.

'I thought I heard English accents!' he cried, strolling over and sitting himself down. He picked up a menu, and ordered the most expensive dishes there. When he had finished eating, he smiled, got up and left, forgetting to pay his tab, and leaving it to us!

Once the routine of setting up was established, I had my days free. I sloped off, as is my wont, and went to a suburb called Manley, where I found a delightfully secluded beach. How marvellous, I thought, when all the other beaches are so crowded, to stumble across this one. I changed into my costume and had a lovely swim, then lay out on the pale sand to dry. As I drifted off to sleep I was aware of a heavy thundering sound thudding through my body. Something large was approaching me, and fast. Clutching my towel I sat up, only for my head to make direct contact with the hugest galloping Great Dane. He slightly swerved from the collision then gambolled gaily on. My face was not so happy.

I went back to the hotel, getting some strange looks on the bus, and when I finally saw myself in the mirror it was a horrible sight. My cheek and forehead were black and red, my eye had all but disappeared into my skull and my lips looked as though I had injected an overdose of collagen. As I started work that evening I explained to Ba what had really happened and told her about the wonderful deserted beach I had discovered.

'You fool,' she said. 'Why do you think it was deserted? Manley Beach is famous for shark attacks!'

Gulping, I prepared the tea and took it round to the actors. Peter Eyre was my first dressing room stop. His jaw, already low (Peter has a famously long face) dropped to chest level.

'Boyfriend beat me up,' I said.

'Really?' His chin reached knee level. 'What boyfriend?'

'Blind date,' I said. 'He's Danish.'

I moved on to the next dressing room. Ever after Peter imagined I had some secret life. I did not correct him. Other people in the company got the two stories a bit mixed up and thought I had been attacked by a shark. I let them think what they liked. There's nothing like a bit of mystery!

CHAPTER 6

Sydney had been a triumph and we were fêted by the local actors (including a young ingénue called Pamela Stephenson, who was playing Solveig in an endless production of *Peer Gynt* at the Opera House) and invited to many parties. On the last night's curtain call, someone threw a gigantic thing like a cabbage at Glenda. Apparently in Australia it is a sign of great respect. Who knew? I shall remember that if anyone ever throws a cabbage at me.

And so we flew on. While most of the company rested in Hawaii for a day's break, the stage management had to push on to Los Angeles to set up. LA was amazing and the Huntington Hartford Theater, a vast converted cinema, was right in the thick of Hollywood, on the intersection of Hollywood and Vine.

We stayed in a weird hacienda-style hotel called the Magic Hotel of Hollywood Hillcrest. It was two storeys high in peeling pale pink stucco, and built around a flaky turquoise pool. Far from being magic, it was tattered and worn and resembled the seedier scenes in *Day of the Locust* with a hint of the Bates Motel. But I adored it.

So far on the tour my dress sense had not received plaudits. In fact I was still wearing that same Laura Ashley floor-length smock from those far-away T.I.E. days. I also sported a viridian green coat which I think I had had since school. Constance Chapman had taken me aside and explained that if I wore nicer things I might have a queue of men waiting round the block. Ba and Fidelis, with whom I shared an apartment in the hotel, said they didn't want to walk along the street with me. One day I found them sniggering quietly among themselves and knew something was up. When I made my way downstairs to get the car into work, I noticed something floating in the pool. It was the pink brushed nylon shortie negligée which I had been given by my mother, who in turn had been given it by a friend, for jumble.

'The coat is next,' said Fidelis.

'And the Laundry,' said Ba. The Laundry was the name everyone had christened the floral smock, as when wearing it I resembled someone who had walked through a washing line.

There followed a ceremonial drowning party. And something about it made me very happy. I was moving from one stage of my life into a new one and it would start with the clothes. So far, whatever the weather, I had toured the world dressed as a small boy-scout's jamboree, topped with a thatched roof. I was called Giant Haystacks, not after the wrestler, but because I looked like a giant haystack. But, from now on, things were going to change.

As it happens, this sartorial revelation coincided with the company's discovery of a shop on Hollywood Boulevard which made print-to-order t-shirts. A competition was decreed.

Glenda's first was 'Acid Hedda'. Tim West had 'Heddaward VII', while Patrick Stewart, who played the role of the philandering Eilert Loevborg, had a more intellectual one based on his character's journey, which read 'EL loves HG, TE, HG, EL'. While we were in Sydney, someone had come to the box office and asked if the show advertised actually had 'Glenda Jackson . . . in the flesh?' (as though they might put on instead a cardboard cut-out in the role), so Glenda wore another with the logo 'In The Flesh'. Next, Glenda, who, whenever there was trouble with the theatres or the management, made a joke of crying 'I won't go on!' put that on her t-shirt. The following day we all wore one by way of chorus, which read, 'She won't go on!' Fidelis was given one with 'Adeste Fidelis'. Glenda made her a replacement emblazoned 'Troublemaker' and then Glenda made one for me in white with gold lettering which said 'BEST'.

As it was such a special present, the next morning I put it on, daringly, without the usual set of cardigans and smocks to cover my shape. For the first time since I was a child, on my top half I wore just a t-shirt, and ventured out into the hotel.

I had only walked a few corridors when I passed the producer, Paul Elliott. He looked down at my breasts and gawped, 'Yes, they

ARE the best.' I turned on my heels, went back to my room and changed back into the black all-covering bivouac.

That for me was the end of t-shirts for many years. Thank you, Paul. (For your information, Glenda was furious.)

Glenda arranged for us all to have a VIP tour of Universal Studios. The VIP bit meant we were driven round the attractions – the flash flood, actors rehearsing on the set of some soap opera (which I think might have been a library-type room in *Marcus Welby M.D.*). We were shown Lucille Ball's dressing-room door, the phoney Main Street, the actual house from *Psycho,* all from a small jeep, taking routes round the back alleyways, away from the general public.

As we cruised through the back lot we sped past a kind of rubbish dump of toppled pillars, broken chairs and an old cart across which flopped in three slices, a huge tattered rubber shark. Pam yelled for the driver to stop. My escapades with sharks were now company business and it was decided I should pose with this prop.

'What film is this from?' I asked the driver.

'Oh it's just some B picture,' he replied. 'It'll probably never make the UK cinemas. No real stars. Unknown director. Just a rubber shark. It's going to be called *Jaws.*'

Since then many replica sharks have been made to appease the public's taste to see the 'original' shark from that mega-successful film. But I am probably the only person outside the cast of the film ever to have posed with the (albeit tattered) genuine article.

After the show one night, Glenda's debonair actor friend Peter Bromilow invited us to the launch of some motor-bike christening party, which consisted of hundreds of leather wearing mustachioed blokes in tartan shirts, squealing a lot as they revved up their Harleys. Connie and Jennie even got to ride pillion. They sped off into the night for what seemed like hours and we feared we might never see them again. It was a sultry and such a happy night. Ten years later I wondered how many of those hilarious boys had survived the first wave of AIDS which swept through California in the 1980s.

Glenda threw a party and asked us all who we would like to meet and then invited them. Fidelis asked for Elvis, but sadly didn't get him, but almost everyone else you had ever heard of did come. I almost fainted when Greer Garson came over and graciously introduced herself. There was George Segal, Susan George, Sarah Miles, Julie Christie, Richard Dreyfuss, Ryan O'Neal, Elliott Gould, Ellen Burstyn, Paul Newman, Joanne Woodward, Roddy McDowall, Art Carney and Bette Davis again. It was that night that I realised that Hollywood stars seemed to have something in common. They were all tiny, with huge heads. It was like being at a munchkin's ball.

Every night we played in Hollywood, it was my job, after the show, to bring the visiting stars through the wings directly to Glenda's dressing room, bypassing the long snake of autograph hunters.

I escorted them all: Bea Arthur, Barbara Stanwyck, Irene Worth, Walter Matthau, Ruth Gordon, Marsha Mason, Nick Roeg and Theresa Russell, Patrick McGoohan, Jon Voight, David Tomlinson, Cloris Leachman, Fred MacMurray, Douglas Fairbanks Jr, Gregory Peck and Jack Lemmon. (Much later in my life the subject of Jack Lemmon would almost bring me to blows with Sir Laurence Olivier's son-in-law – see Chapter 30.)

Obviously there were so many stars in Hollywood that people expected to see them everywhere. One day, sitting in a café with Glenda, Connie and Peter Eyre, an autograph hunter pounced.

'Miss Jackson! How wonderful. I loved you in *A Touch of Class*.' He passed her his autograph book. 'Miss Chapman. You were so marvellous in *O Lucky Man!* And *In Celebration*.' The autograph book moved along. 'Mr Eyre, how fantastic was that film *Mahler*? You were great in it.' Peter signed.

Then the film fan turned towards me, thrusting the autograph book under my nose. There was a long pause.

'But *you*! *You* are my *absolute* favourite.' He grinned. 'Truly. I mean it.'

Glenda, Connie and Peter swung in my direction, waiting to hear about some great film role I had been keeping secret from them. The fan continued: 'To have appeared in all those sexy Swedish films . . .'

Glenda, Connie and Peter gasped. Could it be true? Little Celia, the walking thatched tent, was a secret porn star?

'And then, to come here to Hollywood and do the musical of *Lost Horizon*. You're incredible. I love you . . . Liv Ullmann.'

It was around this time that Peter Eyre got the idea that I should put on a tight sweater and go sit in Schwab's Pharmacy and wait to be discovered. I passed on that one. It might have worked for Lana Turner (and, in a comic send-up, for Lucille Ball) but it was the tight sweater bit I couldn't face.

More celebrities were to be discovered another way. We visited Forest Lawn cemetery and they were all there: Gracie Allen, Errol Flynn, Humphrey Bogart, Clark Gable, Jean Harlow, Spencer Tracy. Even if they were all under the sod.

The place was not only remarkable for having the world's largest collection of famous dead people, it also had the greatest collection in the world of, well, let's quote the old brochure: 'genuine replicas' and 'authentic reproductions'. Within a few square acres of California you can find an 'exact copy of the original' church from Stoke Poges (of Gray's elegy fame), 'an accurate reconstruction' of the kirk i' the heather from Glencairn (where wee Annie Laurie worshipped), 'a faithful replica' of Longfellow's New England meeting house and 'the only exact reproductions in the world' of all the sculptures of Michelangelo. Well!

There was also something which claimed to be the largest oil painting in the world, but no doubt by now that record has been broken. It was a hilariously grim canvas of the Crucifixion, which looked more like people gathering for a pop festival on a black clouded hillside one rainy British afternoon than anything from the Bible.

The whole company had been warned not to go out alone after dark. Hollywood was dangerous, we were informed. There was some local serial killer or rapist on the prowl. I can't recall if it was the Hollywood Slasher, but everyone was talking about some mysterious criminal lurking. On top of this, at that time Hollywood Boulevard, a street between our hotel and our theatre, was notoriously menacing. However, some people won't be told. Unable to get to sleep in the early hours one morning (remember we would rarely get home from work till after 11pm or well after 12pm if we ate out) Fidelis and I decided to try an all-American thing which we did not then have back home: the all-night supermarket.

Feeling like characters from the recently released film *The Stepford Wives*, we drifted round the deserted neon-lit aisles in slow-mo with our trolleys, choosing biscuits with strange names and garishly coloured cereals which we had previously only seen in advertisements in imported American comic books.

At the check-out Fidelis and I were busy excitedly comparing our exotic purchases when the person behind me in the queue, a six-and-a-half-feet tall handsome African-American said, 'Say that again.'

So I said, 'I've never heard of sugar-sprinkle Twinkies, have you?'

'Gee, I love your weird accents,' he said. 'Say it again!'

He chatted to Fidelis and me for a while and then escorted us back to the hotel, telling us he was a musician and that his name was Moses. We bumped into him a few days later on Hollywood Boulevard and he walked us to the stage door, where he gave us both a delightful smacker on the lips. He happened to be wrapped all around me as Glenda quietly slid past on her way into the theatre for the matinée.

A few minutes later, while setting up the prop table, a call came over the tannoy. 'Miss Imrie and Miss Morgan to Miss Jackson's dressing room. Immediately.' Glenda gave us both a stiff talking-to and really earned one of the nicknames she had garnered during the tour: Nanny Jackson.

As we sheepishly turned to leave she said: 'Oh and by the way you *are* both going to join me tomorrow, aren't you?' The following morning we were due to leave LA.

We nodded eagerly, fearing that our little kissing episode might have lost us a place with the rest of the group known as 'The Girls'.

So next morning, bright and early, we took our places along with Glenda and 'The Girls' i.e. Tim, Pam, Connie, Ba, and Peter, in the VIP enclosure at LAX to board the Faberjet. This jet was owned by George Barrie, composer and owner of the cosmetics company Fabergé. He had produced *A Touch of Class*, Glenda's last Oscar-winning film and, while she was in America, he was lending Glenda his own private plane.

Who knew people travelled like this? There were squashy sofas, a piano, and a chef with a huge knife preparing sushi in a rather flamboyant way. I prayed we didn't hit turbulence.

But a few hours later we landed safely and taxied onto the private lane at Dulles Airport, Washington DC. As the jet came to a stop the doors burst open and in marched several uniformed officials.

'OK,' said a tall one, in shades. 'Where are the guitar cases, the drums?'

We all shook our heads.

'The instruments,' he said slowly, knowing we were from England and therefore might not understand the language. 'Where. Are. Your. Instruments?'

Glenda rose. 'We have no instruments. We are the Royal Shakespeare Company.'

The macho customs man took an aggressive stance.

'Is that a rock group?'

He had the evidence before him. He peered round at those present: 70-year-old grandmother, Constance Chapman; stout, bald Timothy West; languid, balding Peter Eyre; prematurely grey, embonpoint Pam; three timid underling girls and growling Glenda, in no make-up, at her fiercest. He shrugged and left, taking his posse with him.

'I don't want any trouble from you Brits,' he shouted as a parting shot. 'You can get off now.' It was that Special Relationship at work again.

In Washington we saw all the famous sights. The Capitol, the Jefferson Memorial, the Lincoln Memorial. In fact with all those white pillars, it felt strangely like walking round the top of a wedding cake.

A VIP tour was arranged for a private visit to the White House (present incumbent Gerald Ford, who was at the time away from Washington). The only problem was the visit clashed with an understudy rehearsal.

I took the professional option and skipped the rehearsal. After all, I could practise my lines any old time but how often would I be invited inside the White House? (N.B. Up-and-coming young hopefuls, you'd better not copy my example. I was a *very, very* bad girl!)

Fidelis and Oz did their duty and missed out on a fabulous day. I think they both felt bitter about it for the rest of the tour, and possibly to the present moment.

The whole company however did make it to a special visit to the Senate. We were shown the snuff boxes inside the door. 'For the Senators from the Southern States' we were informed, so naturally I took a sniff. Then we sat down to lunch, and I was passed a basket of delicious corn bread. It was explained that this special corn bread was also always served to please the Southern senators. It made you wonder which side had won the Civil War.

Halfway through the meal, John Glenn, the astronaut, came and sat at our table. I was really excited to meet a real-life spaceman. I could barely contain myself. But then he went on to tell us the complete (and I mean complete) history of corn-bread. I drifted off after about three sentences, because the strange thing was he was really, really dull.

I thought about it later and realised that to be good at the job of sitting in a space capsule whirling round the earth at enormous speed, and not knowing if you'll ever make it back to earth, you would have to be pretty calm and unimaginative or you'd have a nervous breakdown before you even took off.

Despite the fact we were working very hard, and partying too, as we were invited everywhere, on our Sunday off we decided to zip up to New York on an express train which had twirling seats.

The minute I got out into the New York streets, I felt as though I was walking on an electric carpet. That city buzzes like nowhere else on the planet. Even in the hotel, when I drew back the curtains and flung open the window and could see nothing but the brick work of the adjacent building about 10 inches away from my nose, I didn't care.

We went to see Ellis Island, the Empire State Building and Sardi's. We went up the inside of the Statue of Liberty because in those days you could. We even took in a Sunday matinée performance, something never seen at that time (or for many years to come) back in the UK. The show was Bernstein's *Candide* and it was amazing. The ensemble production took over the whole theatre, auditorium and all, with actors swinging on ropes over your head and the most incredible singing and dancing. After that we took tea at the Algonquin. It was even fun having supper at the now defunct Luchow's, though, being a vegetarian, German is not my favourite cuisine. But, for that night only, how I wished I ate meat, just so I could order the Schwarzwälder Pfifferlinge, or, at a pinch, the Schlemmerschnitte. Heaven knows how we fit all those adventures into one day and still got back to Washington in time for the Monday night show, but we did.

One evening in Washington, Glenda asked Ba, Fidelis and I if we would go to her suite immediately after the show where we were to arrange the table and cook a dinner for some very important backers whom she wished to impress. Well, what else is there to do in Washington at 11.30pm?

The ingredients for a huge vegetable pie were waiting there in the kitchenette. On a sideboard in the dining room was the wine, which needed to be opened and left to breathe. We really enjoyed paying back Glenda for the kindness that she always showed us, and all assembled in her suite as soon as the show came down.

Fidelis runs a tight kitchen. When cooking she has all the manners of Fanny Craddock and all the charm of Gordon Ramsay, and delegates in a similar way. She commandeered her own corner, while I was sent to the cold counter to prepare the pastry. While Fidelis beavered away at the vegetable filling, chopping and beating and stirring away like all three weird sisters in one human form, I diligently rubbed butter into flour. Ba meanwhile opened the wine and poured us a drink 'to be getting along with' while she laid the table, setting out a beautiful array of cutlery, china, glasses, candles, bread baskets, even little saucers with iced butter pats.

I downed the first glass before I even started adding the water to my pastry mix, and by the time I was thumping it into shape on a bread board I was three sails to the wind.

As my head whirled, the aroma of the vegetable filling became intoxicating, and Fidelis was yelling for a casserole dish to be brought to her. I started to panic. I was nowhere near ready, plus I couldn't find a rolling pin.

'Use a bottle,' barked Fidelis. 'It'll do as well as anything.'

I saluted and careered across the room, polishing off the remains of the wine in order to gain its bottle. Ba was putting on music and creating mood lighting and we were all feeling rather high.

'Right, my part is done!' cried Fidelis, turning off the electric ring and presenting me with a casserole dish full of delicious pie-filling. 'Once the pastry is on, just shove it in the oven.'

Bing-bong! The warning doorbell.

I could hear voices cooing with pleasure at the lovely table. Fidelis and Ba had gone into the other room to shake hands with the Very Important People.

I'm not sure what actually happened next, but it did involve putting the pastry on the top of the casserole dish and placing the completed pie into the piping hot oven.

So, I joined the others, gleefully accepting some more wine from Ba. Pam and Glenda were there now, with two very smart intellectual-looking people from New York who were discussing the ins and outs of Scandinavian play-writing.

After twenty minutes the guests took their seats at the table. Fidelis went into the kitchen to get the pie and I heard a gasp. Ba and I flew in after her.

Fidelis's face was black. 'What is *this*?' She was holding out the pie.

'Uhoh,' I said, swaying from side to side. 'I sort of forgot to roll it out properly.'

Fidelis put the pie down. Instead of the usual honey-coloured flat crust, my pastry balanced on top of the dish like a 3-D map of the Lake District. In some parts it was paper-thin and burned to a cinder, in others great mounds of uncooked stodge reared up out of the mixture like beige whales about to blow.

'What are we going to do?' Ba was pulling up her sleeves. 'Shall we go straight to the salad?'

'Don't look at me,' said the perfectionist, Fidelis, glowering in my direction. 'You can serve it.'

'Mmmm! Smells delicious,' cried the female would-be investor. 'Glenda told me about your famous vegetable pies.'

'Yes,' said Glenda. 'They are such good cooks. I'm so lucky.'

Ba was giggling. Pam stood in the doorway, mouth wide open, her face alight with the dreadfulness of our situation.

'Celia,' she said, most observantly. 'You're drunk!'

Pam picked up the pie. 'Come on,' she said. 'Everyone's getting impatient.'

So we took our seats at the table, and Pam served. Perhaps unsurprisingly, instead of the usual rolling conversation, as people bit into their first mouthful, everything went rather quiet.

American socialites are very good at maintaining a bright façade, whatever the circumstances. The lady kept on smiling, grimly. The atmosphere had become rather tense. I was out of it, trying very hard to control myself for I feared that any moment I would roar with laughter.

'When do you move on to Toronto?' asked the gentleman, steering safely away from the subject of the food on his plate.

'Sunday,' said Glenda.

But the pastry couldn't be ignored for long, even I knew that! I noticed that the smiling lady, who reminded me of a Yank version of Joan Bakewell, had finished eating the pie's filling and was busily steering great hunks of half-cooked pastry round and round the plate as though it was some kind of Scalextric set.

'Mmmmmm!' she murmured after a few moments. 'This pastry is so delicious . . .'

Everybody looked earnestly in her direction. Did she have the successful way of excusing herself from eating it?

'This pastry is SO delicious,' she repeated. 'I'm going to *have* to leave it all.' She laid down her knife and fork.

Exploding with silent laughter, I slid from my seat and spent the rest of the evening beneath the table, shaking and wiping away tears of hysteria.

CHAPTER 7

We took the Faberjet onwards to Toronto, landing on a cold, bleak April morning. When we landed, Glenda offered us a lift into town. She looked out of the limo's window and growled, 'We came to Toronto. But it was closed.'

We all took a walk to work. There was nobody about. It really did seem as though the H-bomb had gone off and no one had let us know. We were trying to find the theatre.

'It can't be far,' said Pam.

'It'll be that one there,' said Fidelis laughing and pointing to a garishly neon-lit palace which looked more like Tivoli Gardens at Christmas-time than a theatre showing Ibsen.

We all laughed politely. But as we got nearer we stopped and gawked. There were our *Hedda Gabler* posters, surrounded by flashing fairground lights. It seemed unbelievable, but we really were playing here. We entered the stage door and were greeted by the owner/manager Ed Mirvish.

'Hi there! I'm Honest Ed.' He spoke in that quick patter associated with auctioneers. 'And here are your vouchers for 10% off burgers at my nearby Honest Ed's Hamburger Emporium'. We smiled wanly as he passed them round. 'You'll never need to eat anywhere else,' he told us.

And he was right. In fact it was pretty difficult to *find* anywhere else, for everywhere you walked in Toronto you could see his name in blinking lights. There was Honest Ed's Fishbar, Honest Ed's Italian, Honest Ed's Warehouse, Honest Ed's Chinese, Honest Ed's Discount Store.

After a few days we eventually found the entire population of Toronto. They were hiding underground, where there is another complete city. Then a couple of weeks later the sun came out, the temperature went up, and they all migrated up to the open-air version.

Meanwhile we all did the sights, Yonge Street (which everyone you met took pains to tell you was the longest street in the world), a park with a lake full of dead fish and the Niagara Falls, which was noisy and wet and not worth the bother.

One day, strolling along the longest street in the world, we passed a porno cinema going by the delightful name of Minsky's Elite Films. In one of the photos displayed outside we recognised an actor we knew, last seen in the Romans' Season at the Royal Shakespeare Theatre, Stratford-upon-Avon. The film's poster sported the logo, 'This film cannot be shown in England.' Well, talk about red rag to a bull.

Pam, Fidelis and I went in. We climbed a steep staircase at the top of which was a woman peering out of a tiny red-lit window.

'Three, please,' said Pam.

'Will you be wanting the nude body rub?' the woman inquired politely.

'No, thanks,' we said in unison. 'Just the film that's banned in England.'

'Through there.' She indicated a plastic strip curtain leading into darkness and went back to her magazine.

We strode through the gap, then all fell together in a heap on the wooden floor. No one told us there were steps! Giggling like jabbering idiots we felt our way to the seats, a motley collection of chairs arranged in something like rows, and sat down to enjoy the show.

The film that was showing, a short, prior to the main title, had no sound. To cover the silence a John Lennon LP played very loudly. 'Imagine no possessions, I wonder if you can,' droned John, as up on screen a frumpy looking woman sat on a grubby mattress and unpacked her shopping. She'd obviously been to the grocery shop and had bought a courgette, a carrot, a cucumber and an aubergine. She then started to fondle these vegetables, rubbing them lovingly across her face and boobs. When it came to the aubergine we all expressed some doubt that she would be able to reach the climax of her act.

'The one thing you can't hide,' wailed John Lennon. 'Is when you're crippled inside.'

Naturally we laughed. We were still laughing when Fidelis emitted an unlikely little squeak. Looking down, she whispered, 'They're not mine' as we saw two unidentified hands were cradling her breasts. While she tried to extricate herself another pair of gnarled old hands whipped round and grabbed my own ample bosom. So, sadly, we left the cinema faster than you can say Yoko Ono, without ever having seen a glimpse of our friend performing an orgy in a bath-tub of baked beans.

It wasn't all bad though. Glenda got us invited to a concert given by Jack Jones (known to all as JJ). She sat at a table with Ella Fitzgerald and JJ's then girlfriend, *Straw Dogs* star, Susan George. Afterwards we were all invited up to JJ's suite where I picked up Ella's scarf when she dropped it. 'Thank you, sweety,' said Ella, and I realised she was almost blind. Susan sat Ella on a huge throne-like chair from whence she started giving JJ notes on his performance. I sat at her feet, totally in awe. (And glad I wasn't getting the notes.)

A few days later we were all invited by Ella to attend an orchestra rehearsal. I was amazed that only Glenda, Pam, Fidelis and I took it up. And so one afternoon the four of us sat together at the back of an empty auditorium and watched Ella Fitzgerald sing, conduct and chat with the orchestra. We had to keep our eyes on the time as we had a show to get to and eventually, during a break, while the orchestra were all annotating their scores, we tiptoed down the aisle towards the pass-door beside the stage which was the only available exit, via backstage and out. When we were about four feet away from her, Ella picked up the mike and stooped towards us.

'Every time we say goodbye . . .' she crooned, à cappella, giving us a sad little wave. '. . . I cry a little. Every time we say goodbye, I wonder why a little . . .'

Ella Fitzgerald had sung just for the four of us. Who else could boast anything as wonderful as that? It was one of the most memorable moments of my life.

As the weeks rolled on, a slightly hysterical note infiltrated the company. We sensed the end was in sight, for it was next-stop London. It had all been so marvellous, but shortly we would be back in the normal world. Everyone in some way was changed by that tour, and going back to the UK meant you had a choice: you could return to how it was before you left, or you could bring back the new you, and surprise (possibly horrify) your friends. Many of us broke out in some way or another.

At Glenda's birthday bash, near the end of the tour, all kinds of things happened. Glenda's husband, Roy, arrived and offered a drink to Andy Phillips, the lighting designer of orange juice fame, who was over for the Toronto set-up.

'Help yourself,' said Roy gently, from behind the bar.

Andy, ebullient and unpleasant as ever, smirked and, eye to eye with him, replied, 'I already have.'

The whole room went silent. Somebody gasped. Roy left the party and Glenda disappeared after him. He immediately packed his bags and left for England, having discovered Andy's love letters in Glenda's handbag.

Ba was talking earnestly in the corner with Tim, Fidelis was on the floor under a grand piano canoodling with Patrick Stewart, Connie was flirting outrageously with the latest in the string of young pony-tailed boys who became her constant devoted companion in each city, Oz was lovingly examining all the wine labels, and I sat on the windowsill and kissed David Jones, the handsome deep-voiced director of the RSC. I do remember seeing Peter Eyre's eyebrows disappear up into his shiny scalp while his mouth formed a perfect O.

Connie gave me a wink. 'Atta girl,' she said quietly.

David was a sweet man, and I was extremely fond of him. We stayed very close till his sudden and untimely death in 2008. Only a few weeks before he died I accompanied him when he attended an alumni event at Cambridge University.

★

And so the *Hedda Gabler* company left Toronto on a warm Sunday evening at the end of May 1975. As the plane circled Heathrow, Glenda looked out of the window and said wistfully, 'who'd ever think England was really *so* green?'

We were all quiet. For five months we had lived life to the full and now we knew we had to go back and face the music.

The London run at the Aldwych was very different. We were no longer the strolling players, discovering new lands, breaking free from the moorings of our past.

We were just another Royal Shakespeare Company West End run. Except that the RSC didn't really treat us like the regular company. It was more like being a visiting company from out of town who were rather annoyingly renting their theatre. And the motley crew, who had wandered the earth, eating, sleeping and working as one for almost a year, dispersed. Husbands, wives, girlfriends and boyfriends appeared, proclaimed ownership of their partners, whined a lot about how happy we seemed, and the magical bond between us was loosened.

When it all finally came to an end, I was the only member of the company to stay on with the RSC, understudying and stage-managing again, on David Jones's production *The Marrying of Ann Leete*, starring Estelle Kohler and Mia Farrow.

As usual I brought round the biscuits. Estelle renamed me Nelly Pert. On the first night I bought Mia a little trinket which was relevant to her lines in the play. I had bought three things, as I was undecided which to give her. So on the second night I gave her another, and then, just before the third show, the last. On the fourth night, when I entered empty-handed, she looked at me aghast.

'Oh no, Celia!' she said in her lilting LA accent. 'I can't go on if I don't get my little gift.'

She was serious. My gifts had become part of her pre-show ritual. Most actors understand the demands of superstition, and how awful it is if they are broken, so I rushed out to the newsagents and bought a packet of wine gums and presented her with one stuck to a prop ring like a jewel. And for the rest of the run I made sure I was prepared for the nightly delivery of her amulet.

Mia was always very gentle and sweet to me. Her husband, the conductor, André Previn, left quite a different impression. He was rather short with me, and was frequently seen lurking in cars outside the stage door, watching Mia leave after the show. It seemed that things were not going well between them at the time and I felt quite sorry for her.

When my contract ran out, I felt it was time for a real change. So I walked into Vidal Sassoon's Chelsea salon and got rid of the thatch. I went in looking like a hairy pyramid and came out resembling the George Du Maurier illustrations of Trilby O'Ferrall. It was a huge improvement and confidence booster.

However as winter descended, I had had a few months on the dole and found myself with nothing but the slog of heading back to the old treadmill of rep. I got myself another panto, this time in Derby, playing A Citizen of Transylvania in *Sleeping Beauty*. (I know, Transylvania! What were they thinking? I promise you Dracula was in there somewhere too.)

It was all rather disconcerting. I'd been round the world, had met and even worked with some of the most famous people alive, and how much further had I travelled professionally? Well, I was back in the chorus and it was pretty dire stuff to boot. One of the dance routines took place immediately after the traditional dame's cookery school scene, which in this production involved both water and cornflakes. Most nights as I high-kicked in my shiny dance shoes I would slide about on the mess while everyone danced around me. I constantly ended up down near the footlights, on my arse.

It was on just such a night that Fidelis arrived to see the show, up from her home in Birmingham. She had brought an old university pal of hers: Victoria Wood.

CHAPTER 8

I got to know Victoria over the next few weeks during the winter of 1975/6, while I was at Derby and afterwards out of work. A gang of ex-Birmingham University students regularly gathered round the TV at Fidelis's to watch Victoria perform her fortnightly song on *The Esther Rantzen* show. One time she had a wardrobe disaster. She arrived at the studio to be told she was not allowed to wear trousers. She possessed no long dresses. I owned nothing else. I raced to the studio with one of my long gowns and returned to Selly Oak to watch it on TV with the others.

We were all in the same boat, trained and practised but unable to find much work so there was lots of spare time – Victoria's TV job was only one day every other week. We struggled from job to job, barely keeping things together, surviving on anything which came in – painting and decorating someone's flat, babysitting, cleaning. Inflation was raging. Petrol prices had soared and people feared that before long it would reach the unthinkable level of 50p a gallon! Along with our dole money, I remember we received butter tokens. You took them along to the grocers who exchanged them for a slab of cheap butter. Very odd!

There were regular power cuts. We'd all sit around having sing-songs at the piano, or having our fortunes read by candlelight. Bored a lot of the time we'd all go out and spend the day rowing on the lake in Cannon Hill Park.

One day, I went with Victoria, Fidelis, Pam and Adele Anderson (later of the singing trio, Fascinating Aida) to attend a charity football match at Stratford-upon-Avon to see Noele Gordon of *Crossroads* doing the prize-giving. We were entranced to see that Miss Gordon's turquoise suit was magnificently accessorised with matching shoes, bag, hat and even handkerchief.

In the long, hot summer of 1976, we discovered a real ration book cookery pamphlet in a junk shop and got together to make the wartime recipes. We got togged up as land-girls, and nurses, factory workers and even a soldier, and sat in the garden for an austerity party. It was the first of many such gatherings.

As winter moved in, along with the power cuts, the Birmingham gang moved on. Fidelis sold up her place in Selly Oak, and moved to Clapham, together with Stewart Permutt, Robert Howie, me and a few others.

A few months later, I donned dungarees and drove a lorry up and down the M6 helping Victoria and her boyfriend, Geoff Durham, aka 'The Great Soprendo', move their worldly goods from a big Victorian flat in Edgbaston to a little terraced house in Morecambe. The little house had steep stairs. The lorry didn't have a tailgate. What fun we had with that piano . . .

As spring started to burst, I got the wonderful news that I had been chosen to spend the summer in a Shakespeare double bill at the Regent's Park Open Air Theatre. I was to play Jaquenetta in *Love's Labour's Lost*, Mistress Quickly and Alice, the handmaiden of the Princess of France, in *Henry V*. At last I was playing decent parts in a theatre which actually mattered. As it happened, that summer it rained perpetually, and frequently we spent shows hovering under trees while the audience stood about sipping mulled wine in a nearby tent.

Unlike normal theatres, there was no lighting in the corridors leading to the stage, which were mere dirt-tracks through bushes. Louise Purnell played the leads in both plays and, as it happens, both Princesses of France! Most nights the pair of us stood shivering in the leafy wings waiting for our cue, and the renowned actor Esmond Knight, who had appeared so famously in Olivier's Shakespeare films and also in one of my all-time favourite films, *The Red Shoes,* had to pass us on his way to the stage. But Esmond was blind. He had lost his sight while on active service in the Royal Navy, during the battle to sink the *Bismarck*, and therefore was quite a hero to us all. Each night he felt his way to the stage using Louise's and my breasts as a kind of handrail. We said nothing.

The job not only gave me, at last, a decent credit on my CV, it also won me a new great friend, Frank Baker, who was simply marvellous in the role of Costard, my stage beau.

As the damp summer ended, I was in high hopes but after many auditions I was offered only one job, and that was back in the chorus. This time my hoofing was to be at Exeter Rep in the Cole Porter show, *Anything Goes*. However, now that I had proved myself in Shakespeare, I felt sure that I was also in with a chance of staying on to play one of the handmaidens in the following show, *Antony and Cleopatra*. But when I went to the director he told me 'absolutely no way' because the role of Charmian was already cast and I couldn't play Iris because I was too large.

That same phrase! An arrow to my heart! Too large! Not again!

Feeling quite desperate, I packed my bags and prepared to go home and join the unemployment queue, when the girl who was about to start rehearsing the role of Iris suddenly collapsed with appendicitis and I was summoned to the director's office. Even though I had lost no weight, he told me, as he begged me to stay, that I was utterly perfect for the role, and said he couldn't imagine why he hadn't asked me in the first place. Which all goes to show, never believe a word any director says when they turn you down.

Better still, when my stint waving a fan down the Nile came to an end I was asked to come back to Exeter again, this time to play Hortense, the singing maid, in *The Boy Friend*. Now this was really my kind of part and I couldn't have been happier.

Also in the cast was Lally Percy, my friend from Worcester Rep days, and we had great fun in our 1920s' make-up and frocks. Though I was only in the crowd dances, I was very thrilled to be back singing and dancing, and threw myself into performing my solo 'It's So Much Nicer in Nice' with almost indecent abandon.

Despite all my best efforts, when the show was over it really was back to unemployment. Rather than joining the dole queue, I signed up to be a waitress at the Shakespeare Tavern, a kind of Elizabethan-theme restaurant near London Bridge, where the servers wore ye-olde costumes and sang ye-olde songs while doling out dreadful-looking 'authentic' ye olde food from milk-maid-style buckets worn across our shoulders on wooden yokes. Guests paid a lump sum for the event, which included experiencing the 'genuine replica of an Elizabethan banquet'. They could have all the food and drink they could cram into their greedy mouths. Frequently the visitors ate so much they were sick all over the table and if it ever happened at one of mine, I would always find some frightfully important work in another far-flung corner of the room!

One of my fellow wenches was the fabulous Anita Dobson, later to achieve fame as Angie on *EastEnders* and to marry Queen guitarist, Brian May. Together we wailed out choruses of 'Sweet Lass of Richmond Hill' and 'Greensleeves', and were told off by the management for adding 'unnecessary' harmonies, descants and trills.

The pay at the Shakespeare Tavern was abysmal, really no more than a pittance for turning up, because we were expected to earn our money through tips. Trouble was, the kind of people who had forked out to attend an event as grim as this tended not to tip at all. After all, it was advertised as an evening at an 'all-in' price, and naturally they took that definition quite literally. It was Anita who advised me to pull down the front of the frilly blouse an extra inch and thus double our evening's wage. On a very good night we might go home with £6, other times we slaved all evening and barely made up our tube fare home.

During the day I worked as a nanny to Frances de la Tour's two children, while she was out filming *Rising Damp* and her husband, Tom Kempinski, was up the end of the garden in a shed writing *Duet For One*.

It was an incredibly dispiriting time, with no acting work, scratching a living any way I could, and it seemed to last forever. I got a few one-day parts on TV, in series like *Shoestring* and *To The Manor Born*, playing a supermarket check-out girl who says chirpily, 'Mornin' Mrs fforbes-'Amilton!' as she whips the lavatory roll from the conveyor belt, inquiring loudly the price, from a nearby till, much to the embarrassment of Mrs F-H (Penelope Keith).

At the time I rented a room in a house in Clapham, sharing with Fidelis, the playwright, Stewart Permutt, and two or three ever-changing others who came and went as work decreed. Pat Doyle, now a famous composer of music for films like *Sense and Sensibility*, *Wah-Wah*, *Calendar Girls*, *Harry Potter* and *Gosford Park*, stayed briefly with his wife, and woke us all in the middle of the night to tell us that there was a UFO circling the house, though it must be said that only he saw it.

We joined the Starlight Club, a wonderful camp cinema in the bowels of the Mayfair Hotel, where they'd play magical double bills like *The Women* and *Stage Door*. During the interval you would sit in your pale blue plush seat while being served delicious finger sandwiches from a silver platter. Now to me that really is what going to the cinema should be like, not rolling up at these horrid soulless multiplexes, where you suffocate from the stench of 2000 people cramming buckets of popcorn into their drooling gobs while they swill it all down with three gallons of Coke.

One September, while Fidelis was away working on a long contract at Glasgow Citizens' Theatre, Stewart and I decided to throw a dinner party to celebrate his birthday. He happens to share the date with my dear pal Sian Thomas and theatre administrator, Mavis Seaman, so they too were invited, along with a few other of Stewart's friends.

We proudly cooked everything ourselves. The menu started with avocado. Sadly we bought them that morning and by the time we came to serve them they were still rock hard. We followed this with a vegetable stew. To tell the truth we took so long sculpting our way through the brick-like avocados, with images in our minds of Michelangelo hacking through travertine marble, that when we eventually got back to the kitchen the carrots, potatoes, leeks and celery had all merged into one beige slop. The final coup was a simple dish of home-grown blackcurrants with cream.

After the event we phoned Glasgow to describe the evening.

'Blackcurrants?' asked Fidelis, with a quiver in her voice.

'Yes. From the garden.'

'Blackcurrants are finished now,' said Fidelis, oddly quiet. 'They fruited in July, remember. We ate them all.'

'No,' I said. 'There were plenty left.'

An ominous pause followed. 'And where *exactly* in the garden did you pick these blackcurrants?'

'They were all over the place,' said Stewart. 'Under bushes, near the roses.'

'How tall were the plants upon which you found the berries?'

'Oh,' said Stewart and I, miming it out to each other. 'About six inches . . .'

'Thank God I'm in Glasgow,' said Fidelis. 'You've just served your guests deadly nightshade.'

As it happens no one was even sick. I suppose we were lucky in having drenched the little black berries with cream. Come to think of it, they were rather bitter, and not very tasty at all.

But neither, it seems, was anything that evening. For a friend of Stewart told someone who told someone who naturally told me, 'You know Celia, do you? She's quite good fun, but, whatever you do, never ever accept an invitation to dinner. She is the most ghastly cook.'

During my out-of-work spells, I was bored so started lots of evening classes. I think I managed only one night doing pottery because the teacher kept telling me off for talking. At psychology of criminology I lasted much longer, and I could still tell you a thing or two about Kretschmer and Somatotyping. I was a real whiz at Tae Kwon-Do, which is a bit like ballet with aggression, and galloped through the belts and tags. I can even boast a Level 2 certificate in driving a powerboat.

I had been inspired to do sculpture by seeing the work of Bernini in Rome, but had failed to enrol in time. However it turned out that life drawing, which was the nearest thing I could find, was utterly exhilarating. The teacher sat a naked person in front of us and then set a timer. We had two minutes, three minutes, five minutes, one minute – and in the allotted time had to flesh out the whole body in black charcoal on grey sugar paper. It was great drawing at such speed. My portfolio grew thick.

I showed my work to Fidelis's mother, an artist who had trained at Liverpool Art School and, when she wasn't painting herself, taught painting at Salisbury Art School. She oohed and aahed. She held them out, squinted her eyes: all those things you see people do in art galleries.

'Keep going,' she said. 'You have a keen eye and a great sense of line.'

I was thrilled. I took the portfolio to my own mother, hoping for the same effect.

I told her to shut her eyes and laid a few of my best efforts out on the floor for her to see.

'Open up,' I said, beaming.

She looked down.

'Ooogh! Bledther, bledther, bledther,' she said, shutting her eyes and making that childhood noise of disgust. 'No thank you. Bledther, bledther, bledther . . . Take them away.' This was the last time I consulted her on my artistic efforts.

Next I took up upholstery. At an auction I managed to find the shell of an old Victorian walnut parlour chair, which I then upholstered in a regency satin stripe – robin's-egg blue and cream. It took weeks. I did the webbing, the strapping, the stuffing, cut the fabric to size, tacked it into place, and glued down the silk braid to cover the rough edge.

To this day, no one has, to my knowledge, ever sat on this chair. I am far too proud to let anyone's bottom descend upon it. All these years later, it still stands in my bedroom where I can gaze lovingly upon it during moments of self-doubt and think, well, if nothing else, *I upholstered that chair.*

Finally the call came from my agent, telling me I had landed my first leading part on TV. I was to go Port Isaac in Cornwall, which was pretending to be Scotland, where James Warwick (Tommy from Agatha Christie's *Partners in Crime*) and I were to chase around the heather in a new sci-fi thriller called *The Nightmare Man*. Both the director and writer were ex-*Doctor Who* creatives and the show gathered quite a cult following. I was also able to pay reverence to my doctor father by using what I remembered of his accent, and playing a pharmacist (wearing a white coat, anyway).

CHAPTER 9

Coincidentally the Scottish theme continued for some time.

Soon after filming on *The Nightmare Man* ended, I went to work for the first time at the world-renowned Glasgow Citizens' Theatre in the Gorbals, just up the street from where my paternal forebears had lived 70 years earlier.

The Citz at that time was famous for a tight ensemble of rather exciting actors, performing classic plays to an incredibly high standard, with sensational costumes and ravishing sets and all done on a very low budget. The theatre itself stood in the middle of an acre of nothing, empty waste land, where once ancient tenements had stood, behind it more scrubland dissected by an elevated railway, with trains rattling along carrying heaving wagons of industrial goods along a narrow viaduct. The arches beneath were filled with garages and seedy bars where if you were lucky you might catch a cabaret act like 'The Hillhead Hillbillies – Western music with a tartan flair', 'Pauline and her Performing Poodles', 'Snakey-Sue – she can charm you!' and 'Moira – the midget with the mammoth voice'. Well, it was the 1970s, when you were still allowed to call a spade a shovel.

The dark brooding streets were littered with broken glass and flying pieces of torn paper. Piles of rubble were usually interspersed with several smouldering bonfires. Tramps slept in corners, Alsatian dogs roamed in packs and there were many rats, alive and dead.

But step inside the theatre and you entered another world. It was a palace of red, black and gold, with gorgeous nineteenth-century stone statues, glittering chandeliers, gilt caryatids and pink elephants. The scarlet walls were hung with huge black-and-white photos of Citz's productions. Everyone front of house (except Sheena, the ancient and formidable Queen of the Bookstall) always smiled. Sheena always looked like a furious bulldog. You daren't ask her if she'd enjoyed the show for she would inevitably answer, 'No. I hated it!' The actors seemed to radiate a kind of wild glamour and the company driver, Big D, a huge bear of a man who bore a striking resemblance to Desperate Dan, frequently appeared in plays as a peasant or lackey. Everything about the place seemed larger than life.

The company was run in a different way to other theatres of the time. The actors were all paid the same, and the shows' programmes listed in alphabetical order every person who worked in the building, from the night-cleaners to the directors. I am very sad that the Citz, as we knew it, is now no more. It was a fabulous, if mad, place to work.

Every seat in the house cost 50p, at the time the going rate for a local cinema ticket. So we ended up playing nightly to packed houses made up from all strata of society. If you looked down into the stall seats you might see an intellectual sitting next to a young hairy biker, along from a lady pensioner, beside a punk. If you were too slow or boring the audience slow-clapped you. If they were uninterested or affronted by you they walked out. Sometimes people heckled, on really bad days they booed.

There truly was nowhere else like it and it was utterly exhilarating.

The Citizens' was the only theatre in the country to hold open auditions, advertised in *The Stage* newspaper, so everyone had an equal chance to go for two minutes before the scrutiny of the three directors: Robert David MacDonald, Philip Prowse and Giles Havergal. I had tried five times to join the company. Year after year, I waited in line at the open auditions. I sat on pavements outside West End theatres from before dawn to be sure I would get a chance; I stood for hours in the wind-tunnels surrounding the Roundhouse, to make certain of having my two-minute opportunity. And during those magical two minutes, between literally hundreds of others doing the same, I prayed I could somehow win the attention of the three directors.

God knows what it was that finally caught their eye, as the first role I was offered was as a belligerent young girl in Goldoni's eighteenth-century Venetian farce, *The Good Humoured Ladies*. The cast included David Hayman (now of *Trial & Retribution*), Jonathan Hyde, Sian Thomas, Rupert Farley and Celia Foxe – of whom more anon.

I followed this up by playing Clara Eynsford-Hill in Shaw's *Pygmalion*, with Tim McInnerny (Percy in *Blackadder*) as my brother, Freddie, and my younger friend Fidelis playing my mother! The late Robert David MacDonald was brilliant playing Professor Higgins, and Johanna Kirby was that rare thing – a totally convincing Eliza Doolittle, both as cockney rough and posh lady.

Fidelis and I were slight outsiders in the company because once *Pygmalion* opened everyone else in the show spent their days rehearsing *The Maid's Tragedy*, a bleak Jacobean play. Our sense of being left out was compounded when one day a member of *The Maid's Tragedy* cast went berserk and held up all the other actors in the corner of the rehearsal room, while swinging a prop sword and reciting the Lord's Prayer at the top of his voice. He called on Allah and God the Father to bring retribution on Satan, or, as we all knew him, Giles Havergal, one of the three directors of the Citizens' Company.

Naturally, Philip Prowse, the third director, who was actually taking that rehearsal, had sidled out of the room the moment it was clear genuine danger was looming. It was he who had raised the alarm. When Giles heard the news, he emerged from the front-of-house office, pale as a ghost, his ears waggling up and down, and went promptly up to the rehearsal room and offered himself up in exchange for the release of all the actors.

The ambulance men arrived but refused to enter the rehearsal room without backup, so the police came too, and after an almighty scuffle the poor boy was taken in and sectioned. Though he had spent weeks telling everyone he was from Persia, it turned out his parents were a quiet couple from Brighton, and, to compound the mad conundrum, two girls who both believed they were engaged to him came up to Glasgow and met each other for the first time over his hospital bed.

Of course there was no other subject of conversation in the backstage canteen for days. Some of the former hostages were sympathetic to the hospitalised actor, others furious that their lives had been put in danger or rehearsals had been interrupted. But we had absolutely nothing to contribute to the general discussion, as, in the canteen or the corridors, we'd barely even passed the sword swinging fellow.

So instead, Fidelis and I drove off into the country to see the regional sights. One day we passed a nice hotel by a loch which advertised a lovely-looking Sunday evening buffet and we resolved to go there the following Sunday for tea and supper then stay over (so that we could drink and not drive) before returning to Glasgow early Monday morning.

Very excited, we arrived just after lunch, informed the hotel's concierge that we were vegetarians and checked into our rooms, then went down to the lounge for tea. The place was jammed with braying Young Conservatives, so we fought our way towards the log fire, hoping to sit there and have tea and scones. It was useless. I decided to go out around the loch for a walk, but Fidelis preferred to stay in the warm, to brave the cacophony of chinless wonders, and perched in a corner by the fire to read.

By the time I returned from my misty evening stroll, darkness was falling and we went eagerly to the dining room, only to see a sign: 'Buffet Supper Tonight Cancelled: Reserved for Young Conservatives only. Other hotel guests please go to rear dining room for à la carte menu.'

We discovered it was too late to check out. If we did we would be charged for the all-in supper and room price anyhow. So, really depressed, we made our way to a dreary dank dining room, with loudly ticking grandfather clock, and were served from a dire set menu which included lukewarm green pea soup which came complete with lumps of dried green-pea-soup powder and stale rolls with little plastic packets of margarine.

Knowing we had lost the money for the room, we were tempted to leave anyhow and head back to Glasgow for a decent curry and our own digs. But by this time a heavy fog had descended and to drive through winding, mountainous country roads would have been hazardous in the extreme.

We picked at the revolting food, sat by the dwindling fire for a while with glasses of whisky to excise the taste of the horrible dinner, and then in the darkness just before dawn we checked out and returned to Glasgow, feeling really cheated.

That evening when we arrived at the theatre, we were told to go straight to see Giles in the director's office. I suppose we must have thought we were due to be asked back to be in another play, or that two actors had fallen sick and would we take over their parts tonight, something like that. What we were not expecting was an arrest warrant!

Giles came and spoke to us in the corridor, saying, 'Tell me EXACTLY what happened at the Marie Stuart Hotel'. We explained that we had not been to the Marie Stuart Hotel but another hotel nearby, and started to rant on about the Young Conservatives, the buffet and the vile dinner.

'No, I'm not interested in that,' he said. 'Tell me about the robbery.'

'Robbery?' we said in unison.

'Late last night, you left your hotel in the early hours, went up the road to the Marie Stuart Hotel, smashed a window, then entered the hotel and hit a chambermaid over the head with a candlestick.'

We laughed. But Giles stood glowering over us.

'You were identified,' he said. 'There is a police officer in that room.' He pointed towards his office door. 'He is waiting to arrest you. I just thought I had better hear your version of the events first.'

'How were we identified?' I asked.

'The staff at the Marie Stuart Hotel remembered you both coming in for a drink at tea-time, to case the joint.'

'Case the joint?' we both repeated.

'They knew it was certainly you two, after the staff at the Marie Stuart Hotel told the concierge at your hotel,' said Giles. 'Two women with rucksacks . . .'

Fidelis let out an indignant scoff. 'Never in my life have I so much as laid my finger upon a rucksack.'

'Two women went to the bar at the Marie Stuart Hotel,' Giles continued in a sombre tone. 'They knew it was you because you ordered orange juice.'

'Orange juice?' we chorused.

'You ordered orange juice because you are vegetarians. The concierge told them.'

We both stood there goggling at him in disbelief, waiting for him to say 'April Fools', although it was November.

'I am a vegetarian, nonetheless, as anyone who knows me can tell you, when I go into a bar I generally ask for a whisky,' said Fidelis. 'I wouldn't spoil my palate or waste my money on a pub orange juice, thank you, Giles.'

'Well, I did walk past the Marie Stuart in the afternoon,' I said meekly. 'But I didn't go inside.'

'And I never left the lounge of our ghastly hotel,' said Fidelis. 'As a room crammed full of five hundred of whatever is the Scottish for braying Hooray Henrys will bear witness.'

'Did you commit this robbery?' demanded Giles with all the vigour of Perry Mason.

'No!' we shouted.

'Well!' Giles gave a shrug. 'If this is how you both want to play it . . .'

He opened the door into the room where a huge policeman stood waiting. Giles led us in and said: 'Here they are.'

We stepped forward into the room. The policeman glared at us. He looked into our faces, then down at our feet, then back up to our faces. We both stood like statues. My mind was racing. I suppose everything really did fit the picture, being disgruntled about the dinner, leaving the hotel in the darkness of early morning. How could we prove we were innocent?

Then the policeman asked us to lift up our feet and present our soles. We obliged. The policeman threw his head back and roared with laughter.

'I knew those old biddies were mad,' he said. 'I have a shoeprint. The perpetrator had huge feet. I'm pretty certain it was a local youth well known to us. But all those old girls in both the hotels were adamant that you two were totally suspicious characters, shady, dodgy and odd. And you were utterly damned by being vegetarian.'

For a few weeks in the spring of 1980, I played a stripper in *Seduced* at The Royal Court Upstairs. It was there that I made another great and lasting friend in Larry Lamb. For my role I was taught the art of how to remove clothing by a hilarious real-life stripper called Ziggy Stardust. Stripping was quite a daring thing for me to try, but the time had come to have a bash and Ziggy helped me wonderfully. In the end I just pretended to be her and copied everything about her, from the way she smiled, through the tones of her marvellous husky voice, to the roll of her gait. It was the best and only way to make sense of the part. For the opening night, she gave me a gorgeous embroidered jacket which became a kind of talisman, and I still wear it on every first night.

As it was my first London production, I knew I simply had to make the most of my appearance in the show. So I wrote letters to practically everyone in *Contacts*. Few replied. But one letter did come.

'I rarely go out in the evening as that is when I make my transatlantic phone calls, but please phone my assistant to make an appointment to meet me.' It was signed Michael Winner.

So I phoned, and he invited me out to his spectacular house in Kensington and I found him highly amusing and very good company. He invited me to screenings in his private cinema and took me for spins in his pink Rolls Royce. When I was away he would send me newspaper cuttings which had amused him. The headlines included, 'Man changes sex to keep lesbian wife who fled with nanny' and 'Wife cuts off de-facto husband's penis and throws it from moving car.' You know the kind of thing.

As winter drew in, I was called back to the Citizens' to play the Good Fairy in *Puss in Boots*. Not only did the Citz have the low price policy where seat prices were by now 75p, but to top that, the previews were absolutely totally free to allcomers.

When the curtain went up for the first free preview I will never forget the roar from the poorest Gorbals children who packed the theatre. Then the cheer they let out at the curtain call quite undid me and I burst into tears, blubbing like a wain while trying to bark out my rhyming couplets of joy.

Every time I had an entrance I popped out of a smoke bomb in my sparkly pink frock, tossing up handfuls of glitter. For four weeks, everywhere I went I left a trail of pink glitter. No matter how assiduously I bathed or shook out my clothes, the glitter seemed to keep coming. It followed me round shops and onto buses, into people's homes, and along the street. If I had wanted to, I wouldn't have been able to hide because anyone could have known where I was simply by following the sparkling track. I was invited to stay by some of my father's relations, the only ones I'd ever met, in their posh house in Bearsden. Every time I left the room they had to bring the hoover out to remove my sparkling pink residue. I felt terrible.

Incidentally the Broker's Man in *Puss in Boots* was played by the hilarious Pat Doyle, and Alex Norton, DCI Burke in *Taggart,* dragged up to play the dame, while the eminent music historian, Derek Watson, a published authority on Liszt, Bruckner and Wagner, was the musical director. Thanks to pantoland, to this day he is still always referred to as Uncle Derek. Glasgow audiences were like no other. They cheered hard, but they also pelted us with boiled sweets when they were bored, during love duets particularly.

We performed a Christmas Day performance and three shows on Boxing Day. It was hard work, but it was heaven.

My digs at that time was a room in the flat of Clare Crawford, a lady in publishing. It was a lovely flat in a very respectable area. In Glasgow there are places called closes and most buildings have them. A close is essentially the stone stairwell leading up to the flats. There is no gate and a close is open to everyone at all times as it is considered part of the street, and is served by street lighting. One night, when Clare was away, after the show, I returned home at around midnight, leaving the usual glitter track behind me. Suddenly a man appeared on the landing above me, and, passing on his way down, asked me for the time. I pulled up my sleeve, looked at my watch and told him. Next thing I knew he had slammed me up against the door and was holding a knife to my back. I was fumbling away, trying desperately to get the key into the lock, pointlessly ringing the bell at the same time. It's funny how at these times the simplest things seem so hard. Time appears to bend and seconds last for hours. In the terror and panic I had somehow forgotten to shout.

Then I remembered and at the top of my voice let out a wild holler, enough to waken anyone. The man fled. I got myself inside, locked up behind me and shaking, phoned the police. They didn't seem all that interested. 'An actress?' It was as though my profession made it somehow understandable that I had been attacked, as though actresses somehow asked for it.

Because of appearing in the panto, I was in Glasgow for Hogmanay. Having heard all about the famous Scots festival, and being particularly superstitious about seeing in the New Year, I was very excited to have a go at doing it the 'real' way. How many years had we all gathered round the TV at home and watched Jimmy Shand and Andy Stewart raising whisky glasses and dancing jigs to accordion bands, while announcers informed us Sassenachs that Scotland was the home of the biggest and greatest tradition of New Year celebrations? And now here I was right at the heart of it all, to experience that unique excitement for myself.

When my last show of the day was over, I linked up with Jane Bertish, Jim Hooper and Fidelis Morgan who were rehearsing Brecht's *Fears and Miseries of the Third Reich*, the show which opened after the panto, and together we went to Gibson Street for a curry. There were no other diners in the usually bustling restaurant.

The waiters hovered ominously, snatching our plates away with unseemly haste. At about 10pm, the lights were turned off and we were none too subtly given the bum's rush. Feeling pretty unimpressed by the Scots hospitality we set off into town to join the merry throng of revellers.

The West End streets seemed strangely quiet and the bus was almost empty. We got off in the town centre and found an off-licence where we bought some champagne to pop at midnight. As we strolled along St Vincent Street, we listened. Glasgow had never seemed quieter. What was going on?

We turned into George Square. No one was there. Well, not quite no one. There was a huddle of six people a little further along. We approached them, hoping that perhaps they knew what was happening, and could tell us where the famous Hogmanay celebrations had been hidden. The only trouble was, the huddle consisted of the same waiters who had only just chucked us out of their Gibson Street restaurant.

At ten minutes to midnight, we knew that nothing at all was going to happen. We strolled through the deserted city down to the river. Gripping our plastic cups and bottle, we stood on a bridge and popped the bottle at midnight. Magic did happen when, on the dot of midnight, all the Clyde ships sounded their whistles.

Knowing we had seen the best of what was going on, we hailed a taxi to the first of the three parties we'd been invited to. The invitations all read 'after midnight'. We noticed that the streets were now buzzing again. How bizarre! Where had all those people come from?

When we arrived, we told our host about our weird experience and how the streets of Glasgow had looked as one might imagine it after an attack by neutron bomb. He told us that the Scots' Hogmanay tradition was not what foreigners believed it to be, but was similar to the English Christmas Eve. People gathered quietly with their families (or as our host put it – 'oor ain folk') for a formal meal and then, as the midnight bells rang, toasted one another with whisky. Once midnight was rung then all hell broke out. For only then were visitors welcome. Once the New Year arrived, it was customary to wander from house to house, bringing drinks, presents and pieces of coal. The parties often lasted into the dawn, but they only started at the 12 bells.

This was 1980. Since then, the local Scottish tourist boards, sensitive to the incoming crowds of people like us – foreigners who know no better – have organised enormous firework displays and concerts and the fantasy Hogmanay has become true. But it's worth knowing that what is now announced as the 'traditional Scottish Hogmanay celebration' is in fact a more recent invention than the personal computer.

★

After New Year, I was lucky enough to be asked to stay on and play the part of Françoise in the Philip Prowse/Robert David MacDonald adaptation of Marcel Proust's *À la recherche du temps perdu*, wittily entitled *A Waste of Time*.

One of the extras in the show was a lanky boy who had just been expelled from the Central School of Speech and Drama. He camped about and wore so much stage make-up he looked less like a nineteenth-century Parisian man-about-town than someone attending Carol Channing night at the Vauxhall Tavern. It was his first job. Despite not having a single line in the whole script, which was thicker than a phone book, he managed to infuriate half the cast and lure crowds of paparazzi to swarm outside the stage door chasing up excited rumours of an affair with Bianca Jagger. His name is Rupert Everett.

The company was packed with wonderful actors. The late and sadly missed Stephen Dartnell played Proust so movingly, with stylish support from Robert David MacDonald, Giles Havergal, Sian Thomas, Fidelis Morgan, Di Trevis, Jane Bertish, Patrick Hannaway, Robin Hooper, Andrew Wilde, Jill Spurrier, Angela Chadfield and Rupert Farley. (As it happens, Alan Rickman was also meant to be in it, but walked after the read-through, having decided his role as Charlus wasn't big enough. I think he later regretted having missed out on being part of that era-defining show, though we did spend a few evenings out together eating pakoras in Sauchiehall Street.)

After the first run-through, Robert David MacDonald came to us one-by-one and calmly resting his hand on each of our arms in turn, cast our characters, basing them on people in his own life.

My role, Françoise, was Proust's Nanny/nurse-maid. 'And you, Celia, are my mother.' I remember the weight of his hand and I remember the weight of that honour and responsibility.

One of my scenes involved herding a gang of chickens across the stage, then catching one of them, which was obviously doomed to be dinner. Philip had made the decision to use real chickens, having been reliably informed that they would be very obedient. Naturally during rehearsals we did the scene with imaginary chickens and it went awfully well.

On the day of the technical rehearsal, real poultry was delivered to the stage door and when the moment arrived, the stage management unpacked them and let them out onto the stage for the scene.

Well, to say I didn't control them would be an understatement. I ran, they leaped in the air, cackling. I tried to round them up, they dispersed with what seemed to be military efficiency.

'Let's go back,' drawled Philip from his seat in the stalls.

The stage management gathered them and put them back into the wings and the scene was reset. Next time it was worse. One chicken waddled down to the footlights and glared into the auditorium. I caught it, while the other chickens performed poultry polkas behind me.

'Stop!' Philip stood up. 'Celia, dear, the idea is you have to round them up and catch one. It's not difficult.' That was easy for him to say.

'I just need a few goes,' I said, shielding my eyes from the lights, trying to see him in the darkness. 'I know I can do it, I just need . . .'

'Reset!'

We went again. The chickens seemed to calm down, and I felt wonderfully confident.

The cue arrived. The chickens ran on. I pursued. Once I got near them, they made a mad dash and darted about all over the place, while I staggered after them, then, united, did an about-turn and returned to the wings from whence they had come. The final catastrophe came, when all four birds, as if to show me who was boss, decided to stroll on nonchalantly, then as soon as I set foot on stage behind them each dashed for refuge in their seemingly pre-discussed new hiding place. Unfortunately this hidey hole was beneath the heavily petticoated silk dresses of the quartet of octogenarian duchesses (including Queen Sheena of the front of house bookshop) playing cards up stage left. Panda-bloody-monium.

Cards, brandies, lorgnettes, fans, fowls, feathers, sticks, gloves and garters flew up into the air all at once.

'STOP!' screeched Philip. 'Celia, you've had your fun. Now it's cut.'

Even without my chickens, the show ran for almost four hours. On the first night, the curtain went up on a full house of almost 2000 people, and we took our final bows to about 15 of them. But word-of-mouth from those few must have spread, because for the rest of the run there were queues round the block and the show was successful enough to be revived the following year and taken on a tour of Europe (by which time Rupert had been promoted to a decent speaking part). By then, I was elsewhere.

Once Proust rehearsals began, I moved out of the room I had rented in Clare's flat, as Sian Thomas had already reserved it. Searching for digs is a nightmare. It's the shortness of the tenancy combined with the rogues and vagabonds reputation of the acting profession that makes finding decent places to stay both scarce and very, very expensive. Try it tomorrow. Phone and ask an estate agent if there's a furnished flat for one person available for six or eight weeks, without a huge deposit. It's still the same. Add that you are an actress temporarily up to work at the local rep and listen to the laughter.

The only room I could get was on the fifth and top floor of a tenement in Park Road. The ground floor housed a seedy Indian take-away restaurant and the close provided a walk-up for various prostitutes' working flats. My flat consisted of two attic rooms (a bleak, dark bedroom and a kitchenette) and a loo. The plumbing was minimal: no bath, no shower, just the kitchen sink, which only had one tap, and a cold one at that. There was no heating, except a small electric bar heater which I bought myself. I used the theatre to wash and shower. There was nothing to cook on but a single electric plate. When the temperatures dipped, as they did wickedly that winter, the solo tap completely froze and there was no water to be had at all. Digs are always pretty dreadful, but this place really took the Highland Shortie.

During the nastiest cold spell we all turned up at the stage door every day with white frosty eyebrows (and, for the men, white beards too). While sprinting from the car-park to the stage door, even the snot froze in our noses. Temperatures were rumoured to be minus 23 degrees. It was perishing.

One night I was fast asleep in my chilly bed when there was a tremendous thundering on the door. I couldn't imagine what was going on. It must have been around 4am. I didn't open the door because I was frightened that it was in some way related to the prostitution business thriving elsewhere in the building, or maybe thugs or pimps demanding their money back from a previous tenant. I needn't have worried about opening up though, for, next thing I knew, the door had been kicked in and four policemen stood over my bed.

'Miss Celia Imrie?' said one. 'Get some clothes on and come with us.'

Oddly enough the first thing I thought was that something terrible had happened to my mother. I was bundled off to the Maryhill police station (no sight of Taggart), and put into a dirty grey room where an officer told me he needed to ask some questions about the man who had held a knife to me in the close outside Clare's flat a few weeks beforehand, during the pantomime.

It was a strange way of getting statements, but it *was* the 1980s, and a species of Gene Hunts obviously also existed north of the border. Clearly the occupation of the other inhabitants in the tenement where I rented my grim rooms dictated the alarmist attitude and lack of respect shown to me by the police.

Back in London during the summer of 1980, Celia Foxe, who one day I discovered was also called Ceal for short by her friends, and I got together. We brought in Fidelis and Stewart and put on a revue. We called it *Performing Ceals*.

Stewart and Fidelis wrote together under the pseudonym Sadie Shanklin. Celia Foxe and I played all the parts, including dirty old men and babies. I particularly enjoyed a confessional monologue about being fat ('I first discovered I was fat when I was about 15. Up till then I thought it was just a phase I was going through . . .'), and a gruesome but hilarious song in the style of 'D-I-V-O-R-C-E', in which I dressed up like Dolly Parton, in a white rhinestone jumpsuit and huge peroxide wig. The four of us made the set and costumes ourselves, we also did all the publicity and rehearsed in the front room of the house in Clapham.

The show played to packed houses at its first venue La Bonne Crêpe, a theatre café in Maddox Street, but the critic from *The Stage*

Primrose Day, 1947. Mums and Dads' wedding with Brownies and piper in attendance

With Mums and baby Kit

Petunia (Juliet, left) and Daisy (me) reaching up for the stars with knickers falling down

'Tuesday's child is full of grace'. The statuette of a little ballerina given to Mums when I was born, and which became my inspiration

In the drawing room at Crubie in about 1966. Standing: Juliet (Jukes) and Andrew (Anchor). Sitting, from left: Rosalind (Rosa), Katherine (Kit), Judy (the dog), Nanny (Pop) and a skinny me

Dancing to Mussorgsky's *A Night on a Bare Mountain* in the choreography competition, 1968. I came third

First *Spotlight* entry: Understudy to Beauty?

A modern day Madonna and Child. The controversial Shelter poster, photographed by Donald Silverstein in 1971

'Now then, let me tell you a story . . .' 'Miss Keen' with children at Theatre in Education, Edinburgh, 1972

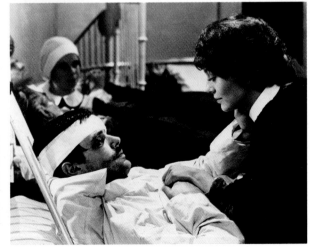

In the background. With Simon Williams and Lesley Anne Down in the original *Upstairs Downstairs*, 1974

Me and my pals hit The Pitts. Stewart Permutt (left), and Fidelis Morgan

Jaws, the one and only original, also known as Bruce

Sightseeing on *Hedda Gabler* world tour, 1975, at Universal Studios (above), and Niagara Falls (left)

Standing, left to right: Connie Chapman, Ba Penny, Fidelis Morgan, Glenda Jackson and Peter Bromilow. In front: Pam St Clement (left) and me

War Time Ration Book Party in Selly Oak, 1976. Standing: Steve and Virginia. Sitting, from left: Sheena, Victoria Wood and me

Performing Ceals Revue, with Celia Foxe (now Celia Melia)

Tube Party, 1980. Evening dress and Disney hat, with Jo Cameron Brown

Shy Di, BBC Scotland's *31 Take 2*. New Year's Eve, 1981

Nightmare hair, nightmare coat, *Nightmare Man*, 1980

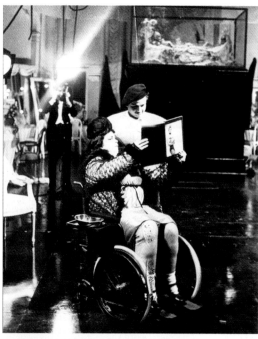

Custom of the Country, The Citizens Theatre, Glasgow, *c*.1983. Rupert Farley and me padded out in a Hollywood staging of this Jacobean tragedy

I'm the good fairy ... Oh yes I am. *Puss in Boots* panto at The Citizens Theatre, *c*. 1980

Else Queen, one of my favourite roles. In *Cloud Howe*, 1982

In heaven in 'the shop'. Mrs Overall with Miss Babs

Darling Buds of May. Mrs Perigo in the Glynis John dress

Another favourite part with two of my favourite people in *A Dark Adapted Eye*, with Helena Bonham Carter and Sophie Ward, 1994

Mr White Goes to Westminster, and I go on the back of a bus

Miss Jewsbury with her oboe, filming *Oranges Are Not the Only Fruit*, on Morecambe beach

Me and Harold P in *The Hothouse*. This Chichester Minerva Theatre production went on tour and then came to the Comedy Theatre, London, in 1995

gave it one of the worst reviews I have ever read. He claimed he would rather be hit over the head with a spiked club than sit through the show again. Nonetheless the next day there he was, sitting in the theatre bar after the show, seemingly just to taunt us. Celia Foxe and I confronted him, and some of the audience came to our defence. The nasty little man then made another rude remark, and before we knew what had happened Celia had emptied her glass of red wine over his head. In solidarity I grabbed the bottle and finished the job, while the remaining members of the audience stood behind us and cheered.

When *Performing Ceals* was revived at another venue a few weeks later we used *The Stage* quote in the centre of the flyer, and surrounded it by glowing plaudits we had received from such marvellous professionals as John Gorman (of The Scaffold and *Tiswas*), Wayne Sleep, Ingrid Pitt, Joanna Lumley, Michael Winner and Peter Bowles. It might have been unimportant in the annals of British Theatre but it remains one of my favourite jobs.

When we got bored, Stewart, Fidelis and I cooked up themed parties. We threw a *This is Your Life* party for Pam St Clement, at a time when she was one of the last people on earth who would have had such a thing in reality. Special guest star was a pair of yellow rubber gloves, for at the time Pam was very famous in Italy where she featured on huge advertising hoardings sporting a pair of Marigold gloves. We had a party too on the Clapham bandstand, where my mother, as ever, played the fiddle. She adored the violin, and actually once possessed a Stradivarius which went by her name. During the war she used her skill performing as a member of the Voluntary War-Time Entertainments, Southern Command, and I still have her framed certificate to prove it. She loved to whip out her other fiddle at parties and lead everyone in a jolly jig or two.

We threw parties on the Isle of Wight for the Cowes Week fireworks, the Garlic Festival, the Island Steam Fair and the August powerboat racing. We also created what I believe was the first party of its type on the Circle Line – a tube party. In those days people were allowed food, drink and cigarettes on the London Underground.

We had bottles of champagne, and boxes of snacks. Guests, in compulsory full evening dress, were instructed to join the party in the second to last carriage of the Circle Line train that arrived at their particular station after 8pm. And naturally, (understanding my own constant fear of being trapped) everyone was absolutely free to alight at any time. Most of the ordinary people travelling looked at our carriage full of laughter and shook their heads in disapproval, but a gang of Australians with back-packs sauntered down to us and accepted a couple of beers. 'Geez,' said one. 'You Londoners are fun. We were expecting lots of grey faces, not an Ozzie welcome like this!' When we passed through Westminster for the third time a gang of tipsy middle-aged MPs got on and teetered right down into the part of the carriage which we had commandeered. We expected trouble, but instead they held out their hands for glasses of champers, which they downed in delight, toasting our ingenuity and telling us they wished it could be like that on the tube every evening coming home from a hard day in the House. It was a great party and a delightfully cheap way of having a fantastic and slightly edgy laugh, and all the while we kept our fingers crossed that the transport police wouldn't come and cart us off. Nowadays of course they would. Boo!

Soon I found myself packing my bags for Scotland again. This time the northern reaches of Caledonia claimed me when I was cast as Else Queen, a cheeky maid who gets raped, in the TV adaptation of the Lewis Grassic Gibbon classic *Cloud Howe*. This really was a break. It was certainly the best part I had ever been offered, and was just the sort of thing I had been praying for.

On the train up I had a pre-booked seat at a table but a Chinese family of four were split up so I offered them my place. I then walked through about five coaches to find a seat for myself. After a couple of hours I was bored and went back to my suitcase to check on my script and filming schedule. I opened up the case, had a good rummage till I found the correct pages, and various pieces of correspondence that would entertain me for the remaining three hours, and then returned to my faraway seat.

A little while afterwards the train pulled in at Carlisle for what I thought was the usual two-minute stop. But the train did not pull out again. I was starting to wonder what the delay could be when I looked up to see two uniformed members of the transport police peering down at me.

'Is this the woman?' asked one of them.

I looked around. They surely couldn't mean me. Not another brush with the law? But one of the Chinese family (the ones to whom I had given up my seat) was cowering behind him. He nodded inscrutably. The policeman tapped me on the shoulder and said loudly, 'You must come with us.'

I stood up, protesting that I had a job to go to and couldn't miss this train. He yanked me forcibly by the arm and I was bundled out of the carriage, off the train and into the station manager's office.

'You were seen stealing from a suitcase,' said the transport policeman.

'I haven't touched anybody's suitcase but my own,' I said.

'You were seen, sidling into the carriage and stealing.'

'Take me to the case,' I demanded. 'I'll show you. It's my own.'

We climbed back onto the train. By this time all the other passengers onboard were squeezing their faces flat against the windows to see who or what was holding them up. Head held high, I walked the policemen to my case and opened it.

'But can you prove this case is yours?' asked one of the policemen.

I pulled out my knickers. The Chinese family were still there in the carriage, pointing at me as though I was an animal.

'These are my knickers, constable,' I said, now in a fury. 'And this is my brassière. Shall I try it on for you? That should surely solve the matter as it was made to measure, especially for me by Rigby and Peller, corsetières to Her Majesty the Queen.'

Although there was no compelling non-circumstantial evidence, after a few minutes, for some reason, they finally believed me, and let me go back to my seat. The train moved forward. For the rest of the eternal journey all the nearby passengers talked about me in a subdued hum.

We arrived in Aberdeen over an hour late.

A few years later I told famed film director, Alan Parker, the story of being taken in for questioning for stealing from my own suitcase, and he said it would make a marvellous short film. Anybody like to try?

The location base for *Cloud Howe* was in Edzell, a village just outside Aberdeen. The script was great, and kept to the classic story. And the whole show was extremely well acted and directed. The only problem was that I, along with Hugh Fraser (Captain Hastings in *Poirot*), Donald Douglas, Vivien Heilbron and the rest of the cast had to wrestle with the bizarre Aberdeen accent. In Aberdonian the word 'handbag' becomes 'hondbog', 'going' becomes 'gayun' and the phrase 'he sacked my pianist' is too rude to say aloud.

We were dedicated to getting it right and I believe our on-screen accents were all pretty good – so good in fact that no one who lived south of Pitlochry could understand a word of it. I believe in some regions, for the sake of clarity, the series was actually subtitled. My role, though, had everything I could wish for in a character: Else Queen was funny, brave, loyal and tragic. To this day it remains one of my best loved roles.

Scottish TV at this time was particularly strong. The Glasgow BBC of the day produced some excellent comedy, out of which had come Pamela Stephenson, Tracey Ullman, Emma Thompson and Richard Wilson, so when I was offered a part in the end of year comedy revue, *81 take 2*, I was very excited.

The company included newcomers Robbie Coltrane and Rik Mayall. We covered all the big events of 1981. I played the Queen doing *Desert Island Discs* picking eight versions of God Save the Queen. I also played her daughter-in-law Princess Diana getting married, making various attempts at the full name of her spouse-to-be, all done as though she was playing a dumb crambo-style parlour game. I also had a stab at Helen Mirren doing an award acceptance speech and Noele Gordon singing a teary torch song on getting the news she had been sacked from *Crossroads*.

I then returned to London for Christmas. It was only a few days after the New Year's holiday when I got news that I had made a big breakthrough and had been offered the role of John Nettles' girl-friend in the hugely popular TV series *Bergerac*.

The show was top of the TV tree, so there were banner announce-ments in the press, 'Celia's Busting Crime!'

CHAPTER 10

Bergerac had been running for ten episodes, shown on Sunday nights in the autumn and winter of 1981. It had some of the highest ratings on British TV, regularly commanding audience figures of over 15 million. My role came with the unlikely name of Marianne Bellshade and I was a high-flying financier to millionaires.

I arrived in Jersey alone on a flight from London, landing on a dank evening and I went straight to my B&B. I was excited and rather thrilled to be playing in such a prestigious TV show and staying so near the sea.

Ms Marianne Bellshade did not appear till the second episode of the second series which meant that I arrived on the set a few weeks after filming on the second series had begun. On top of that, most of the cast and crew had also been in the previous series.

The day before I was due to start work on episode two, I hired a bike and cycled out to the set for lunch. I got lost and by the time I got there naturally everyone finishing off episode one was a bit too preoccupied to greet me. The few people who weren't busy didn't have a clue who I was. So I hung around at the back, feeling embarrassed and quite out of place. It was not a good beginning. I was the lone intruder, an outsider in a settled world.

I was also having serious qualms about the script as I had to deliver lines like 'I'm just doing my green-fingered bit' when caught at my window box with a trowel in my hand. No line was necessary there, and if I really *had* to speak I would have preferred to say something plainer, like 'Hold on a sec'. The trouble with these fancy lines, which were so fashionable at the time, is that they drive the performer towards a kind of diabolical acting style, where every other phrase is spoken as though it is written in inverted commas. It is false, stagy and something I loathe to watch. I have to confess I felt very un-comfortable at being expected to do it myself.

During the next few weeks, I investigated Jersey and found some bits rather grim. Pretty scenery is all very well, but the tax-haven aspect of the place disgusted me. I hated the high walls protecting ultra-rich people who would not deign to pay British tax, while still enjoying all the privileges of British life. Bars and restaurants seemed to be crowded with loud-mouthed swaggerers, reeking of money and booze, all tight-lipped and often seeming as miserable as sin.

One week into the job it was my thirtieth birthday, which co-incided with the first TV screening of *Cloud Howe*. I got permission from my landlady to use her kitchen and baked a cake, then dropped vague invitations to the whole cast and crew. I didn't say it was my birthday but simply invited them all to come and have drinks with me in my digs.

I waited in my room. No one came.

Next morning I ate some of the cake for breakfast and fed the rest to the seagulls. My confidence was at an all-time low. I was trapped on this island, not enjoying the work and seemingly all alone, with months of it looming ahead of me. So when one of the cast, let's call him George Peters, suddenly turned to me and said, 'By the way, has anyone said to you "Welcome to Bergerac"?' I felt an overwhelming surge of relief.

George came to my room and tried to teach me how to deliver these unspeakable lines. One thing led to another and we started an affair. But, if anything, that led to the job becoming even harder.

When the series ended and we broke for the winter, I returned home to London. One day, standing in a Clapham newsagents', the Fijian proprietor turned casually and said to me, 'Oh hello, Celia, you're in the paper today.'

I was young. Naturally I bought a copy. Walking home, I read the page three headline, 'Busty Bergerac Bird Gets the Boot!' That was how I discovered I had been sacked.

That afternoon, the producer, Robert Banks Stewart, met me. He said 'Don't be upset. This could be the making of you. I know you've got lots more up your sleeve.' But at the time it seemed like the end of the world.

George tried to continue the affair but, now I was home among my friends, I realised it was all wrong. For a start George was married and he was part of an ongoing world from which I had been rejected. I avoided his calls. But this only led to him calling me over and over, the two house phones ringing all night, waking everyone else in the building, whether I was there or not.

After a few months of it, I moved out of the Clapham house because I realised I was the cause of everyone else's sleepless nights. One poor girl had come to me in tears because she was working for her finals examinations for her degree course, and she had not slept for days as George kept incessantly phoning her and asking for me.

When I told George I wanted to end the affair he would not believe me, and I didn't help matters by occasionally feeling sorry for him and agreeing to meet up. He started to contact members of my family. My mother was not at all amused.

I told George that I was really serious and that the relationship must stop, but he started following me around. I would go to the supermarket only to find a note on my windscreen. One night I went to the theatre. Shortly after the play began, George entered the auditorium and made his way to the empty seat in front of me, then, to my enormous embarrassment, sat backwards in his seat, facing me, with his back to the stage. I was mortified. I couldn't wait to get out of town.

So when the offer came, I jumped at the chance of going back up to Glasgow Citz to be part of the experimental weekly rep season. In two months we did Shakespeare's *The Merchant of Venice,* Shaw's *Arms and the Man,* Fletcher & Massinger's *The Custom of the Country,* Coward's *Sirocco,* the Marquis de Sade's *Philosophy in the Boudoir* and a new play by Robert David McDonald about the life of the Jacobean playwright, *Webster.* The company was a fabulous, tight ensemble which included Robert Gwilym, Ron Donachie, Laurance Rudic, Ciarán Hinds and many other members of the regular Citz company.

Seemingly undeterred by any memories of putting us on stage with wildlife, Philip Prowse directing, decided to use real pigeons in the Second World War set production of *The Merchant of Venice*. Someone had informed him that pigeons would be hypnotised by the glare of the stage lighting and would strut about in pigeon-like fashion, giving a very effective reality to the Venetian street scenes.

The stage management sat outside in the rubble of the Gorbals with boxes attached to pieces of string and captured as many birds as they could in time for the opening.

The technical and dress rehearsals went swimmingly. The pigeons were beautifully behaved and gave a genuine touch to the scenery.

I played Jessica, and disguised myself as a member of the Hitler Youth to escape with Brownshirt Lorenzo, played by the late great Johnny Doyle. Bassanio was an SS officer, and Portia a blonde high society Italian collaborator. Ron Donachie's Shylock was stoned to death in the shadows of a bridge after he left the (kangaroo) court. The sheer brutality of the production held back no punches, and never once went for the dubious 'charming light comedy' aspect of this strange play.

At the first preview, all seats free but nonetheless an official performance, we took our positions and the show began. Curtain up. A Venice street, water reflecting up onto spooky buildings.

Ciarán Hinds' Antonio, Bassanio and the others came on and made Shakespearean deals with Shylock in the busy street. Enter the pigeons.

While we belted out the verse, behind us, the pigeons got a bit over-excited and started a frantic mating ritual. The male birds thrust out their chests and gobbled while trotting briskly after the females, who in turn ran like hell round the pillars of the set to escape them. Their very earnestness was impossible to upstage.

Within minutes the play changed from a Venetian tragedy to a Whitehall farce. The audience grew hysterical.

And yes, the pigeons were cut that night, before we even reached the interval.

A few days later, the Citz company left on a tour of Italy, playing *The Merchant of Venice,* Goldoni's *The Impresario from Smyrna* and de Sade's *Philosophy in the Boudoir.*

We all flew out to Turin where we were hosted by the Teatro Stabile and played in a huge ex-cinema as part of the city's twinning celebrations with Glasgow. The Italians were very hospitable, although the theatre itself had its problems. A few weeks before we arrived many people had been killed in a fire in a Turin cinema. The blaze had been caused by the wall hangings going up in flames. Stringent precautionary laws were brought in. As the theatre we were playing in was a converted cinema, all the satin curtains which had lined the walls (and which had acted as sound-proof cladding) had been removed, as were the carpets, the upholstery and anything else which was judged as potentially flammable. The ceiling, floor and walls of the auditorium were now bare concrete. To compound the sound problems there was pneumatic drilling going on in buildings either side of the theatre and, in some wooden-floored rooms above the auditorium, Madame Piedmontese's infants' tap classes pounded away with rhythmic regularity. We all got onto the stage and found it very difficult to be heard.

By the end of the week when we were coached down the autostrada to Parma to take part in the fantastic Parma Theatre Festival we were quite hoarse.

During the journey I sat at the back of the coach. Some of us got very worried when loud groans and wails started coming from towards the front of the coach. It sounded like someone dying of appendicitis. Luckily it turned out only to be the actress, Jill Spurrier singing along to the peculiarly new invention – her walkman!

We arrived at our lodgings in Parma, which we had been told were in a luxurious posh Catholic boarding school. The ex-Catholics among the company had already started buzzing but we gaily ignored them, taking them for doom-mongers. But we should have realised, for they had all actually attended posh Catholic boarding schools. They knew that the word 'luxurious' never came into the equation. They also knew that the posher the school, the harsher the conditions.

We were led through airy painted halls and up a grand marble staircase. Lovely! The monks who escorted us seemed gentle and genial. What on earth could be the problem here? It was gorgeous. Then the welcoming monk ushered the 25 of us into the sleeping quarters. We stood hunched together in one huge bleak room, with white walls, gabled ceiling with beams, and a flagstone floor. It was sparsely furnished, lined on either side with 15 very basic iron single beds.

But the horror didn't end there. At the end of the room was an open washing area. It comprised a row of white sinks and four toilet cubicles all proudly facing out into the room. Not one of the lavatories had a door!

Some members of the company started shouting for the Equity deputy, others huffed and puffed while they searched high and low for the company manager who had booked the place. Naturally he had taken one look at the see-all sanitary corner, thought about the personalities in the company who were expected to use it, and bolted. Jane Bertish, usually the most sanguine of women, flung herself on one of the beds and burst into howling sobs.

It would have been marginally better if two of the directors didn't have a strong streak of the ascetic running through them. David and Giles' eyes were brightly gleaming at the prospect of sleeping in this gloomy austere dormitory. I wondered if they might not suddenly call for whips and hairshirts all round, so that we could all flagellate ourselves while we were at it.

Philip Prowse, however, was already standing outside on the pavement sunning himself, drawing deeply on a cigarette while he waited for a taxi to whisk him off to a four-star hotel.

The next two hours were grimly hilarious, as every member of the company tried desperately to find local hotels with spare rooms. It was festival time. Nearly everywhere was booked out. We all had to share, not only in twos, but threes and fours. But at least, as they say in all the best brochures, we now had use of private 'facilities'.

The Parma Theatre Festival was hosted by the magnificent Colletivo di Parma, who also performed, showing fabulous productions of *Henry IV* and *Macbeth*. Our fellow guest companies included troupes from France and Holland and the famous Peter Stein Company from Germany. We were not too happy to discover that the German actors had all been very amused by the tale of our proposed lodgings, having been put up themselves in single rooms at the luxury five-star hotel right next door to the theatre (and all paid for by the state).

But however basic our eventual accommodation, it was absolutely great working among such prestigious international theatre groups, sitting in the Italian sun and eating wonderful food while exploring such a beautiful and historic town. And, boy, let me tell you, you should taste that local cheese! The supermarket stuff isn't a patch on the parmesan which is freshly cut from huge truckles in cave-like shops in the town.

Soon after I arrived home, I auditioned for Liverpool Playhouse, to be in *Alfie*. It was Oscar-nominated film director Alan Parker's first ever stage production. Adam Faith, the 1950s' pop heart-throb, was to play the title role, and I landed the parts of the Doctor and Ruby, the roles taken in the original film by Eleanor Bron and Shelley Winters.

On the first day Alan stood before us in the rehearsal room.

'Well,' he said in his lovely cockney drawl. 'I'm used to saying "Action" to get things going.' He looked round the assembled group. 'So what do I say here, "Off you go, darlings"?'

Adam Faith was quite a short man, and I am quite tall. So when the designer put me in a blonde beehive and high heels, as Ruby, it was already on the cards that mirth would inevitably ensue.

The set was designed in true 1960s' style, and Ruby's flat was decorated with a cabinet topped with the typical naff ornaments from those times, including a 10-inch-high Spanish lady flamenco dancer, castanet-wielding arms held aloft. Beneath her frilly black-lace-layered skirt the doll had long pointy plastic legs like chopsticks.

One night as I sprawled on the sofa for the smooching scene, Adam threw himself down upon me with slightly more vigour than usual. He managed to thrust my whole body back into the cabinet. Adam/Alfie then turned towards the audience and did his little three-line, 'haven't I done well this time' monologue, then got back to the smooching with me/Ruby, after which I had to rise gracefully from the sofa and slow dance with him. We already had to fight not to get a laugh in this scene, as I towered over Adam.

But this night I staggered to my feet and got the biggest laugh of my career. The plastic Spanish dancer had toppled from her shelf onto my head, and her pointed feet had taken firm grip in my blonde beehive. She reared up with me, and, for the rest of the scene, stood at a jaunty angle on top of my head, waving her castanets with glee. I tried to shake her out but with no joy. She clung on, smiling and vaguely quivering in my nest of hair while we tried to finish the rest of the scene.

Adam and I slid about, clutching each other, facing upstage to wipe away tears, crying with laughter and quite unable to speak any of our lines. It is moments like this that make actors forever entwined in blissful memories.

Adam never knew that at the age of 10 I had written to the *TV Times* to get his signed photograph, which I then displayed on the dressing table in my bedroom beside my photo of Rudolf Nureyev.

It made it all the more shocking, when, a few years later, standing in the green room at Glasgow Citizens' Theatre I read in the paper he had died suddenly of a heart attack. He was so full of life it seemed impossible.

On the weekends during *Alfie*, I went off on 'jaunts'. Whenever I work away from home I always try to, even after the episode of the Marie Stuart Hotel. This time I drove out into North Wales, past towns with unlikely names like Mold, and the unpronounceable Gwernymynydd and discovered a small village going by the name of Loggerheads. I bought as many postcards as I could and sent them off with a one short message, 'It's my Sunday off. Am at Loggerheads with the rest of the cast.' Most of my friends in London wondered how I could possibly have fallen out with everyone.

When the Liverpool run was over, I returned to London and accepted an invitation from Stewart and Fidelis to come back to Clapham for supper and a laugh. I parked up outside a supermarket with an off-licence department (in those days many did not) to purchase the obligatory bottle of wine. When I emerged, I found my windscreen washers had been pulled off and my side mirrors smashed. I thought it must have been kids or vandals and drove on.

Stewart, Fidelis and I cooked and ate our dinner and were sitting in the back room, catching up and having a very good laugh when, just after midnight, the doorbell rang. It rang and rang. Someone seemed to have their finger stuck on the bell-push.

The someone was George. He was very drunk. Still holding the bell down, he started shouting obscenities through the letterbox. I couldn't face another row and hid in the back room while first Fidelis, then Stewart tried to persuade him to go away.

'You've got her locked in the cellar,' shouted George. 'I know Celia really wants to see me and you two are preventing her.'

I lurked in the kitchen and watched Stewart as he told George not to be absurd, go away and sober up. If I really wanted to speak to him, Stewart said, I would phone him tomorrow when he was more clear-headed. Then George shouted that, invited or not, he was coming in.

'Open up, Stewart,' he hollered. 'If you don't let me in, I will kick in this door and there will be murder and mayhem on the streets of Clapham.'

He spoke in a quivering voice that sounded as though he was playing in a Victorian melodrama.

'George, you're being ridiculous,' said a weary Stewart through the door. 'Please go away.'

'I repeat, Stewart, unless you open this door at once I will kick it in.'

Stewart sighed and said, 'All right then, go on.'

Unfortunately George did just that. First his fist crashed through the beautiful stained glass nightingale panel. On the second thrust he knocked the door right off its hinges. Then, like a raging bull, George stormed the house, punched Stewart to the floor, pulled the phone from the wall and smashed a bookcase into splinters. He galloped through into the kitchen, grabbed me by the hair and dragged me through the hall and out into the street.

Luckily, during the letter-box obscenities, long before the door was smashed in, the neighbours had called the police, so, within minutes, a posse of police cars arrived on the scene. George was bundled into one car and we were taken to the station in another to make statements. Hours later, when we were done, the interviewing officer led us along grey corridors out into the dawn. We passed a large lecture room with a porthole. Through it we saw George, sitting in the centre of a gaggle of young policemen, who listened in rapt attention while he was obviously regaling them with tales of the fun he had playing a cop on TV.

A policeman took me back to Clapham. As I climbed into my car I said to Stewart, 'I feel as if I've been hit over the head with a ten-ton truck.'

Stewart screamed with laugher as I drove off, still reeling at how horribly our festive reunion evening had gone, thanks to me. I was tired and shattered. I drove slowly, and arrived an hour or so later at my room in Fulham. But when I got to the front door, I did not stop.

Parked outside was George's car, which I had last seen outside the house in Clapham when I was carted off to the police station. I couldn't believe that the police had released him so quickly, especially as they had assured me I was safe from him for that night. I was even more shocked that George had been allowed to get into a car and drive off, when he was so clearly very, very drunk.

I turned my car about and drove back into town, then parked up behind the Tate Gallery and slept on the back seat till the gallery opened. I spent the day inside, sitting on benches, staring listlessly at paintings, hiding from the world. My coat and handbag, containing my purse and my script, were still in Clapham. After dark, when the gallery closed, I made my way south of the river to retrieve them. I only planned to spend a few minutes inside, for the following morning I was due to start rehearsing for an international tour of *The Merchant of Venice*.

But I needed to talk about the events of the previous night and of course to apologise for all the destruction and trouble I had inadvertently brought about. By the time I went to leave, armed with my things, the house was surrounded by journalists. They had apparently been there for most of the day, ever since George had made his mid-morning court appearance. At the exact moment I had arrived, they were not there. Perhaps the newshounds were taking a personnel changeover, or gone off on a tea-break, or for a pint or whatever. Maybe they had simply been sitting, waiting inside their cars, and had seen me go into the house and were now hot on the trail and ready for the chase. As I opened the front door to leave, the whole street was heaving with camera-toting paparazzi. I slammed it shut and went back into the living room. Then the phone rang.

It was Fidelis's sister telling us to turn the TV on to BBC 2. We did. Jeremy Paxman was holding up a copy of the following day's edition of *The Sun*. There was an old publicity shot of me on the cover. I was wearing some sparkling boob-tube and grinning inanely. 'Busty Bergerac Bird in Door-smash Drama', Paxman dolefully intoned. He then held up the *Daily Mail*. Another inappropriate photo of me. 'Crash!' Paxo read, 'An Inspector Calls for a Lovers' Tiff.'

By now the journalists were hammering on the door, flapping the letter box, shouting through it and generally re-enacting the events of the previous night. It was unbelievable. But *Bergerac* was the top TV show and two people connected with the show getting into a fracas was too good a story for the papers to resist.

We sat inside, not knowing what to do next. The phone rang again. This time it was one of the neighbours, Lesley Joseph, now famed for her wonderful TV character Dorien in *Birds of a Feather*. She had seen the crowd of journalists outside, and tomorrow's head-lines on TV, and offered to come round with a bottle of wine and emergency supplies. A few minutes later she arrived, and eventually got us laughing at the absurdity of the whole situation.

I couldn't think how I was going to get out of the house to go home and get a decent night's sleep before I arrived at rehearsals, which started next morning.

Then Lesley came up with a brilliant idea. I was to stay in Clapham for the night and if by 7am the journalists had not gone we would press ahead with 'Plan Lesley'. After a few drinks, Lesley went home carrying a plastic bag which contained odd pieces of quite notice-able clothing which we had all chosen while rifling through the wardrobes and boxes of stuff left over from *The Performing Ceals*.

Next morning, bright and early, Lesley pushed through the

journalists. She was wearing the costume we had constructed, a bright blue tracksuit, covered by Stewart's slightly garish paisley shirt, and high stiletto heels. On her head clung the silver-blonde wig I had worn as Dolly Parton, and perched on her nose was a pair of thick *Coronation-Street*-Deirdre-style horn-rimmed specs, which Celia Foxe had sported in a sketch in *The Performing Ceals*. Lesley was also wearing fluorescent pink lipstick and blue eye-shadow. She held up a pint of milk and a loaf.

Once inside, she hastily got out of my great escapee costume and donned her own clothes. After a few moments I emerged wearing the same lipstick and eye make-up, wig, tracksuit and shirt Lesley had worn to come in. I sashayed straight through the huddle of journalists without one of them giving me a second glance.

I arrived at the Portland Place rehearsal room to find another gaggle of pressmen waiting for me to arrive there, and again swaggered through them, unrecognised.

Once safely inside I changed back into my ordinary rehearsal clothes. I sat in a corner and read the day's papers. George had admitted to the magistrate that his actions had been indefensible. After imposing a £300 fine, the magistrate had told him, 'Your actions are not only indefensible they are disgraceful. A man your age knocking down a girl's door because you can't have your own way! Go away and behave yourself.'

I phoned my answering service at lunchtime and picked up a message from Michael Winner. 'Thank you, darling Celia. You've given me the best laugh in months.' What a way to start a new job!

Poor Stewart, I later heard, was very disappointed that in not one of the newspaper accounts had he been name-checked, and, despite gallantly defending me, having been punched in the face and knocked to the floor for his efforts, he was only ever referred to as 'a male dinner guest'.

So here, to make up for that slight, I would like to make it plain. 'The male dinner guest was brave, hilarious, talented playwright, Stewart Permutt. My friend and hero!'

CHAPTER 11

In 1984 I was playing Nerissa, assistant to Portia, in *The Merchant of Venice*. The tour, directed by Pip Broughton and organised by the Newbury Watermill Theatre, was to take in all the great cities of India: Bombay, Delhi, Madras and Calcutta. Up the Khyber Pass, then onto Pakistan: Lahore, Peshawar and Karachi, then to Kathmandu, and finally to Baghdad, Iraq. What a thrill!

I had to get all kinds of jabs and visas. For my Baghdad visa it was necessary to provide my 'father's father's' full name. Who knew? I phoned my mother to ask.

'You're going to Iran?' she inquired.

'No, Mums. Iraq.'

'Not Iran?'

'We can only go to one.'

'Why not both?'

'Iran and Iraq are at war at the moment, Mums.'

There was a long pause. Then she said, as though she had mislaid a hairpin, 'Oh damn!'

We performed some previews of *The Merchant of Venice* at Newbury, before gathering at Heathrow to leave for Bombay. Unbelievably, some journalists were waiting for me at the departure gate but they were driven off by the indomitable casting director, Marilyn Johnson.

I was overwhelmed by India, the colours, the light, the sounds, the smells. On the first day someone stole my walkman, but somehow it didn't seem to matter. Amid poverty such as I was witnessing everywhere, why not share things about a bit?

I made friends with a little street urchin who sold single cigarettes. His eyes were luminous and his bright smile could have lit a room. That night I went out onto my sixteenth-floor hotel balcony and took in the magnificent panorama. Then I looked down. Directly below me, curled up asleep on the pavement, lay the boy.

Instantly I understood that the miseries I thought I had been going through back home were just so much meaningless piffle. In India, a land of such deprivation, where some people possess *literally* nothing, you never see people wandering around feeling sorry for themselves. It is a huge lesson to us all.

The company travelled on the famous Indian railways, which were a delight. I gorged myself on the delicious snacks served from the station platforms. I was amazed when I discovered that one member of the company had refused to eat anything Indian for the entire tour and fed himself entirely on egg and chips. What a waste of an experience!

We visited the Taj Mahal, which I thought, honestly, an overwhelmingly sad place. I felt as though a dark heavy weight had been dropped on my shoulders.

I bought myself saris and swathes of beautiful fabrics, and gorgeous glittery jewellery and pens. Everything in India seemed to sparkle and fizz with life.

After the delights of India, it was all-change for Pakistan. We were all given a strict rulebook of laws to follow. No short sleeves, no singing in the street, things like that, and frankly I was not delighted. As we drove from the airport to the hotel in the company coach I gazed from the windows. The joy I had witnessed in India was nowhere to be seen.

Then the bus driver suddenly declared that if we were willing he was going to take us on a slight detour so that we could see the magnificent theatre in which we were due to play the following night.

'We have specially commissioned a great local artist to adorn the building with a portrait of your extremely beautiful leading lady,' he said. In her corner seat, the actress playing Portia quietly glowed.

'How wonderful,' she exclaimed. 'Let's go see it!'

So we did. The bus trundled along, then turned, and there, floodlit for the world to see, was the portrait, done in the usual ultra-dramatic Fauvist oranges, yellows, reds and greens of Asian cinema art. The face was about 50 feet tall and 30 feet wide. It was magnificent. A glorious close-up. The only trouble was that it wasn't a portrait of Portia at all.

It was a portrait of me! Little bit-part Nerissa!

I slid down my seat and sat in the dark, biting my lip and giggling for the rest of the journey to the hotel, imagining my back roasting from the indignant vibes I could imagine emanating from the leading lady's corner seat.

After the vegetarian culinary ecstasies of India, Pakistan came as something of a gastronomic shock. Everything was meat, meat and more meat. Even bread was soaked in meat juice. The few vegetables you could find were unrecognisable grey things from tins. You could only tell carrots from peas by the shape, and even then you couldn't quite be sure. It was vegetarian hell.

I wandered the streets with my dear friend, Jack Galloway (who played Bassanio). As a woman it was impossible to walk alone. Even in those days the place really was pretty scary. I was spat upon once, and why do you think that was? Because I was displaying my wrist! Although I had Jack at my side, men stared at me as though I was a creature let loose from the zoo. But I wasn't going to be confined to my hotel room because they thought it was a woman's place to be hidden.

And for all this prudery about female skin and the belief that we should stay at home, Jack and I discovered a street lined with skimpily clad 13-year-old girls in gilded animal cages like you might find in a circus. It was one of the most shocking sights of my life. And, the worst thing was, we knew there was absolutely nothing we could do about it.

On the first night of *The Merchant of Venice* in Karachi, President Zia came to see the show. Hours before the play started, well before the half-hour call, by which time we were obliged to be in the dressing rooms making up, the whole backstage area was crammed with huge gorilla-like men carrying machine-guns.

When we made our way to the wings we couldn't move for these terrifying bodyguards. Our cues came and it was often difficult to get through the barrier of artillery. They seemed to think that by wanting to get past them onto the stage we were being troublesome and dangerous. Sadly I didn't have the Urdu for 'Get out of the bloody way, you great big oaf'. Or on second thoughts, perhaps it was lucky I didn't.

After the curtain call, instead of dispersing back to our dressing rooms we were ordered to stay on the stage. Then the guards joined us and we were rounded up like criminals and poked into line by machine guns. It felt like a cross between *Sunday Night at the London Palladium* and execution by firing squad.

President Zia strolled placidly along the line, nodding and staring at each of us in turn, as though he was inspecting us for freshness. When he stopped before me a shiver went up my spine, and my hair stood ever so slightly on end. His black eyes terrified me. They were the same eyes as my old doctor, William Sargant.

As he vanished out of the building, along with his dreadful army of fat bodyguards, I felt extremely upset that while in India we had missed out on meeting Mrs Gandhi. She had cancelled her own visit to the show in Delhi, when she discovered we were already engaged to meet this spooky man a few weeks later.

When the company moved on to Peshawar, we were placed in a rather run-down old world Raj hotel. Nevertheless, it didn't stop me going into the fantasy of being in a black-and-white romance, pretending to be Ingrid Bergman lying under my mosquito net.

On the first morning there, I was in the shower when my breakfast arrived. I knew well that in this country it was not possible to answer the door in my towel, so I shouted politely to the waiter to come in, and please leave the tray out on my balcony. A few minutes later I heard the door click to as he left.

I came out, looking forward hugely to my breakfast. I arrived at the balcony door just in time to see a great black crow flap down from the sky, pick up my boiled egg in his beak and fly away. I ran out and stood there half-naked, shouting 'stop!' but to no avail. I lost my egg, but, thinking about it later, realised a) what an asbestos beak that thief must have had, and b) I was lucky not to have been arrested for gross immodesty on a dilapidated hotel balcony.

At our next venue, the capital city of Nepal, I bought some colourful stripy cotton trousers which were much admired later back at home. Most people asked where I got them and it was fun to be able to tell them with nonchalance, 'Oh, these old things? I bought them in Kathmandu.'

I was not sorry when we left Pakistan, more so leaving Nepal, but I have to confess that there is only one thing I remember at all about our next venue, Iraq. And that is how very disappointed I was to find that the Hanging Gardens of Babylon was just a lot of old dirt, with not a dangling plant in sight.

Before we touched down at Heathrow, it unnerved us to learn that in many of the places we had played, tragedy had struck: a fire in Madras, more bombs in Iraq, a plane crash killing President Zia and soon afterwards the assassination of Mrs Gandhi. Ten weeks before, at the start of our tour, the Indian government had been quite right in predicting trouble ahead. Apparently they had warned us and had tried to stop us boarding the plane. We never got the message.

When I got home, having travelled through such a bazaar of cultures, I felt I had changed. But one thing hadn't. George Peters was still waiting.

One night I was in Chelsea on my way to a Tae Kwon-Do class (I am an orange belt, by the way). I knocked at Arthur, my teacher's door. There was no reply. I paced up and down, waiting, when suddenly George emerged from a shady side alley and chased me along the street. We fought, and he held me up against the spiked iron railings. I screamed. A lady in a nightgown came out of her cream stuccoed house and asked if everything was all right. George let me down from the railing and beamed. 'We're fine,' he said, putting his arm around me.

When the woman had gone I threw my car keys at him and told him I needed a moment and if he went to my car I would come and join him in a few minutes. I walked calmly away, then darted round the corner, and ran furiously along the street until I reached Jane Bertish's door in nearby Ebury Street.

Jane had been in the Proust and weekly rep seasons with me at Glasgow, and lived in a house crammed with actors. Though I was welcomed in by Jane, Gary Oldman, Sean Matthias and Johanna Kirby, Jane's normally placid dog, a golden cocker spaniel, went mad at the very sight of me. He stood quivering at the top of the stairs, barring my path, growling and ferociously baring his teeth, as though I was some terrifying monster from the deep. When I took a step forward he lunged at me. It took about half an hour before I was able to get into the room. I suppose he could smell my fear.

Early the next morning I went to Liverpool Street Station and took a train to my mother's house in Suffolk. True to form, it was only a few hours before George arrived, driving my car. My mother asked me what I really wanted from the situation and I told her I had had enough. If that was what I wanted, she told me, she would deal with him once and for all. She instructed me to go upstairs and stay there. I obeyed.

'I want to see Celia,' said George, presenting her with a bunch of flowers.

'She doesn't want to see you,' my mother replied.

'But I am going to marry her,' he said.

'You are hardly in a position to do that.'

'But I'm going to get a divorce,' said George.

'Divorce or no, I tell you, Mr Peters, you are utterly unsuitable as a husband or anything else for my daughter.'

She handed back the flowers. And I do believe that at that moment George finally decided to give up on me, and look elsewhere.

For all my erratic and bad behaviour I am pleased to say we are now, years later, friends.

During all this kerfuffle I had got the call from Victoria Wood. She had a commission for a new TV series and wanted me to be part of it.

The main part of the show was made up of little sketches, many mocking things currently on TV. For instance, Duncan Preston and I played a couple of *Play School*-type actors, all primary colours and keenness.

Some of the other sketches seemed to be pretty near to my own recent life story, one verse of a song referred to me as being chased about by a married man, which made me feel a bit edgy. However, as time went by, I relaxed. Victoria, Julie Walters, Duncan Preston, Susie Blake and I formed a fantastic working bond and we threw ourselves into the whole project with carefree abandon. It was also a tremendous pleasure to be working with one of my all-time favourite actresses, Patricia Routledge.

My first sketch in the show was on location and was about an elderly working class woman (played by Connie Chapman, my old friend from the *Hedda Gabler* world tour) who came into a large amount of money playing the football pools. In my smart business suit I was to pull up outside her house in a Rolls Royce, rush across the road, knock on her door and tell her she had won the pools.

We filmed in a typical northern street, a row of identical terraced houses. As cameras rolled I leapt from my limousine and bounded across the road to the house. I knocked, and, as the door opened, I bellowed the line, 'Congratulations! You just scooped the jackpot, four million pounds.'

In front of me stood a bewildered Asian family. I had knocked on the wrong door!

The production company were left having to explain to the disappointed family that it was only a TV show and that this thick actress had made a bit of mistake, and sorry, no, they hadn't actually won the pools at all, not a penny.

Julie Walters must be the funniest woman on the planet. In the sketch where she played an elderly waitress serving us soup, and spilling most of it on the floor, Duncan and I spent the entire rehearsal time hysterical with laughter. You can clearly see that the laughter continued into the finished show. When it came to the take, neither of us dared look at one another or at Julie. We seem to perform every line, face turned down, speaking into our plates. To stop laughing I had to bite my tongue. In fact by the time the scene was over I had bitten myself so hard my mouth was full of blood.

When the *Acorn Antiques* sketch first turned up in the read-through I confess I was worried. Although we knew each other socially, the only theatre thing Vic had seen me do professionally was fall flat on my arse in the chorus in the Derby panto. Miss Babs demanded a certain kind of terrible amateurish acting. Some others in the company were refugees from *Crossroads,* the actual bad soap upon which *Acorn Antiques* was based, and I suspected we were all there because Victoria thought we were the real thing, i.e. really hopeless actors.

But *Acorn Antiques* became my favourite part of the show, and we all played it to the hilt. We understood the point of it: *Acorn Antiques* was a parody of cheap soap opera with very low production values. But the crew were bewildered. At the first camera rehearsal it was hilarious to watch the befuddled cameramen exchanging mystified looks. Why were we all so hopeless? Did we not know our lines or the blocking? Why the missed cues, the useless props, the swinging scenery? No. The crew didn't understand it at all, and were visibly appalled, fearing someone might blame them for not pointing out the obvious mistakes.

Then suddenly it clicked. After a while they were putting in their own suggestions: wobbly panning shots, bashing booms and out of focus close-ups. It was marvellous controlled anarchy.

And once the live audience was in, the sketch took off beyond anyone's wildest imaginings and soon the *Acorn Antiques* series of sketches alone achieved a cult following to rival *Star Trek* and *Doctor Who.* But, unlike the Trekkies and Doctor Who-ites, it must be added that our fan-base had probably not only never encountered an anorak in their entire lives, but probably sported a closet more akin to habitués of Shirley Bassey Night at Madame Jojo's.

I've often been asked on whom I based my portrayal of Miss Babs. Many people cite the *Prisoner Cell Block H* governor, Erica Davidson (as played by Patsy King). It is amazing to watch how similar our characters are, but in fact I didn't get to see *Prisoner Cell Block H* till after we had finished making the first series. I was riveted when it came on late one night in 1985 when I was visiting the Isle of Wight. The show was only shown locally in the TVS region and we didn't get to see it in London for a further few years.

Governor Davidson certainly had a wonderful way of opening almost every scene. She was inevitably discovered at a filing cabinet where she was either putting in or taking out a blank piece of paper. The hair is similar too. But strangely that was a simple coincidence. Miss Babs came first.

Obviously my main study was my memories of the camply marvellous Noele Gordon playing Meg Richardson in *Crossroads*.

One day when we filmed an episode of *Acorn Antiques,* the shop, for no apparent reason, was turned into a health club. Naturally, as the staff, we had to wear sporty costumes. Before the final take, Duncan and I went to Julie's dressing room and stared at her green leotard. We stood there laughing until we got over it. We had seen it. We resolved that now when we saw Julie wearing it during the filming of the sketch the sight would not throw us.

In the scene, Victoria, Duncan and I were squashed together on a two-seater sofa. Miraculously at the moment that Julie entered, wrinkled tights, lumps and bumps rippling through the viridian green, we held firm. But then momentarily one of us expressed a slight shudder of laughter. Pressed together, as we were, that shudder went through all of us, and it became unbearable. Back and forth it went, as each of us in turn tried to control their irrepressible giggling fit.

'Cut!' yelled Geoff Posner, the director.

We started again. But it was no use. The three us laughed and laughed, sparking each other off in a kind of perpetual motion of hysteria.

'Cut!'

'Action!'

Suppressed laughter.

'Cut!'

'Action!'

Hysterical laughter.

'Cut!'

'Action!'

With so many retakes, time was running out, and poor Geoff was driven to distraction. It was the only time I have ever heard a director actually yelling over the intercom. In the end he gave up on us and the sketch had to be recorded, willy-nilly, with the three of us sniggering helplessly into our chins.

It surprises most people, me included, to realise that if all the *Acorn Antiques* sketches were played end to end it would run for only about 40 minutes.

I loved playing Miss Babs (thank you Vic) and once the show was on TV, I discovered I had a whole new line of fans. Only last week I was informed that in certain circles unless you know at least two scenes of Miss Babs off by heart you cannot call yourself a real gay. To this day camp men stop me in shops and eloquently deliver one of my old cues, then wait expectantly for me to reply with my old line. It's amazing. Twenty years on they know the script better than I ever did!

My next role, strangely enough, was onstage at Hampstead, playing a nun in a closed order. The *Coronation Street* writer, Martin Allen, had written the script of *Particular Friendships* and to help my research he arranged for me to go off to spend a weekend on retreat in a convent. The Sisters of the Precious Blood welcomed me. As it was a silent order I could not speak to anyone, nor they to me. Within the convent only one hour's talking per week was permitted. So that particular Sunday the Mother Superior agreed that the nuns would talk to me for half of their allotted hour, and for the other I could tell them about my life as an actress. As a special concession I was also allowed to go for a long walk through the cornfields with a novice nun.

The sweet young novice explained to me the hardships and difficulties of being a nun, and how also you could not just accidentally stumble into the job, for it was exceedingly hard to be accepted into a convent full-time. Many were the trials you had to undertake before you could pass into full orders. She told me an example of one older novitiate who had failed the trials three times, which meant she was not permitted to have another chance. Three tries was the limit. After that, it was felt they would be unsuited to a life in the convent, but could serve more effectively by taking up a useful role in the lay community.

Having been told this, the woman had left the interview room and gone to the local corner shop where she bought a skipping rope and hanged herself. When the novice got to this point in the story I exclaimed loudly, 'Jesus Christ!' I had to spend the rest of the walk apologising for my sin of blasphemy.

The nuns must have forgiven me, though, for they carved me a small wooden cross and gave it to me as a parting gift. I still carry it.

From Hampstead Theatre Club I was lucky to get a season down at Chichester and spent a lovely summer playing opposite Edward Fox and John Wells in Christopher Hampton's *The Philanthropist*. I only had a small part and for me the real lure was a show I was to do concurrently in Chichester's studio theatre, at that time a tent in the grounds. The play was *Revelations*, a Debbie Horsfield two-hander, in which I played a roller skating queen from Eccles.

From my old nanny, Pop, I borrowed a caravan in Wittering, and enjoyed taking daily swims in the sea before rehearsals.

Unlike most theatres, Chichester always casts months in advance. They had given me the dates, and so in the interim, when I was offered a revival of *When I Was a Girl, I Used to Scream and Shout* at the Edinburgh Festival, I was disappointed to see that it clashed by one week. I knew I could not do Edinburgh as it overran into the Chichester rehearsals.

A few weeks later, having already turned down the revival, a play very dear to my heart as I had been in the original cast at the Bush Theatre, I was informed that Chichester rehearsals were to start one week later than originally planned. By now it was too late to go to Edinburgh.

On top of this I arrived to start work at Chichester only to be told that I was not going to be paid for the week they had decided not to use me. I was incensed. I turned up in the office and demanded my week's pay. But, instead of relenting, Mr Gale decided that I should be punished for my persistence and he took away my part in Debbie Horsfield's studio show.

Hearing that news, I was fit to pop. What a nerve! It was the real reason I had come to Chichester. Plus the fact that I had already slogged through days preparing for it. I had spent hours wobbling along the back streets round the theatre on roller skates, screeching as I slammed into pillar boxes and knocked over old ladies out shopping.

I refused to obey him and give up my role, and that was that. At the same time, neither did John Gale have any intention of relenting. Either I could play the part *or* I got that missing week's money.

It was a standoff as fraught as the gunfight at the OK Corral. Whenever we saw one another in the theatre we passed tight-lipped without a smile or hello.

One day with no warning, John Gale invited me to lunch. At the end of the lovely meal he passed me a small manilla envelope. I opened it to find the missing week's pay. I was relieved and thrilled.

A few days later I played the first night of Debbie Horsfield's show in the tent. I confess that my roller skating never did come up to decent standard. I was supposed to be a champion skater but I was so bad that the crew had to push me onstage. Once moving I sailed across the stage only able to come to a halt when I bumped into something. And I most certainly could not talk and skate at the same time.

How did Barbra Streisand do it?

Howchermagowcher?

CHAPTER 12

Scotland called me back again, this time in the form of the film *Highlander*. As I adore filming I couldn't have been happier, and this film had the most incredible stars. On the night of my arrival in the hotel in Fort William, I was told there was a farewell party taking place for Sean Connery, who had that day finished all his scenes. I rushed to the room and entered just as Mr Connery was leaving. We met in the doorway.

'Who are you?' he asked, his gorgeous eyes crinkling into one of those famous heart-melting smiles.

'I'm Celia,' I gushed. 'I think you're absolutely wonderful. I start filming tomorrow.'

He gave me a wink and said: 'Pity you didn't start two days ago.' Have you ever nearly fainted with simultaneous delight and disappointment? I have.

Next day found me in full rustic wench costume, complete with a long flowing red wig. I was introduced to the star, Christophe Lambert, an incredibly good-looking young Frenchman. The script stipulated that he was to lift me up onto his horse to kiss me goodbye before he goes into battle. I took one look at him and knew that this was never going to happen.

Christophe is perfectly formed, but tiny, and thin as a skinny-malink. I suggested it would be more suitable perhaps if *I* lifted *him* onto *my* horse. No one laughed.

In the final cut of the film you will see that no attempt at all is made to get me into the saddle. I simply grab his small but perfectly formed calf and run alongside him, while delivering the dialogue which I should have been doing as we galloped along together.

Ah well. As gorgeous Christophe might have said, quel dommage, mais tant pis.

One morning while I was waiting in the hotel foyer for my car to take me out to the set, a man asked me to follow him. He was wearing a tunic, kilt, leather wristbands and had long hair and a beard, with cross-gartered leggings and all the costume accoutrements as worn by every actor and extra all over the *Highlander* set, so I simply presumed that, on top of his usual duties, one of the official drivers had been dragged in to do some work as a supernumerary. I climbed into a somewhat smellier car than usual and off we went. The hairy man seemed strangely angry for a location driver, and was speaking to me in a very oddly loud and belligerent way about Scottish politics and the laws of Ancient Scots, in particular the Picts.

Like most actors en route to the set, I was actually off in that other world within my head, trying to use the time silently to go over my lines. I tuned out from the irate stuff he was spouting. I remember vaguely hearing the word 'kidnapped' a few times, and thought he must be referring to the Robert Louis Stevenson book of the same name, which I knew was set round these parts. I glanced at my watch, and started to wonder why it was taking such a long time to get to the location. The usual ten-minute drive had already taken us more than twice that time. I looked around. I didn't recognise the place, but then I was a stranger and had only travelled the route a couple of times beforehand. However, although we had hit no traffic, we were very late, and seemed to be getting into some pretty remote countryside. Still he ranted on.

We drove past a sign, 'Fort William 30 miles'. Thirty miles? That was way too far out. The location couldn't have been more than 10 miles from the hotel. It was only then that I realised that something was not at all right. I started listening to the driver's harangue with a new keenness.

I asked the bearded man who he was. He said he was a clan chief from the Pictish Society. Kidnapping women, he said, was something of a tradition among the Picts and that he was kidnapping me, a woman, as many Picts had done before him. Then he lost me again with a long rant about retribution of rights for the despoiling of the land. As we drove further and further into the mountainous wilderness beyond Fort William I became terrified. By now people on the set (among them the second assistant, the make-up and costume girls) would have noticed I had not arrived, but they couldn't possibly have imagined the truth of my whereabouts. And, remember, this was long before the days of mobile phones.

I looked out of the car's window at acres of bleak moorland rising steeply up into purple craggy peaks. We were miles from civilisation. There weren't even any wee cottages nearby with wooden gates and smoking chimneys to which I could run, imagining myself to be the fugitive in a remake of *The Thirty-Nine Steps*. I could only stick inside the car and pray. I tried to sound and look very sympathetic to the modern-day Pict's noble and ancient cause. Luckily, I had watched many episodes of cheap cop shows on TV and so when, after some time, we passed through a small village and stopped at what must have been the only red traffic light for miles, I did the clichéd thing. I jumped out of the car and ran with all my might. I found the village Post Office, where I made a call to the Assistant Director on the film and was eventually rescued back to the set.

After that I spent the rest of my *Highlander* time with a bodyguard, to protect me from marauding Picts, or should I say nutters.

Highlander went on to become a cult film, which after some time was followed up by a cult TV series, which I did not appear in.

I came back to London, thankfully in one piece, to play an army wife, along with lovely Liverpudlian, Alexandra Pigg, in *The Last Waltz* at the Soho Poly. I was most impressed by her scene in which she has to be sick. Vomiting in all its forms is one of my total phobias. For instance if anyone on a bus looks a bit green I'd prefer to get off and wait for the next one rather than risk witnessing an eruption of vomit. Alex's sound effects were so realistic it was bloody hard not to start vomiting along in sympathy. I don't know how I lasted the run.

When the BBC asked me to take part in a TV *Master Class on Acting* most of my friends advised me not to do it, saying that, at a time when I was just starting to establish myself, it would make me look like a student again. But the opportunity of working with Michael Caine, who was to take the class, proved irresistible. I would like to be able to say 'Hello' the way Michael Caine does on screen. Sounds like nothing, but I tell you it's an art.

Michael Caine was much bigger than I expected. He has a kind of space around him and you would not miss him in a crowd. And like most of the mega-famous people I have met, you could see a mile off that he was a star. It's a funny thing. I'm not sure whether it's the aura of success which comes from being rich and famous, or whether that aura is the thing which made them rich and famous.

Minutes before the show started, I met Michael in a small anteroom outside the studio. We could hear the nearby hum of the excited studio audience waiting for us to come out.

'How do you keep yourself from looking nervous on screen?' I asked, adding, 'Do you *get* nervous?'

He waved his hand and said, 'Save the question for the camera.'

As we walked through the black drape into the studio I noticed a sheen of perspiration glistening on his upper lip. He never really replied to the question when I asked it again. But I had already seen the answer for myself. I heard a rumour afterwards that the night before he had tried to get out of doing the show. And yet now the show has turned out to be a huge hit, especially in America.

Michael taught us a few essential tips which no one has ever got time to share with you on a professional film set, and which for some reason are also ignored at drama school.

1. Don't blink in a close-up.
2. Work out your continuity and props (like cigarettes, gloves and handbags) the night before in your hotel room.
3. In a conversational close-up shot, when the other actor is standing next to the camera for eye-line, instead of looking into their eyes, slightly cheat it. If they are standing to the right of the camera (from your point of view) you look with your left eye into their left eye. i.e. bringing your face more

fully into the shot. By doing this you cheat your eyes to favour the camera.

4. Buy yourself some Gold Spot if you're having a kissing scene. Spray yourself. When the other person opens up to say 'what are you doing?' spray it into their mouths too.

For the next few years, it was a revolving door of *Victoria Wood Shows* with the odd television guest part in regular series like *Taggart* and *The New Statesman* thrown into the mix.

I also played on stage. The role was Natalia Petrovna in Turgenev's *A Month in the Country*. Rehearsals were difficult. The director was not so fond of women, and I struggled with the role, my first lead in a classic play. We opened in Richmond. Early on the morning following the opening night, I got a phone call from my leading man. 'Oh dear, Celia,' he said. 'Might I take you out to lunch?'

'Why?

'Well . . . Your reviews.'

Talk about a punch from a velvet glove.

After the call I went straight to the corner shop and read the reviews, heading first for the paper he had told me was the worst. As I stood there reading, shaking and hot, I realised that the critics were not wrong. They were describing exactly how I felt about the whole thing. I was not happy and, they were absolutely right, I was not good.

That evening I found myself driving blindly along the South Circular Road, hoping that the car would be involved in a crash, anything, just so that I could get out of doing the performance. I know that is a truly terrible thing to say, but I was in despair.

Every night was the same. I spent the whole day anticipating with horror the evening to come and did the play in a kind of funnel of fear. Although we toured, I remember nothing about the towns we visited, Poole, Bath, Cambridge, Aberystwyth, except for the daily horror of dreading going in to do the show.

Since then I have never read my reviews until the run of the play is over.

★

The famous hurricane hit the south of England in October 1987. Like most people, when I was awoken to the sound of crashing chimney pots I hadn't a clue what was happening. At about 2 o'clock in the morning the phone rang. It was Fidelis's mother calling me from the Isle of Wight.

'Celia,' she asked in a quite business-like way. 'Is this The End of the World?'

Funny that she thought I would have had the gen on whether or not this was true, especially as she was more likely than me to be in on the knowledge, as she was at the time the resident fortune teller on Shanklin Pier. (In fact Shanklin Pier blew away that night and she was henceforth out of a job, so she was partly right.)

Down the phone-line I could hear Bonchurch trees crashing down and the huge and very heavy ship's bell, which I knew hung outside in her drive, ringing itself.

'You should see the garden, Celia,' said Fidelis senior, in her lilting Liverpool accent. 'It's as though the trees are dancing.' While pandemonium reigned around us, I settled under the stairs and we talked, trying to keep one another calm.

Fidelis junior was away on tour with Paines Plough way up north in Barrow-in-Furness. The north was not hit by the hurricane. Next morning in her hotel room she watched the wobbly BBC TV news, broadcast by torchlight from what appeared to be a garden shed, and naturally tried to phone home to check everything was all right. The operator told her that it was impossible to get through to London as it had been devastated by an earthquake. 'Thousands dead,' he had said, with some authority.

In fact the worst that happened to us in Clapham was that the garden fence blew down and the phone and electricity were cut off.

I had been asked by the author Margaret Forster to play Elizabeth Barrett Browning, in a small programme for TV, and for my research I naturally read the poetry, but also took myself off to the manuscript room of the British Library, still at that time housed in a front room of the British Museum. I sought out Mrs Barrett Browning's handwriting, always a good clue to character, as I had learned all those years ago in my psychology of criminology classes. I was disappointed to see that her writing was tight and pinched. It seemed to me typical of someone who sat on a sofa moaning.

In the next cabinet was a display about a hurricane which had hit the United Kingdom. Having only just got things back into order in Clapham, I was interested to take a look. The strange thing was that the display was actually about a hurricane which had hit Britain on exactly the same date two hundred or so years before. Beside it was another case about an even worse storm which had hit Britain in 1703, killing more than 8000 people and bringing down not only millions of trees but toppling lighthouses, whole villages, wrecking thousands of houses and tearing the roof off Westminster Abbey. Ours seemed quite tame by comparison.

Apart from the handwriting, all I knew of Elizabeth Barrett Browning's life had come from seeing an amateur production of *The Barretts of Wimpole Street* many years before. Little did I know that I was about to be decked out with a wig that made me look like a demented cocker spaniel, and that most of my scenes were actually *with* a demented cocker spaniel. The dog playing Flush and I lay on the daybed together while I recited poems and called for glasses of porter. At this point the amateurs had brought in a neat little glass of something which looked like sherry or port. But no, porter was nothing like port. Who knew that E. B. B. was in fact a Guinness drinker?

Next up was a total change. I managed to get a role in a film called *Murder on the Moon*. How it came about was pretty strange. I had gone up for the interview and they were unsure. I remember standing on the brink of the set at Bray studios being discussed and having to wait for approval. The actor Brian Cox was already in it. He had seen me doing a Scottish accent in *When I Was a Girl, I Used to Scream and Shout*. The director asked him if he thought I could do American and Brian said 'Well she can do Scots so hire her'.

It was a kind of Cold-War-sci-fi-murder-mystery directed by Michael Lindsay-Hogg, and my main scene was with the film's star, Amazon goddess, Brigitte Nielsen, recently ex-Mrs Sylvester Stallone. Brigitte and I got on like a house on fire and discovered pretty early on that we shared both the same birthday and the same bra size.

We both played spacewomen on an international space station on the moon. As we all know, in space you are weightless, so the requirements of our scene necessitated special effects. We had to be suspended on wires to create the illusion that we were floating about in the air. While the cameras and lighting were set up we stood together and watched a couple of men demonstrate how the contraption would work. The men were hoisted by the thigh and shoulder and seemed to be flying along together, horizontal to the floor.

Brigitte and I chatted merrily as we climbed into our silver space-suits, and we took our positions facing one another, and the suspended hooks were attached to special hidden loops on our thighs and shoulders. The moon-office backdrop was in place, and a group of burly men retired to their corners to winch us up.

It was an odd sensation. First your shoulders seemed to be grabbed from above then your legs pulled out from behind you. Then, belly towards the ground, slowly but surely, up you went. The winch was designed to hit a certain point at which we would both be in the right horizontal position to start shooting the scene.

We got there and looked at one another, ready to go, awaiting only the word 'Action!'

But the start signal did not come. We remained aloft, swinging gently, while the technical crew gathered round, staring at us and scratching their heads.

'Uh oh!' said the cameraman. 'Better get them down again. There's no way I'm ever going to get their faces into the shot.'

Unfortunately the position they had winched us into left us both suspended at an angle, tilted with our feet up high and our noses very much nearer the floor, as though we were heading for a direct crash into the surface of the moon.

'We're going to need more weights for their ankles,' yelled a technician.

When the men had rigged it up, they had not allowed for the extra gravity force provided . . . by the weight of our bosoms.

CHAPTER 13

It was my birthday and I decided on a festive tea party in the lovely old great room called the Foyer in Claridges. The Foyer was an enormous elegant palm court with glass domed ceiling and a string quartet playing in the corner. Sadly the hotel decided to 'improve' the place, and split it up into lots of horrid little poky rooms, so it's no longer there.

Only a few people were due, among them Jane Bertish and her then boyfriend, Gary Oldman, both at the time Citizens' Theatre actors. Knowing Gary's reluctance to put on shirts and ties, I had made sure that both Gary and Jane knew that if Gary didn't turn up wearing a tie he wouldn't get past the doormen. They would turn him away or give him the chance to borrow a used tie from their collection in the gentlemen's cloakroom. It would be far better if Gary wore his own.

'No,' said Gary. 'I won't wear a tie.'

'If you don't, Gary, you won't be let in. It's the hotel policy.'

'I'll get in,' said Gary.

'Not without a tie, you won't.'

'I won't wear a tie,' he said as a parting shot, 'but I will come.'

The party was in full swing when at the far side of the room we saw Jane arrive.

'Who the hell has she brought?' someone asked, sotto voce.

Ambling along beside Jane was a stylishly made-up lady in a floral dress. She was all lipstick and earrings. The lady lifted an elegant gloved hand and gave us all a little wave. As they came nearer we realised that the lady was Gary.

He had managed to break the precious Claridges' tie rule, by arriving in drag!

*

I received a call telling me I had been chosen to be the new voice for Audi, the German car maker. They told me that they had decided the product was in need of a woman's touch. I thought to myself, 'I hope to God this isn't the one that Geoffrey Palmer does with those incomprehensible foreign words at the end'.

They played me the silent film in a small voice-over studio. It was pretty good. All shot in the rain, the ad was full of atmosphere and came over rather like a French art house movie. The plot concerned a father who was rushing through terrible weather to the hospital, where his wife was giving birth.

I was given the script and headphones, in order to watch it again and rehearse slotting in the voice as the timing markers on the screen flashed past.

They replayed the film while I spoke the script. Everything was going fine, and I was skilfully negotiating myself past all kinds of hellish phrases like 'cleaner catalytic converter'. Then came that fateful moment when (as actors do) I was subliminally reading one sentence ahead.

There it was, looming at me, the Geoffrey Palmer phrase – those famous three words, 'Vorsprung durch Technik'. Well, German was never my strong point. Let's just say we did quite a few takes.

I then took what was meant to be a relaxing week's holiday in southern Italy. I had hired a villa between Rome and Naples which looked great in the ad. I arrived to find it was a breezeblock building in the middle of a wine factory. The principal Rome/Naples autostrada ran alongside. All the ground within the compound was concrete, with a huge drain running down the middle which was a dark red, as though a massacre had taken place the day before. The whole place stank of stale wine. The swimming pool was a single lane affair where you could swim and flip yourself around and swim back but two people couldn't do it at the same time without crashing into one another.

I panicked. I had asked friends to come out and join me and this was going to be very embarrassing. I went to the manager and told him I wanted to leave and I'd like my money back, but he was adamant that I had no right to compensation.

I thought I'd go mad if I stayed, so decided to move on, waving the money good-bye. A fellow renter of an adjacent 'holiday flat' gave me a lift to the station. He was pretty annoyed at the state of the place too.

I took a train down to Naples, and decided I would explore the Amalfi coast. I went by bus. What a terrifying journey that is, as the enormous vehicle, intermittently blaring the horn, careers along at breakneck speed round hairpin bends on tiny little roads, jutting out like shelves on the sheer cliff face. I don't think I have ever clenched my teeth for so long at one sitting.

As we neared Amalfi, the heavens opened. And this was no ordinary storm. The sky was black and the rain came down like curtains of sheet glass.

I hadn't booked ahead but had read the guidebook and decided on a hotel. I went into a café to use the pay phone. The café manager told me that the hotel I had picked was recently closed, forever. I tried another, it was full. And another. This one had lost its fire certificate and was shut indefinitely. The café man suggested I try asking at the tourist office along the way.

I left the café to discover that the water in the street was now knee-deep. I held my suitcase in my arms like a baby and waded through the orange muddy flood. Naturally the tourist office was also closed.

Back at the café, the only place still open, the water had now come in, reaching the height of about 10 inches. I sat on a table with my case and knew I had to move along again, but I was not intending to return on the bus along that hair-raising coastal route. I would rather go overland and reach Castellammare di Stabia, which had looked good from the train. I sat on my table island for some hours till the flood subsided a bit then caught the first bus out of town.

This time we took a pretty road out of Amalfi and upwards into the mountains. Once we reached tiny bendy roads again, the driver picked up speed. Along we hurtled, on roads as perilous as the one on which I had come into town. Only this time if the coach happened to come off the road, instead of tumbling into the sea we would be plummeting headlong down into a craggy ravine.

As we neared the top of the mountain, the bus screeched to a halt. The road was steep. We were at an angle of at least 60 degrees. Behind us a sheer drop.

Leaving the engine still turning, the driver got out of his seat, put on his jacket, and then left the bus to shout at someone in the road ahead. I bit my lips raw with anxiety. The road was water-logged. I could see mud outside. The engine was running and there was no one at the controls. Behind us lay infinity.

After five minutes which felt more like five hours, the driver came back.

He yelled in Italian that we all had to get out NOW. The road was blocked, plus there was a mudslide coming and we could easily be dragged backwards into the ravine.

Have you ever got out of a bus in two seconds flat? I did it in one.

The village we had unintentionally arrived at was buried under 4 inches of reddish mud. It was like wading through a giant bog. I tried to walk balancing my case on my head. The mud was hell to get through as you kept getting stuck or leaving your shoes behind.

After a 500-metre slog, clambering across displaced boulders and fallen trees, we were put onto another bus. This one pulled out pretty smartish and we now tackled the downward slopes towards Castellammare di Stabia.

I have never skied. But that bus certainly had a good try. We careered downhill at alarming speeds, while intermittently skidding through torrents of ochre tinted mud. I thought my last moments were upon me. I bent down into the braced crash position, and there, scribbled in felt tip pen on the back of the seat in front of me, were the words, 'I love Gary Oldman'.

Gary was not at all well-known at this point, and yet here, only a few days after his appearance as a housewife at my party in Claridges, was his name on a bus up a mountain in the middle of a mudslide in Italy. It seemed bizarre. I thought for a moment that I must be dreaming. Or that the bus had actually crashed and I was lying in a hospital somewhere deep in a coma.

When we reached the town that evening, the roads were jammed with JCBs scooping away whole streets of red mud.

I was told when I phoned home that the Italian mudslides were so bad they had been reported on English TV news. The local Italian papers simply bore headlines which read 'Fango e morte' - Mud and death. Fortunately I only encountered the first.

Scores of people had been killed, some in the villages we had waded through, others in cars along those perilous roads. I had been lucky.

I had had enough now of my adventures in southern Italy. I went up to Rome and in a lovely little hotel I hooked up with the friends who should have come to the wine-drenched concrete villa with me.

On the way home I changed trains in Paris, where I bought a *Daily Mail* (the only English paper there) to catch up with the news. The middle-page spread was all about the Audi TV ad campaign having had a revamp. Still shots from the ad which I had voiced were arranged across the page like a storyboard. Underneath, in the written analysis it said, 'The female touch has been provided by a voice-over actress who sounds uncannily like a younger Margaret Thatcher.' I spluttered into my café au lait.

CHAPTER 14

It was around this time that I bought my first house.

I love the sea, and had spent many happy times staying with friends on the Isle of Wight. Property there was cheap and I knew that, at the kind of prices I saw in estate agents' windows, I would be able to both get and afford a mortgage. I went on a long search. I looked round many houses. There was a tiny thatched stone cottage complete with rose garden, a redbrick coastguard's cottage perched on top of a lofty bare cliff and the battered wing of a former stately home. One place was a converted church, complete with graveyard as garden (no, thanks), another was an old Victorian schoolhouse with 'Boys' and 'Girls' carved in stone above the doors. I even looked round the tall elegant Italianate house where Karl Marx had once lived and which, though sunny and bright, was exceedingly depressing. Surprisingly, all were within the range of my meagre budget.

Eventually I settled upon a little town house, a workman's terraced cottage, bang in the centre of Cowes. I viewed it on a dark, dreary December day. I figured that if a place looked presentable on such a direly dull afternoon it could only be marvellous on fair-weather days, and I was right. The other good thing was that it was right in the heart of things. So many places I had seen had perhaps been very beautiful but were horribly cut off. If you ran out of milk it would mean a twenty-minute drive. Who could be bothered? I didn't fancy always drinking my tea black.

I spent a wonderful summer working on the Cowes house. While I chipped away at a fake tiled 1950s' fireplace, which I felt sure was covering the genuine original Victorian one, I wore dungarees, earphones and goggles. I had been instructed to buy a bolster, which it turned out wasn't a large pillow, but a kind of huge blunt chisel which one hits with something called a lump hammer. The first bolster I bought only had a one-inch end. A visiting friend laughed and called it my 'fairy bolster', explaining I would be there for three years rather than three hours if I stuck with it. So I went and got a real one which weighed as much as two large packets of sugar and knocked out bricks by the dozen. Once I got the knack I couldn't help myself. Next, I demolished the front garden wall which blocked out the light. The bolster soon became inadequate and I hired a pneumatic drill to take up the concrete in the garden where I eventually put down a turf lawn. I fixed tiles and grouted. I painted ceilings. I laid lino and carpets. I slept on the bare ship-board floor.

I made myself tea in mugs, and sat gnawing at sandwiches, wiping my mouth with the back of my hand, while admiring my handi-work. It felt just like being a real builder. I couldn't have been happier.

On my self-appointed days off, I would drive across the island to the Shanklin auction rooms where I became quite addicted to bidding for things I hadn't quite planned to buy. I not only acquired beds, chairs and sofas but a whole Spode dinner service, a goldfish bowl, an ornamental planter and a huge box full of assorted brass ornaments – horse-shoes, hand-bells and knockers. Auctions I think are as exciting as going to the races or playing the roulette table.

The house became my wonderful escape, somewhere I could retreat when I had time off. It made me almost look forward to being out of work so I could get back to the little place and go for long wind-blown walks on the beach. To this day I love the feeling you get as the boat leaves the Southampton quay and sets out into the choppy Solent heading for Cowes. It feels as though someone takes a huge load from the top of your head and that you can breathe deeper than you have done for weeks.

So proud was I of my new abode that I boasted about it, and said gaily to everyone, 'It's a wonderful place. Lovely garden. Minutes from the sea. You MUST come down and stay.'

When a party of eminent people from TV and radio decided to take up my offer, I was overjoyed and raced down ahead of them to get the place ready. What I hadn't realised was that, from the way

I went on and on, everyone had got it into their heads that I was the châtelaine of some huge country pile with en-suite quarters for all my guests, sloping lawns running down to the sea, and possibly a pool and tennis courts. So that when two carloads of distinguished friends pulled up outside my little workman's terraced house, with what most people might describe as a back yard rather than a garden, the expression on their faces was (in retrospect, hilarious, but at the time) terrifying.

Let me explain the layout. When you entered the front door, you walked right into the living room which led directly through to the dining room and then through to the kitchen and then the first door you encountered opened into a titchy bathroom. A narrow and perilously steep staircase led to the first floor, which was organised in such a way that you needed to walk through the main bedroom to get, by way of a tiny cupboard door, up the even more lethal stairs to the little top attic bedroom (furnace in the summer, an ice-box in winter). Not one room was what you might call private. And the four-foot square bathroom wasn't really up to providing facilities for six visitors plus me.

As they tried to squeeze enormous suitcases up the terrifyingly steep stairs they smiled grimly. Still wearing my rosy specs, I had failed to see that the house, though utterly darling to me, was not at all suitable as a venue for a country house party.

Continuing to smile through gritted teeth, my guests survived the weekend, but I can still recall the relieved glee in their voices as they said goodbye and escaped into their cars, heading back to London, never ever to return.

Before I bought the house, I had pulled an old cast iron fireplace from a skip and kept it. But it was way too big for the tiny fireplace exposed by my extensive work with lump hammer and bolster, so I left it leaning against a wall in the garden.

Then one day I pushed it tight to the wall to look like a real fireplace. As time went by, I painted the surrounding walls to look like wallpaper and did the whole garden as an alternative living room, with a painted clock on the mantelpiece and painted flames in the grate. My newly laid turf lawn looked like a most luxurious lime-green shag-pile. In the end my garden looked somewhat like the living-room set for a Joe Orton play.

But real work called me back to town, this time in the form of a play at Hammersmith Lyric Studio Theatre.

Matthew Frances, who had directed the roller skating Debbie Horsfield play in Chichester, had formed a new company and was putting on Fidelis's adaptation of Patrick Hamilton's *Hangover Square*. I took the part of the vile tease Netta. To help define the schizophrenic personality of the leading character, George Harvey Bone, played deliciously by Dudley Sutton, the role of Netta was split into two. The other Netta was played by the fab Anne Lambton, and our love interest was played by Ian Reddington, later to be Tricky Dicky from *EastEnders*, both old friends from the Glasgow Citz.

As Anne and I were both playing the same role, we had great long winding metaphysical discussions about which one of us was real, who was who, whether we could see one another, which one of us was in Bone's head and which one was actually in the room with him, how did we change, were we ever both real at the same time . . . ?

After rehearsals were over, Anne and I would sit outside the rehearsal room in the car, and on it would go. Poring over the script trying to make some kind of logical sense to how we approached the part, or should I say, parts. You are real in scene two, me at the end of the same scene, but can we see one another in the mirror? No, but can he see me, and if I'm not there, how did I get into the room or onto the sofa? We were bewildered.

One evening we cornered Fidelis.

'Please', we begged. 'Please explain who is who and which is real and which is in his head, and where is the logic?'

Fidelis smiled enigmatically and said, 'It's magic, not logic.'

And that was it. For the rest of rehearsals we were in heaven. It became our mantra, and still is to this day. 'It's magic, not logic.'

The show was a huge hit. Nightly there were queues round the block waiting for returns. Considering we were just a small fringe company, the play attracted the most incredible list of stars. The Pet Shop Boys came, and Mick Jagger, Lionel Bart, Tony Hatch and

Jackie Trent, Lynda La Plante, Ian McShane, Stephen Sondheim, Michael Winner, everyone who was anything on British TV was there too. The theatre ushers told me they'd never seen anything like it in the whole time they'd worked at the Lyric.

One night a strange rumble of sound went through the audience. We stood in the wings, mystified. There had never been such a sound before a show. Was the Queen in, or Princess Diana, had someone suffered a heart attack, or was there about to be a bomb warning?

The house lights dimmed, the go-green lights came on, music swelled and we went out to start the play. Everything seemed quite normal. That is until we noticed quite a few of the audience seemed to be spending more time facing away from the stage than towards us.

At the interval the news reached us that the cause of this phenomenon was the presence of Liza Minnelli.

For the second half we were at it too, trying to get a squint at this mega-famous star. After the show was over, as we sat in the dressing room taking off our make-up, the door was opened by a stage manager and in walked Liza with a Zee.

'Hello, you guys,' she said, holding out her hand. 'I am Liza Minnelli.' As though we didn't know. She was utterly charming and said she'd recommend the show to all her friends.

Not logic, you see. Magic!

Next I was off again to another glamorous location. Accrington to be precise, where I was to play the music teacher in the TV adaptation of Jeanette Winterson's *Oranges Are Not the Only Fruit*.

The book concerns a young girl being brought up in the shadow of religious obsession. To research my character, one of the few people who stand up against the oppressive dictates of the church, I attended an ecumenical meeting. Before I had the chance to let them know I was only there to research, the regular members swooped forward to welcome me into the congregation. In fact, how do you say it? 'Don't mind me; I'm only here to have a snoop'?

I had heard of Accrington because of the football team called Accrington Stanley, and who, along with Hamilton Academicals, Partick Thistle and Queen of the South had always leapt out at me on those childhood Saturday afternoons when the football results were delivered on the BBC. I, however, believed that the town was actually called Accrington Stanley and so when I told my friends I was about to go up to Accrington Stanley and film a series by Jeanette Winterson I got a few raised eyebrows.

'Wow. Winterson on football!' one person said. 'What a fascinating idea.' I thought they'd gone mad, but just quietly nodded and carried on.

It was cold and bleak in Accrington, and it seemed to rain every day. A waitress at the hotel asked me what we were filming. I told her it was a new novel by a local girl. She turned to me, her mouth wide with delight and said, 'Not Mystic Meg?'

We put on our dreary clothes, scraped off every morsel of make-up, and played the depressive roles, and obviously had lots of church scenes. During them, we had to sing real hymns. However, despite practising them over and over, when it came to final rehearsals, I was always at a loss for the words. I managed to engineer myself a place near the back of the congregation, standing next to Emily Aston, who had the same problem. Over and over the pair of us huddled together, trying to keep out of shot as our lips jabbered away quite out of synch with the others, and we both searched vainly for the words. Every now and then Emily would shake her head at me, pull an 'eeek!' face and giggle.

I have to say it was great to have a co-conspirator. Trouble is, at the time, Emily was only seven and I was old enough to know better.

Unfortunately on this set, the company was rather split. You would often sit in the make-up wagon and hear a gaggle of actresses making rude remarks about the others not present.

I have a tendency to slope off on my own whenever breaks are called. Never more so than when a company fragments, for on those occasions simply by joining a table for lunch you are understood to have taken sides. Picking the wrong table can get you sent to Coventry by the other half of the cast. The whole atmosphere becomes much too much like primary school.

So one wet and dismal day, I picked up my plate of food and tried to find somewhere secluded to hide while I ate. There was nowhere roundabouts where I could possibly go without getting drenched, a cardinal sin when wearing one's costume. So I crept into the wardrobe wagon, and sat among the racks of clothing, peeling an orange. (At this moment it *was* the only fruit.)

In the silence I could hear click, click, click. I had no idea what the sound could be. There would be a pause. A few seconds' pause, then again click, click, click, click, click.

After a few minutes of this continuing, the intermittent quiet was replaced with a little sigh. I'd recognise that sigh anywhere.

'Geraldine?' I said. 'Is that you? Are you knitting?'

'Oh, Celia,' said the series' star, Geraldine McEwan. 'I was escaping.'

'Me too!'

From that instant to this we were great friends. We have since spent a few New Year's Eves together, for Geraldine, like me, enjoys Scottish country dancing to the rousing reels, polkas and jigs of Jimmy Shand.

During the following months, I did a few TV parts in single episodes of established series and a couple of new series too.

The film *Blue Black Permanent* had an Edinburgh location and I was put up in the same hotel where my mother had many years before tried to struggle with understanding the local accent. She had asked for the menu, but instead the waiter had hovered over her and told her what was available.

'Will ye have the clearrr soup?' he intoned in a voice not unlike John Laurie, Private Frazer in *Dad's Army*. 'Or would ye preferrrr the fush?'

My mother looked at him, bewildered.

'Clearrr soup, or fush?' he repeated.

My mother went on looking, hoping for an éclaircissement.

'Clearrr soup, or fush?'

My mother feeling slightly intimidated and anxious not to appear ignorant, decided to be rather adventurous. 'Do you know? I think I'll try the fush.' When a plate of fish arrived she was surprised and disappointed in equal parts.

It was in this same hotel that I sat down for dinner with my co-star.

He was talking about his friend Brian Glover, an ebullient actor who had been a professional wrestler. 'He's an extraordinary man,' said my co-star. 'He makes an absolute thing of going out with really ugly women. It's sort of his thing.'

There was a short pause as he took a spoonful of soup.

'He'd love you,' he said.

The long dinner stretched out ahead of me, as I started dismally on my soup, which might as well have been sand, I knew there was still the main course, pudding and coffee to go . . . How embarrassing.

On my Sundays off, I took myself on the usual day excursions. The first was a great success. I took a picnic and boarded a train for North Berwick. Once there I found the beach and sat down to enjoy my sandwiches. Afterwards I decided to climb a big rocky hill on the beach. I was wearing my best cashmere coat and trainers, and clawed my way up to the top. The view was superb. But then I looked around and thought now how the hell do I get down?

I stood there all alone in the wilderness, as the light started to fail and the tide was steadily rising. A gang of sheep gathered at the foot of the hill, looking up at me and bleating. No one knows I am here, I thought. What will happen? Do I just cling on and stay all night till the tide goes out again and the sun rises? As I got more and more scared the sheep seemed to be laughing at me. 'Nieh, heh, heh, heh!' they chorused merrily.

In the end I knew I must escape, whatever the method. I tried climbing down, but I could not get a decent grip, and in the dark my feet kept missing. So instead of climbing down I just sat down on my backside and slid my way to the bottom, bumping over rocks, skidding through long grass, till I hit the sand. Then I paddled back to shore. My shoes and trousers were muddy and soaked, my best cashmere coat was ruined. Very bruised, I made my way back to Edinburgh.

The next weekend for my Sunday outing I decided to head north rather than south, and, having seen the magical-sounding name Kirkcaldy* on a map, I set my heart on going there.

---

* Which I knew was pronounced kur-coddy.

This time I took the bus. We arrived in the town about an hour after departure. I stepped cheerfully away from the bus stop and walked the short street leading down to the beach. I took one look at the grey, muddy, oily strand, took another deep breath of the industrial stench and that was enough. Holding my nose, I managed to get myself back to the bus stop so fast that the very same bus that I had come on had not yet had time to turn round ready to head back to Edinburgh. Who knew that Kirkcaldy is famed only as the lino manufacturing centre of the world? I ate my picnic on the bus.

Some of *Blue Black Permanent* had been filmed in the Orkney Islands. Many years later I was attending a gala screening of *The Talented Mr Ripley* at a cinema on the Isle of Wight. A man in a tuxedo came up and stood before me, beaming.

'At last,' he said. 'How lovely to meet a fellow Orkadian.'

I looked at the man, resplendent in his evening dress, unsure whether or not to call security. Was he a *Lord of the Rings*-style nutter? Was he about to launch into some strange troll language or tell me long incomprehensible anecdotes about his nights fiddling with little plastic toy dragons, befriending wizards and goblins or slaying orks?

'We Orkadians can always sniff one another out.'

I smiled and took an imperceptible step away. After an eternal minute I plucked up courage and said, 'I'm ever so sorry, but I haven't a clue what you're talking about.'

'You're an Orkadian,' he said. 'And so am I.'

Fearing the worst, I took the plunge. 'Orkadian?'

'We both come from the Orkneys.'

He seemed so happy, I hated to break the spell. But I then had to explain that in fact I actually came from Guildford, my father really was Scottish, but he was a Glaswegian, and the publicist on *Blue Black Permanent* had slightly elaborated the truth when linking me to the Orkney location.

At the end of the job I was whisked from Scotland down to Kent to film *The Darling Buds of May*. I was very impressed with an unknown actress who played the pretty daughter. Her name was

Catherine Zeta-Jones and we worked together again two years later in Thomas Hardy's *Return of the Native*, before she moved to Hollywood and her tremendous and well-deserved success in movies.

I played a haughty lady called Corinne Perigo, and was given a lovely retro floral 1950s sun-dress. I saw a name tape sewn into the seam as I put it on – Glynis Johns. Throughout my childhood, Glynis Johns had been so famous. She had had a ballet background and apart from popping up in so many feature films in the 1960s, of course played the redoubtable suffragette mother in *Mary Poppins*. When I exclaimed my delight, my dresser told me that Ms Johns had worn the dress in the film *Miranda*, in which she played a mermaid. It was in fact *the* dress Miranda wore when she was allowed a day off from being a mermaid and went to town dressed as a woman.

Strangely, on the night that that episode of *Darling Buds of May* was shown on TV, the film *Miranda* was also on, so that evening you could have seen the exact same dress in two features made 50 years apart.

CHAPTER 15

In 1991 I worked again at the National Theatre, the first time had been about four years before in *School for Wives*, this time I was playing Jessica Tilehouse in Edward Bond's *The Sea*. Dame Judi Dench played the lead role, Mrs Rafi. I was her downtrodden companion.

I had encountered Judi a few times before when were both working in separate productions at the National. We did not know each other, but frequently passed in corridors bestowing on one another those polite smiles obligatory between people who recognise, but do not really know each other. Some years previously at the National, I invited her to join in the sweepstake on the other National★ which I was running from the wings of the Cottesloe Theatre. The dame (4-1 on, grey filly, outstanding form, well-fancied) was quick to partake. Judi had been rehearsing Cleopatra, in Shakespeare's *Antony & Cleopatra*.

While I was out buying stage make-up for my own performance, I saw a hideous chart demonstrating, in a kind of painting-by-numbers way, how to put on stage make-up for the role of 'Older Egyptian Woman'.

A wee devil smiled inside me . . . What the hell, I thought. I bought the chart. Under the text I scribbled 'Good luck, Judi, with love from Celia' and sent it to her as a first night card. Next time we met in a corridor she laughed out loud. She told me she couldn't possibly keep all the first night cards she had ever been sent, but she was definitely keeping that one.

Now I was thrilled that we were actually working together on *The Sea*. For the read-through, the cast sat in a large circle. Judi sat

★ The Aintree Grand National Steeplechase.

directly opposite me. In the play our characters had to sing a hymn. Mostly when a song comes up during a read-through it is skipped, and saved for later musical rehearsals when a pianist is present. So when the song came up we both went to turn the page and plough on with the rest of the play. However, the elegantly exacting director, Sam Mendes, had other ideas.

'Carry on,' he said.

We both looked at him, mystified. Carry on with what? We had no idea of the tune and there was no répétiteur to help us.

'Make it up,' he ordered.

In the scene, at a cliff-top funeral, while singing an interment hymn, our two characters competitively try to slip the highest and fanciest descant into their part. Like our characters in the play, Judi and I are ever so slightly on the competitive side. So when we each started embellishing the descants, it didn't take long before we got completely out of control.

Judi sang some notes higher than Yma Sumac, and I'm pretty sure I delivered some complex coloratura trills which incorporated tones that only dogs could hear. Laughter ensued. But we pressed on, singing, wailing, shrieking, all the while trying to suppress our laughter. The song finally came to an end.

When we caught eyes, we realised we had amused ourselves so royally that we had both shed our mascara and looked like a pair of cackling racoons. Unfortunately we now had to complete the play-reading looking like this. As we were sitting opposite one another, every now and then one of us would get a glimpse of the other's eye make-up disaster and it set us off again into uncontrollable giggles.

During the interval of an understudy rehearsal, to which we had been invited, Judi read my programme notes and immediately cross-questioned me on a very early entry in my biography, *The House of Whipcord*. You know what happened next.

When Valentine's Day came along I received not a card but a book. It was in French, a language of which I have only the smallest knowledge. The book was Colette's *Chéri*, which is famously about a middle-aged woman having an affair with a younger man, the son of a friend of hers. Inside was a typed sticker which read 'PEUT ETRE – EN DIX ANS? xxx' ('Maybe in ten years?'). I realised the valentine had come from Sam West, son of my old friend, Tim. Sam and I had certainly spent many flirty days together – it was one of those shows – and I can tell you he is a very good kisser. I put the book on a shelf, looking forward to what might happen in ten years' time, and longing to see whether Sam was going to turn up on my doorstep and put his plan into action. It was strange that he chose this particular valentine, for it was while I was playing in this show that my body clock seemed to kick in and I found myself overtaken by odd flutterings of broodiness.

For the last few pages of *The Sea*, Judi and I were not on stage. There didn't seem enough time till the curtain call to wander back to the dressing rooms, yet it was too long simply to stand waiting in the wings, so we came up with an idea. We commandeered the quick-change cubicle just behind the prompt corner, then took it in turns to buy a bottle of champagne which we put on the props table with a couple of glasses from the canteen. Sometimes I managed to snaffle a bit of lobster for Judi, as she loves it, while I got a few Twiglets for myself. As we came off from our final scene we would leave the stage then sneak into our private hidey-hole and treat ourselves to a micro-cocktail party while waiting for the end of the play.

When we recently met up, Judi and I pondered what we must both have looked like as we staggered on to take the curtain call each night, inevitably three sheets to the wind.

It was also during *The Sea*, that Judi's grey cardigan routine started.

It had been decided quite early on that I looked a bit too young for the grey dowdy old frump I was playing, and, in order to tone me down a bit, the wardrobe department had had a particularly dull grey cardigan specially knitted for me, to give it that homemade look particular to spinsterish types.

Judi's good luck card to me read, 'Excellent use of a grey cardigan'.

Some months later, I won the Clarence Derwent award as best supporting actress for my performance in *The Sea*. Judi sent me another card. 'Congrats on winning award for Best Actress wearing a Grey Cardigan.'

After a few years of playing a string of more attractive roles, I received another card, 'I don't know *why* you are playing all these glamorous parts. You are much better suited to the grey cardigan parts.'

CHAPTER 16

I was back up north next (in Accrington again) to film the TV series *The Riff Raff Element*. The plot concerns a down-at-heel posh family who rent out a wing of their stately pile to a family of new-age hippies from Manchester. My character, Joanna Tundish, had to walk through the woods in the usual country wear, Barbour and wellies, holding a rifle over her arm. When I then encountered Declan, the character played by Cal Macaninch, trespassing on our land, I had to hold up the gun and, keeping him framed in my gun's sight, track him and force him to strip naked. At the read-through I jokingly suggested he come to my hotel room to rehearse in private. As it happens, he did.

One evening in the hotel, celebrating the wonderful Richard Hope's birthday (my on-screen husband), Cal asked me what I wanted most in the world. I replied, 'A baby'.

He said, 'I'll give you a baby'.

'What? Now?' I replied.

'Yes.'

I took his hand and said 'Come on then . . .'

Next day we climbed Pendle Hill. The view was breathtaking, for more than one reason. Everything in the garden, which at that moment took in the Irish Sea and most of Lancashire and Yorkshire, was rosy.

I was very sorry when the series ended. But it was well worth it for the anticipation of the next job.

I am not a great reader. I'm ashamed to say I probably manage one or two novels a year. But the ones I do read stay with me forever. I had read about four of Ruth Rendell's delightfully creepy non-Wexford books before being offered the lead role in a TV adaptation of *A Dark Adapted Eye*. I had also briefly met her once with the writer Hammond Innes at a party in Suffolk, but obviously the chit-chat you can muster at a social gathering is quite different to the conversation in a working environment.

On location one day, I dared myself to approach the rather fearsome baroness and say how much I was enthralled by the haunting grip of her story. Ruth Rendell explained how she came to write *A Dark Adapted Eye*. 'You always hear people saying, "I wonder who the father is?"' she said. 'Well, I thought it would be an interesting idea to explore the question "I wonder who the mother is?"'

In the brilliant plot, my sister, Eden, played by Sophie Ward, has an illegitimate baby, but doesn't want it, so my character, Vera, terrified of scandal and fiercely protective of her beloved sibling, stuffs a cushion up her front and pretends the baby, Jamie, is her own. Some years later, after Eden marries a rich man, has a miscarriage and is told she cannot have children, she comes to reclaim the infant from Vera. She wants the child in order to save her marriage, as her husband needs an heir to bequeath his fortune. When Eden takes Jamie away from Vera, Vera goes to steal him back, and in the ensuing scuffle stabs Eden to death.

I had grown so fond of Sophie. It was very easy to idolise her in life, as I did in the story, because she, apart from being beautiful, kind and radiant, was the ballet dancer I had always wanted to be.

When the murder scene came around, I gripped my prop knife and stabbed Sophie with the frenzy the scene demanded. When the director called 'Cut', I burst into quite uncontrollable tears, and so did Sophie. It was only acting, but I cannot tell you how terrible it felt to do that to someone you care for.

Later on Vera is hanged for Eden's murder. We filmed that day in a grim location, a disused Victorian-built mental institution. Being in such a place obviously rang bells for me and brought back floods of horrible memories of my time as a patient in the Royal Waterloo Hospital under Mr Sargant.

The hanging scene itself was harrowing in every way. The brilliant stunt adviser fitted me out with all kinds of safety harnesses, but even so, as I stood over the hatch and the trap door was released for me to take the deadly drop, I was completely terrified.

I was so tense that, as I plummeted into the dark, my back went out of joint. That afternoon I could not stand upright and by the evening I could barely move. An osteopath was called and, after manipulating me into a vaguely vertical position, he advised me to go to bed and sleep with a packet of frozen peas held against the painful part of my spine. Next morning I took the packet of peas down to reception. There was no freezer in the hotel bedroom so someone at the front desk kindly arranged for it to be put each morning into the hotel freezer.

On the third day I was just drifting off to sleep, the frozen bag of peas nestling inside my pyjamas, when, with a loud bang, the plastic Birds Eye bag exploded. The memory of the stink of that bed, and the sight of my newly green-splattered polka-dot pyjamas will stay with me forever.

In *A Dark Adapted Eye*, my niece was played by the heavenly Helena Bonham Carter. We both share a propensity to laughter, a master's degree in escapology and are both daft about our figures. Whenever we took lunch together it was almost a competition to see who could order the Ryvita, boiled eggs, Tic-Tacs and Diet Cokes fastest. Helena is not only a brilliant actress but also a terrible giggler and she regularly reduced me to tears.

I'm often asked if I was actually pregnant during the filming of *A Dark Adapted Eye*, but I was not. However the filming did coincide with me being taken by storm with an overwhelming yearning. Biological clocks were ticking and I really wanted to have a baby. As the 'mother' of the child it was in my contract that I had to 'breastfeed' on screen with a bare bosom. The plot, with its obsessive babytalk, stoked up all the fluctuating hormones, which were already in danger of running wild, into a passionate unquenchable desire.

One day sitting on a bench between takes, Sophie said to me, 'Did you decide not to have children then?'

My stomach flipped.

'God, no,' I replied. 'It's what I wanted all my life.'

At the time she had a 3-year-old son and a baby, who she was still breastfeeding.

One evening just as the production car dropped her off at her cottage before taking me on to my hotel, Sophie's husband came out of the cottage door, holding their baby. When the tiny child saw Sophie he stretched out his arms towards her and smiled so sunnily it broke my heart. Sophie beamed back. I have never seen any two humans seem so happy to see one another.

My stomach flipped again. I so wanted a baby of my own and I couldn't let time run out.

We completed the film and, although I was sad to see the end of such a magnificent piece of work as *A Dark Adapted Eye*, the time had come to go back up north and film another series of *The Riff Raff Element*.

Filming began in Clitheroe, Lancashire. My only previous knowledge of the town was from a radio series of my youth called *The Clitheroe Kid*, in which wee Jimmy Clitheroe (in fact a little old man with a child-like voice) raced about being naughty.

I discovered that while I had been busily working on *A Dark Adapted Eye*, Cal had not surprisingly found another lover. The new woman in his life came up to stay in the location hotel and from my nearby hotel room I could hear the sounds of their lovemaking. That was grim.

Everything was made much worse because in the storyline of the new series my character, Joanna, was pregnant with Declan's (Cal's character) baby, and I had to lumber about in pregnancy dresses, with a fake bump which was strapped on each morning, and had then to spend all day pretending that Cal had fathered my imaginary child.

The whole episode was agony. What had once been glorious had become a horror story. I did not spend any more time on the set than I absolutely had to. Whenever I was not called for filming I beat a fast track home.

Before filming the second series, I had been to a doctor for the insurance medical, and after an examination he told me I had little chance of conceiving. It was very late days for me, he said, and if I was to have a baby it really had to be within the next couple of years.

One day I went to BBC Broadcasting House to do a radio play. During a break, Benjamin Whitrow, who had regularly appeared in Olivier's company at the Old Vic, and was later well known for his brilliant portrayal of Mr Bennett in the famous TV adaptation of *Pride and Prejudice,* sat next to me in the green room and asked me if I was married.

'Lord no,' I replied. 'I find this business and marriage doesn't go. Not that I would know, never having dared. Work is my great love, and I suppose it's like having two lovers, though generally the human lover gets jealous of the time, energy and thought that I devote to the work. They believe the work is a rival which takes me away from them.' Even as I spoke I thought that I sounded like a pretentious prat.

I had in fact decided at six years old that I would never marry and had told my mother so. 'If I got married, Mums,' I said, 'it would just be me and my husband in a house on our own, and what on earth would we talk about?' I remember that she laughed.

Many years later I told Eleanor Bron the story, adding that my real horror was that the husband would find me boring. She gave me that famous wry look of hers and said, 'Have you never thought that in fact the actual horror is that it is *you* who would find *them* boring?'

Still, the truth is I believed that marriage, the St Thomas's psychiatric ward at the Royal Waterloo Hospital and *The House of Whipcord* all have one thing in common. They trap you. If I ever married I know I would dread the daily sound of the key in the door and the casual expectancy of 'Hello! I'm home!' Whenever I might put the phone down I can imagine the irritatingly nosey 'other half' would ask me oh-so-casually, 'Who was that on the phone, darling?' And I know I would feel like replying 'Mind your own f***ing business, darling.' Perhaps I would come in late after a show and maybe dinner with friends to 'Look at the time! Where on earth have you been?' I'm afraid my temptation would be to turn right round and go out again, this time to a nightclub to dance till dawn. No. That world of cover-up and compromise is not for me.

If I could have really done evening classes in escapology I would have. I can wriggle out of everything, and I have to say that, whenever I am met by any situation which appears to have no exit, my first instinct is always immediately to start looking for a way out. It has not gone unnoticed by the more perspicacious of my friends, Roger Lloyd Pack (Trigger in *Only Fools and Horses*) calls me 'the Dodger' and the distinguished director and dearest friend, David Conville refers to me as 'the Slippery Fish'.

Anyhow, during our marriage conversation I had told Ben that although I never wanted to take that step I absolutely did want a child, now more than ever, before it was too late. Ben asked if I really meant it? We gradually got to know each other and grew very fond. He thought perhaps in time . . .

Quite early on Ben and I walked on the beach one day as I laid out my terms, which were as detailed as Millament's contract scene in *The Way of the World*. As long as he understood I would not ask for anything, I wouldn't want to live with him, or marry him, would never ask for money for the child and I would be responsible for choosing and paying for the child's education, accommodation, clothing and everything else. I might easily have continued in the Congreve vein had I known the role by heart, for I also demanded, 'the liberty to pay and receive visits to and from whom I please, to write and receive letters, without interrogatories or wry faces on his part, to wear what I please, and choose conversation with regard only to my own taste, to have no obligation upon me to converse with wits that I don't like.'

I was trying to be clear and true. Some people might say calculated, but I would say, knowing myself, I was being honest. If Ben could take all that on board, I said, then his offer to fulfil my wish for a child would be wonderful.

We mutually agreed and he has proved to be a marvellous father to Angus.

I discovered I was pregnant just before Christmas Day. I hugged the knowledge to myself. I knew how the announcement of early positive results could end in disaster. When it came to pregnancy it was always sensible to wait till you were more than three months gone before broadcasting the news.

However while driving my mother across Putney Bridge on our

way to Christmas lunch with the family, I posed her a question, 'Mums, would you mind very much if I had a baby and I wasn't married?'

There followed the longest pause I can ever remember in a conversation.

Then she said very quickly and quietly, 'I'd hate it.'

We drove on in silence. That decided me positively not to tell anyone at all till I had seen a doctor for the second trimester check-up.

For three long months, besides me, only one other person knew I was pregnant, and that was the wardrobe mistress on my next job, the Ken Branagh film, *Frankenstein*, because she *had* to know and then adjust my waistline accordingly.

It was great to be working with Helena Bonham Carter on *Frankenstein* so soon after *A Dark Adapted Eye*. I only had a small role, playing Mrs Moritz, the housekeeper and the mother of a girl who had gone missing and was terrified she had been killed by the monster.

One day Ken Branagh, who played Doctor Frankenstein as well as directing, said, 'Celia, here's your homework for tonight. You are to go home and write a speech for yourself. It must be no more than ten lines long.'

I went home to the house in Clapham, which was at the time crammed with published writers, and resisted the temptation to ask any of them for their help. Instead, I went up to my room and scratched my head for about an hour, after which I went downstairs and cooked supper. Then I sat and ate it alone in front of the TV. When it came to writing I realised I didn't know where to start. After eating, I returned to my room and again sat at my desk, staring at the blank piece of paper till it was time to go to bed.

I ate breakfast next morning feeling terrible that I had written nothing, and it wasn't till I arrived at the rehearsal room, when I knew I *had* to come up with something, anything, that I started writing. While watching Helena rehearse, with my fond memories of our work together on *A Dark Adapted Eye,* I scribbled down my paragraph-long speech.

The rehearsal continued. I was up, walking about, doing my bit. Ken made no reference to the homework, so I felt partly relieved that he must have forgotten about it. But he hadn't.

At the end of the day he said 'Come on then Celia. Let's hear it.' I gulped. I knew what he meant. I did the speech I had written.

'Hmmm,' he said. 'Not bad. I can't promise we'll get to film it, but thanks for giving it your time.'

A few weeks later I went home clutching the pages for the next day's filming. I sat down to learn. To my utter surprise there was my own speech. We shot my ten lines in their entirety.

(A year later, I invited Cal MacAninch, to accompany me to the première. In the car carrying us to the cinema I bet Cal £500 that the speech would be cut. So it was with mixed feelings that I greeted the revelation that my whole self-written speech was there in the final cut of a film which starred Robert de Niro. I had got my dream, but lost my monkey.*)

I went for my second trimester test the day before I was due to set off on a weekend trip to Le Touquet with my great pals Rosalind Knight (star of *Gimme, Gimme, Gimme, St Trinian's* and *Carry On* films, and daughter of Esmond from my Regent's Park days), Fidelis Morgan and Sian Thomas. The four of us have made quite a few cross-channel excursions together, usually day trips, frequently including a posh lunch at some little French bistro somewhere in range of the ferry ports and a trip to the hypermarket. On one of these jaunts we not only had the delicious lunch but went for a wander round the wilderness at Fréthun, where they were digging the Chunnel. That was an amazing evening. The Channel tunnel entrance was at the time a huge surreal wilderness, like the surface of the moon, with great excavators driving around in the lamp-lit twilight.

But this time we were going for a whole action-packed long weekend in racy Le Touquet-Paris-Plage.

I told the others that I was pregnant. As we were sharing a pair

---

* A monkey is racing slang for £500.

of twin rooms with an adjoining door, there was no doubt that during the weekend someone might notice.

That evening we went to the Le Touquet casino and luckily we all won on the roulette tables, then went for a special meal in a highly recommended restaurant. We seemed to be the only diners in the place and the management pulled out all the stops for us. The menu was 12 courses long, including 3 desserts. Fidelis and I went for a vegetable menu, Rosalind took the meat one and Sian the fish.

One of the courses was, to our astonishment, a hardboiled egg. Rosalind, Fidelis and I pocketed ours as we were already stuffed and still had 7 courses to go.

When it came to the desserts, despite how beautiful they looked and smelled, Rosalind, Fidelis and I had to admit defeat. To our surprise Sian said, 'You three are mad! How can you refuse them? They look gorgeous.' Then she promptly wolfed down not only her own 3 desserts but the remaining 9 of ours. Altogether Rosalind, Fidelis and I ate 9 courses each, but Sian devoured 21. (And she is still so thin!)

When we left the restaurant, we all spent a good five minutes in the street, taking off belts, unbuttoning shirts and lumbered back to the hotel rather like four groaning Teletubbies on slow-mo.

Rosalind then put in earplugs, donned a swishy black velvet eye mask, à la Lady Isobel Barnett, and retired for the night, leaving Fidelis to read in the next bed. In the adjacent room, Sian and I lay awake and talked about nothing much till we both fell asleep.

I was woken by Sian rushing for the loo. After a few further visits I had to put the radio on to drown out the sounds coming from the bathroom. Shortly Fidelis, in the next room, also woke and crept through the partition, thinking it was me in the bathroom, with morning sickness. Lucky for Rosalind, in her masked and ear-plugged nocturnal state, she slept through the night of vomits.

The next morning, Sian, wan as an arum lily and looking rather like the face in Edvard Munch's painting *The Scream,* insisted on walking round Le Touquet with me. Rosalind and Fidelis scarpered, but always knew where we had been, because there was a trail of vomit in the gutters. Poor Sian! To this day she is still convinced her sickness was caused by a faulty mussel or oyster, but the three of us still suspect it was simple overload.

But, despite witnessing all that, I was never sick myself, not then, not on the rocky boat home, nor at all throughout my pregnancy.

A few weeks after our French trip, Victoria Wood phoned. 'I've written you a part in my new drama, *Pat and Margaret*. You're a neurotic mother with a baby and a nanny at home.'

Reluctantly, I confessed, 'Actually, if all goes well, I will be actually having a baby at the end of July.'

'Oh, Ceal, how wonderful,' Victoria replied. She sounded delighted. 'That's easy, I'll change it to a neurotic mother-to-be.'

This was marvellous, as it meant I could keep working right till the end of my pregnancy.

One of the weird ironies of the show was that, while filming, once again in Accrington, I stayed in exactly the same hotel room that I had in *The Riff Raff Element* days.

Julie Walters gave me my first pregnancy presents, a child car seat and a bottle of champagne.

CHAPTER 17

Around this time, my neighbours in Cowes told me that they were selling up, and an idea came to me. I would buy the little house next door, knock down the garden wall and thereby have a house big enough for me to live in, work in and have my baby, while in the adjacent house I could give a nanny her own quarters including a nursery, without everyone getting on top of one another. I made the deal with my old neighbours and bought the next-door house.

A few weeks later, heavily pregnant, I threw a party, partly to celebrate my birthday and also to toast the successful purchase of the house next door. Among others, I invited my old nanny, Pop, who lived across the Solent in Winchester.

When people at the party asked me about the next-door house I gaily explained to them how excited I was and told them how I had bought it for my nanny.

A while later there was a noise across the garden, a spoon tinkling against a glass, heralding the fact that someone was preparing to make a speech. I imagined that this was going to be some kind of happy birthday malarkey, so stood back and waited.

'Ssshhh, ssshhh! Everybody!' We all fell silent and Pop, my childhood nanny, took a step forward.

'I'd just like to make a little speech to thank Celia,' she said. 'She has just made this the happiest day of my life!'

I was astonished. What on earth could she be talking about?

'Just in case there's anyone here who hasn't heard, Celia has very kindly bought the house next door for me.'

Oh my God! This was a novel way of learning the true meaning of the word 'ambiguity'.

Yes, I had indeed said I was buying the house next door for my nanny. But I had meant the prospective nanny for my unborn child. Now here was a conundrum. What to do or say?

The truth is that I was simply struck dumb and couldn't think of *anything* to do but smile graciously and accept the thank-you. And after that, I simply didn't have the heart to tell Pop there that had been a bit of a misunderstanding over my use of the word 'nanny'.

So Pop duly sold up her house in Winchester and moved in to the house next door to me. And it worked out so very well. A few years later when Mums's second husband, Douglas, died, she was left with nowhere to live. So my mother also moved to the island and lived next door with Pop. So although it was initially an un-intentional gesture, in the end everything all worked out brilliantly. Pop took the greatest care of Mums, just as she had taken the greatest care of us, as children.

Living next door also meant that both my nanny and my mother had many opportunities to spend time with little Angus.

My baby was due in the third week of July. Days passed and nothing happened. I went for check-ups, and nothing happened. I was ordered to come into hospital to see the midwife. Still nothing happened. July came to an end. My friends were up the road enjoying the fun, fireworks and parties of Cowes Week. Nothing happened.

At 10am on 2 August, the gynaecologist informed me that unless the baby made an appearance within the next twenty-four hours, he would schedule an induced birth. I wasn't having any of that, thank you very much. For a start I didn't want my child to have a falsely created astrological time and day of birth. Superstitious, I know, but it seemed wrong to me not to let the child have the birth time it had decided for itself.

'By the way, if it does start happening,' the gynaecologist added. 'Don't rush into hospital at the first sign.'

'How will I know it's begun?' I asked.

He smiled. 'Oh, you'll know.'

I went home and two hours later the labour began. Despite my love for evening classes I had not bothered with the ones about giving birth. I just thought it kind of happened. What could there be to learn?

That same afternoon, the gynaecologist's wife had invited me to tea. After a couple of hours labour, when I was doubled up and couldn't walk across the room, I phoned her.

'I'm awfully sorry,' I said, 'but I don't think I'll be able to make it to tea today, I'm afraid.' I didn't give a reason. But she was a gynaecologist's wife, for goodness sake! Why hadn't I just told her I was already in the throes of labour?

With Katie my sister and Ben I didn't go into hospital till 7pm that evening and refused all drugs, barring gas and air. In one direction the window of my maternity room looked out onto green woods, on the other I could see Parkhurst Prison.

At 10.30pm, the midwife suggested sending for the gynaecologist to give me something to speed things along a little. At that exact moment, the gynaecologist walked into the room. It was nothing special, he was simply doing his nightly rounds. But, in front of me, the midwife asked him to drug me.

'No, no, no, no!' I cried. I was not going to let him go along with the midwife's suggestion.

I concentrated terribly hard, gave an enormous push and a few minutes later the baby shot out like a cannonball.

I took one look at him and I could see the Scottishness of my father in him. I knew he had to have a Celtic name.

Angus William Jake Imrie was born in St Mary's Hospital, Isle of Wight, at 10.35pm on 2 August 1994. He had blue eyes, wisps of blonde hair and weighed 7lb 10oz. Like me, he was born on a Tuesday. Bravissimo darling Angus.

INTERVAL

So many people ask me the same questions over and over that I am going to answer them here. I'm also going to add some trivial facts and a few recipes.

My FAQ list is:
1. What are your favourite roles?
   a. My favourite roles have been, in no particular order, Else Queen in *Cloud Howe*, Vera in *A Dark Adapted Eye* and Mrs Quickly in *Nanny McPhee*.

2. Do you like music – and which artists are your favourites?
   a. I adore music. I am a particular fan of Stevie Wonder, Paul McCartney, Jeff Beck, Chopin, John Mayer, Ella Fitzgerald, Paloma Faith, dance band music, Dusty Springfield, Andre Rieu, Lucinda Williams, ballet music, Duffy, Johann Strauss, Beth Nielsen Chapman, *Tosca*, B.B. King, Carroll Gibbons and the Savoy Orpheans, Bette Midler, Astor Piazzolla, Pat Metheny, Montserrat Caballé, P.J. Proby, Colin Blunstone, Wynonna Judd, Neil Sedaka, Nigel Kennedy, Alice Cooper . . .

3. How do you prepare for any part you play?
   a. Preparing for a part is a strange thing and everyone has their own private tics and obsessions. Naturally it's a case of reading the script over and over, and not only going over your own lines, but working out when you need to be noticed and when you must get out of the way or the story will be fudged. Most actresses seem

to bang on about shoes. But, on or off stage, shoes don't interest me that much. I prefer to choose a perfume to wear for a character. For instance for *Plague Over England* I wore 'Je Reviens', a perfume which reminds me of my mother. I try to listen to music from the era too.

b. If there is anything technical, and, by technical, I would include dancing or singing, I like to get the trick, routine, steps or tune into my head very early, so that I can concentrate on other things.

c. If the character I am to play is or was a real person, I search out people who had connections with them to find out peculiarities that might not be mentioned in books.

d. If there is an accent involved, I not only consult the tapes and voice coaches, but walk around the area, shopping and asking for directions using the accent I am learning. If I get weird looks, I always think that I must be getting it wrong. Mind you, a friend pointed out to me that I might be getting weird looks because people know who I am and are wondering why I am putting on a peculiar voice or imitating them.

Personal trivia

1. I once threw the javelin for Surrey.
2. I share a birthday with Linda Ronstadt, Iris Murdoch, Brigitte Nielsen, Hammond Innes, Rembrandt van Rijn, Ken Kercheval, Inigo Jones, Jacques Derrida, Robert Winston and Marie Tempest.
3. My surname, Imrie, derives from Flemish Weavers and means 'Work Rule' (whatever that is).
4. I share my surname with
   a. a page 3 legend (Kirsten Imrie)
   b. the scale by which doctors rate degrees of pancreatitis (the Imrie Score)
   c. one of the founder-owners of the White Star Shipping

Line, whose ships included the ill-fated RMS *Titanic* (William Imrie of Liverpool).

5. My parents' family mottos were
   a. Mother [Cator] '*Sine labore nihil*' or 'Nothing without Work'
   b. Father [Imrie] '*Evertendo fecundat*' or 'It becomes frightful turning over'. (And I didn't make that up.)

Six-and-a-half favourite films*

1. *Women in Love*.
2. *All About Eve*.
3. *The Women*.
4. Charlie Chaplin's *The Kid*.
5. *Ballets Russes* and *The Red Shoes*.
6. *The Go-Between*.

Five favourite actors

1. Richard Burton.
2. Cary Grant.
3. Jack Nicholson.
4. Roland Young (especially in the *Topper* films).
5. Jacques Tati.

Five favourite foods

1. Chocolate religieuse from France or Maison Bertaux, Soho.
2. Fish and chips (especially from the Rock & Sole Plaice, Covent Garden).
3. Bhel Puri.
4. Baked beans on toast (Branston beans, white doorsteps).
5. Pocket Coffees (delicious Italian sweets – almost impossible to find outside Italy).

Five foods I hate

1. Parsnips.

* I just couldn't leave out two dance films, *Ballets Russes* and *The Red Shoes*.

2. Stollen.
3. Marzipan.
4. Nuts.
5. Christmas cake. (It incorporates all the others, except parsnips!)

<u>Favourite holiday moments</u>
1. Sipping a Campari in Piazza Navona, or indeed any al fresco café in the Centro Storico, Rome.
2. Riding the 'Beast' or strolling down the streets of New York.
3. Going for an early-morning swim in the Mediterranean, anywhere along the French or Italian Riviera.
4. An early-morning bike ride along the seafront from Cowes to Gurnard, with breakfast at the Watersedge Café.
5. Watching the moonlight over the ocean at Bombay.

<u>My chocolate cake recipe with secret icing</u>
110g/4oz butter
110g/4oz granulated sugar
2 eggs
150-175g/5-6 oz plain flour
2 heaped teaspoons baking powder
2-3 heaped tablespoons cocoa powder
Generous pinch of salt
Generous pour of real vanilla essence
(Ground almonds can be added to the mix to make it juicier, so can grated beetroot.)

Mix butter and sugar till smooth, then add the eggs. Next sieve flour and baking powder together with cocoa into the mixture. Add salt and vanilla.

Put mix into greased baking tray and bake at 180 degrees for about 15-20 minutes.

Secret icing
Cocoa and icing sugar mixed together with a cup of espresso coffee and some vanilla.

The secret ingredient in the icing (as Kathy Kirby sang, 'it's no secret anymore!') is the coffee.

Always make at 5am on the morning you are planning to eat it.

Five great British outings
1. The Grand National (or most jump race meetings).
2. The Isle of Wight Festival (John Giddings is a genius).
3. Eating ice cream or tea and toast on the beach at Gurnard.
4. A steam fair (like Carter's).
5. Leighton House Museum in Kensington.

Five most hated phrases
1. Brownie points (unless you actually are a Brownie).
2. Let's settle down together.
3. Bless!
4. At the end of the day.
5. You can't . . .

My cheese straws recipe
(Ten minutes and dead easy.)
1. Use either bought puff or shortcrust pastry. Obviously with puff (my preferred choice) the resulting straws will be lighter.
2. Roll pastry out into a rectangle. Spread with Dijon mustard just as you would butter a sandwich. Scatter well-grated good strong Cheddar cheese mixed with parmesan, over half of the pastry.
3. Fold the pastry over. Spread a bit more mustard and a bit more cheese.
4. Then take a rolling pin and roll till it is back to the original thickness.
5. Cut into narrow strips.
6. Bake in a hot oven (about 180-200 degrees) for five or so minutes. Just keep peeping till the straws have turned the colour you prefer.

7. Sprinkle with cayenne pepper and serve with drinks.
8. If you want to achieve the full Fanny Craddock effect and make them into matchstick bundles, dip the end of each straw into the cayenne pepper. Cut one of the strips of pastry twice as long as all the others and bend round into a circle before baking. You should then push a few matchstick straws through the little pastry ring and serve. Believe it or not, I actually DO this!

ACT II

CHAPTER 18

Absolutely Fabulous is of course an icon in the TV world, so I was very excited when I was asked to play the role of Claudia Bing of Bing, Bing & Bing. Especially as it was my first job after giving birth to Angus.

Jennifer Saunders tends to write most of the script the night before studio day, so learning lines in time for the filming is nerve-wracking. My first episode featured a guest performance from Naomi Campbell, and I have to say she was totally well-behaved. She seemed really shy, reserved and very polite. So polite, in fact, that it was terribly difficult to hear her, as she was also as quiet as a mouse. It was one of those occasions when I wished I'd taken an evening course in lip-reading.

Angus was only a few months old and so I brought him into rehearsals. Joanna Lumley immediately asked to hold him. To this day, in Angus's eyes, that was something akin to having been touched at birth by a saint.

The dress I wore in the show was an original by the designer much lampooned in the series, Christian Lacroix. Lacroix of course is one of the top end designers in the world, and designed among other things the wedding dress for Christina Aguilera. My costume cost over £2000. In today's prices you could easily double that and add a bit.

My hair for the show had to come up to the same expectation and so was done by Nicky Clarke, who had come hot-foot from doing Princess Diana's hair. As soon as I heard this, I asked him to give me exactly the same style as he had just given her.

Only a few months before, I myself had a close encounter of the third kind with Princess Diana. When I was pregnant, I visited Alton

Towers with a gang of pals who were working in nearby Nottingham. The park was busy. Everywhere you went there were eager photographers lurking. I asked what they were searching for and, swinging their cameras around, they told me Diana was somewhere about, with the two princes. Naturally I kept my eyes peeled.

Being pregnant, I was not allowed to go on certain big-dipper type rides, so when my friends went on I leaned against an adjacent wall to watch them, only to find the princess standing right beside me. Though crowds milled about, no one seemed to see her. She stood alone, watching the two boys who were clearly visible in the front car of the ride, with detectives filling the rest of the carriage. She turned, recognised me and winked. It was a marvellous conspiratorial wink, which seemed to say 'I know *you're* here; you know *I'm* here . . . Hello!' I have to confess I fell immediately under her spell, and when a few seconds later she pulled another face at me it gave me the kind of sparkly feeling inside you might have expected to feel if you had met Elvis. I later met Bill Clinton at a charity bash. He had the same effect. It's a true megastar quality.

I was offered a second episode of *AbFab* a few years later. I phoned Jennifer to explain my reason for possibly turning it down. I had a clash of dates and on the studio day, I was due to be in Paris. So I feared she would instantly withdraw the offer.

'What are you working on in Paris?' she asked.

'Um, well, er, I . . .' I stammered. 'You see, I am going to Paris but it's not *exactly* work.'

'So what is it then?'

'Well, as a matter of fact, the thing is, you see, I've managed to get Golden Square tickets at the Bercy Stadium to see Madonna in concert.'

'My God!' she screamed. 'Celia Imrie . . .'

I expected, and deserved the worst. How unprofessional was I? Who had ever heard of such a thing? Disgraceful behaviour! Whoever would put an expedition to lark about at a pop concert before work? Yada yada yada . . .

But instead I heard this, 'Celia! You lucky, lucky thing. Celia!

Madonna, live! Oh, of course you must go to that. Madonna in Paris! Don't worry. We'll work round you. You MUST go to that. Oh, am I jealous!'

Thank you Jennifer.

So I did both the episode of *AbFab* and went to Paris to see the concert. And, yes, Madonna was marvellous.

I love the writer Joan Aiken, and in particular her character Dido Twite, so I leapt at the opportunity of being in a TV adaptation of *Blackhearts in Battersea*. The film provided me with a new substitute for my evening classes for I had to learn how to juggle and also how to operate a hot air balloon.

But by the time I was filming *In the Bleak Midwinter,* a few months after the first *AbFab,* I was in the throes of post-natal depression. To make matters worse, despite having been put together by the same team as *Frankenstein*, the atmosphere on *Midwinter* was not nearly as free. It was all a bit *Carry On Up Your Old Varsity Chums* and I felt quite a fool, not being as well educated as the others.

I find that when many people from the upper echelons of ex-university life gather together, something very strange happens. They all turn into joke-competitors, each trying to outdo the other with humorous anecdotes and one-liners, while you, the non-university ones, have to do an awful lot of grinning, even at times when you haven't a clue what they're all on about. Everyone around you seems to turn into something like a rabid hyena on a joke rampage. It all becomes rather *Monty Python*, and, to be truthful, I never really understood that either.

Talking of university reminds me of a night early on in my time at Glasgow Citz. A gang of actresses went out to dinner at the Spaghetti Factory, the local trendy café of the era.

We sat in a little snug and two of them started comparing notes about where and when they got their degrees. One very talented actress, called Zoe, turned to me and said, 'Celia, where did you go to university?'

I was astonished. I would have thought it was writ large across my face that I had not. I didn't even do A levels. (And I barely did O levels!)

'Leeds,' I replied. It was the only town I could actually say through my rictus grin. No laugh followed. What was happening? I couldn't believe they actually believed me.

'What did you study?'

'Oh . . . Oceanography,' I said, before I exploded with laughter and told them the truth.

Anyhow, into this mêlée of varsity-itis which was *In The Bleak Midwinter,* suddenly erupted the rainbow of glamour which is Joan Collins. On her first day we sat and had lunch, or rather I should say *I* had lunch while I watched Joan take ten minutes to eat a grape. She explained to me how fizzy water was more fattening than still, and made me roar with laughter with a string of hilarious anecdotes and her swishy nonchalance.

After I had waited a few weeks for the phone to ring, Patrick Malahide called. I had played his wife a few years earlier, on *Lovejoy*. He had written a new film, *The Writing on the Wall*, and wanted me to be in it. So I packed Angus into a carry cot and made my way to the location in Germany. It was my only experience working in a multinational cast. We had people speaking different languages, French, German, Czech . . . Yet we did all seem to understand one another.

We also had an American actor on the set who fascinated me. I couldn't take my eyes off him, as he reminded me totally of how my father would have looked as a young man – something which of course I never saw. That actor was William H. Macy.

Back to the theatre next. *The Hothouse* was directed by my long-time dear friend, David Jones, and was written by and starred Harold Pinter. It was exciting to be in such prestigious company, and playing firstly back in Chichester then in the West End.

Harold often took a glass of wine with his lunch, and occasionally nodded off during afternoon rehearsals. One day when he woke up I said, 'Hmmm, that was very interesting.'

'What do you mean?' he replied. ('What do you mean' was something of a catchphrase of his.)

'You were talking in your sleep.'

'What did I say?'

'You said "the tendrils of the vine can twist you to death".'

'Did I?' he replied, somewhat startled.

'No,' I confessed. 'I made it up.'

'Very good,' he said, giving me an old-fashioned look. 'Don't do it again.'

Pinter was always very blunt, which I found quite refreshing. He had no time for people who faffed about, or for social small talk. He also hated wasteful phrases. For instance if a person ever opened a conversation with the phrase, 'How are you?' he always replied, 'What do you mean? Healthwise, financially, what?'

David Jones had an irritating dry cough throughout rehearsals and Harold got cross with him for the constant hack, hack, hack. One day Harold told him he had had enough of the cough, and had arranged an appointment for David to see his own doctor. It turned out to be a lucky break, for David was diagnosed with early stage throat cancer. He underwent treatment right away, and Harold's irritation saved his life.

I had an onstage kiss with Mr Pinter, and I have to say it was lovely. He kissed in a lingering, sensual way. Very sexy! For a while I had quite a crush on him.

I was really enjoying my time working on this play, but then out of the blue something came along to give me a horrible jolt. I came into the theatre one night and there was a letter left for me in my dressing room. It ended, 'I hope you walk out onto that stage tonight and fall flat on your f***ing face.'

It was signed by someone I knew of, but did not know personally. I had however once worked with her husband.

Now I need to go back in time a little . . . Imagine the screen image going wobbly as we whiz back through the years.

A while before Angus had been born, I had done a location TV job set in one of the seedier cities of northern Europe. A senior member of the production crew was himself of European extraction and spoke with a heavy accent.

I had heard that he always invited the leading lady to dinner, and never forgave the ones who turned him down. Solo dinners with virtual strangers are things I try always to avoid. I dread the long silences filled with the chink of china and cutlery, and hours chewing but not tasting the food, while you rack your brains for the next thing to say. So when the invitation inevitably arrived, I thought at first of bringing someone else to help me out. I was swiftly warned by the wardrobe mistress that this would certainly not do. To bring a friend would be worse than turning him down.

So the time for the dinner rolled up. And, like a lamb to the slaughter, I went. But I didn't have to worry about making conversation, for he did all the talking. In fact he told me his whole life story. It was truly heart-wrenching. He talked of being Jewish during the persecutions of the early twentieth century, about his family being gathered up and put into a concentration camp, and his eventual escape to the West. Naturally I was totally awestruck and full of empathy and pity.

The next night was my last at the location, and during the tea break, he invited me to dinner again. I really didn't want to repeat the dining experience with him, so I gaily said, 'Why don't we go to a museum instead?'

I asked the hotel concierge what were the special unique places in town. He gave me directions to two museums, then informed me that on that particular day of the week one of the museums, which he said was an exhibition of kunst, was closed. I was relieved to hear it. Kunst indeed! What would it look like if I took this man to see that? (I later discovered that in German this rather worrying word 'kunst' actually means art.)

I phoned him and we took a taxi together to the other address the concierge had given us. As the cab pulled up outside I couldn't believe what I saw written in pink neon across the front of the building, Sex Museum. Good God! How much worse than kunst was sex!

So he, now quite excited, climbed out of the taxi, saying, 'Oh Celia! What a wonderful idea. This looks fascinating.' I wished the earth would swallow me.

The ground floor display was safe enough. Lots of artefacts from ancient history were exhibited: an Etruscan stone phallus, for instance, then a Grecian vase and a piece of a Roman mural. Thankfully, it was all quite tame stuff. I breathed a huge sigh of relief and assumed that this episode wasn't going to be nearly as embarrassing as I had feared from the first view in the taxi.

Things got rather hotter on the first floor with some pretty explicit eighteenth-century engravings and a case containing some weird battered old condoms made of leather, wax-soaked cloth and lemon rind. But I could still vaguely classify this as art, or history, or something that wasn't *exactly* sex. And I was very relieved that the museum wasn't anything near as bad as I had anticipated.

However I found that floor three was quite a different matter. In fact, it still features in my worst nightmares. At the entrance, you were confronted by a life-size waxwork of a man holding open a mac, to reveal his trousers and pants round his ankles, and displaying what the labels on the ground floor might have described as a gigantic phallus all of his own. There was a phone box, and when you stepped inside it, a speaker relayed the sound effects of a woman giving phone-sex, there were fruit bowls made to look like vaginas and coffee pots with spouts like penises which adorned tall penis-shaped stands. A case of vibrating dildos (big enough for camels), stood in front of a wall displaying photographs and videos of people in every possible (and some frankly impossible) sexual position. And all this came accompanied by the seething soundtrack of a couple having very, very noisy sexual intercourse.

I had come out in a sweat. Not because I thought any of the exhibits in the least bit erotic, but because I wanted so badly to run. I knew, however, that if I did run, the situation could only get worse. In fact *whatever* I did it could only get worse. I managed to get back to my hotel alone, with the excuse I still had to learn my lines for the next day, my last day's filming.

To my surprise and delight, the last shooting day went completely smoothly and I flew back home to London, relieved that the whole episode had ended without incident.

But a few weeks later the onslaught began. Every day I came home to a number of answering machine messages from him. Let's call him Albert.

Beep: 'Hello, darlink,' he said in his unmistakable accent. 'Albert here. I am missing you. Phone me. Lots of love, darlink.'

Beep: 'Only between 10 and 5, OK? Only phone then, darlink. Lots of love, Albert.'

Beep: 'Darlink, Albert here. I'm phoning from the phone box in the pub. I just wanted to hear your lovely voice.' Etcetera.

I was still in the Clapham house and sharing the answering machine with three or four others. They were not always delighted to come home to find they had missed a work call they were expecting because the tape was full of 24 messages all for me and all from the same person and all saying basically nothing.

At the time, I was out all day rehearsing *The Hothouse* and coming home to these messages had seemed very much like still being in the throes of a real-life Pinter play.

When I didn't phone back the number of calls escalated. So I did sometimes return the call. Then one day we seemed to have a meteor shower of calls describing his entire day:

'Good morning, darlink. Albert here. I'll phone you later.'

'Hello, darlink, Albert speaking. Just grabbing breakfast before I set off.'

'Hello, beautiful. It's Albert. I'm in a service station on the M1. I'll phone again when I'm in Manchester.'

He seemed to phone at least every half hour with an update on his whereabouts and what was on his plate at his last meal.

My fellow house-mates, on this particular day, were highly amused. The phone tape reminded them of some musical experiment by John Cage, or some innovative experimental radio drama. Also, it hadn't taken them long to work out exactly who it was on the other end of the line. I phoned him.

'Look, Albert. You really must stop phoning me all the time. I share the house *and* the phone. Someone missed a call from their agent yesterday because the tape was full of your messages. Everyone knows your name because you always leave it. What must it look like to them? And, remember, you *are* married.'

I was fond of him, but I probably should have told him he had got the wrong end of the stick, nothing was going on, nothing was ever going to go on and please would he go away and leave me alone. But you can ask any actor alive whether they would have done that to an esteemed senior member of any TV or film Production crew. It is almost inbred in us never to say anything like this to someone who could possibly change everything about your career, one way or another. Remember, we actors go from job to job, and nothing is ever secure about our futures. We don't tend intentionally to upset the people who employ us.

Next morning there was another message:

'Hello darlink . . . . [long pause] . . . . . Charlie here . . .'
He might have changed the name but oh, dear, the accent! As if anyone wouldn't have instantly recognised that voice.

Many days (and answering machine messages) later his wife's note arrived. I phoned her straight away.

'This really isn't fair,' I said.

She hissed down the phone.

'Look,' I said. 'We need to talk. Meet me in the Regent's Park rose garden tomorrow morning at 10.'

I arrived at the place of assignation, taking Angus (aged 13 months) for protection, with a clear conscience. After all, I hadn't had an affair nor had I any intention of having an affair with the man. I had my own life, including a baby son to look after. I had no designs on her husband. I was very fond of him and had enormous professional respect for him, as I had re-assured him, repeatedly. It was just that he seemed unable to stop phoning me. And phoning me, and phoning me . . .

With Angus oblivious in his pushchair, we were walking carefully through the park, when she began her rant. 'Leave my husband alone.' It felt exactly like being in a French film. Even Regent's Park seemed black-and-white.

'I have no interest in your husband. You must believe me, please. If there was anything, it was all in his head.'

'You're leading him on all the time, wanting him to leave me and run off with you.'

I was pole-axed. Where on earth had that come from?

'No. I never wanted any such thing. He just phones me. It's a fantasy, don't you see? I have never done anything but sit and listen, sometimes for hours on end, while he told me he thought no one appreciated him and that his work wasn't properly recognised. I can understand why you should think something went on but I assure you I thought it was friendship. I just spent hours of listening to him talk, boosting him up, and bolstering his ego.' I think she believed me and, after the meeting, the phone calls stopped.

It's odd that Angus, a sleeping baby, was with me through all that, because now, as a teenager, he seems to have me totally sussed. He will overhear me on a phone call and say 'Why did you say that?'

'What?'

'That you were really looking forward to seeing them when you're not.'

'It's just politeness.'

'Hmmmm!' he will say. 'They won't think that though. Not the way you said it. They'll think they're really special to you.'

Angus, young as he is, wisely put his finger on a longstanding source of anxiety. He has made me aware of the patterns I have neglected to see myself. For fear of upsetting people, I have often failed to tell people the raw truth. On many occasions, I realise, I have put out the wrong signals, but have been too much of a coward to come clean. Instead, when things hurtled out of control, rather than facing up to them, I have hidden behind my closest friends and my mother, leaving them to deal with it, thereby causing great distress all round. If this has applied to anyone reading this, I am truly sorry.

CHAPTER 19

Stewart Permutt and I now lived in separate dingy bedsits and both found ourselves going through a challenging time. I had a young baby to look after and was now living in a vile flat in Streatham. Outside the window was a huge electronically-operated advertising board. All day and all night it went clack, clack, clack as it revolved its way through its four repeating commercial messages.

The flat was dismal and gloomy, and I felt all it needed was an iron fire escape and some old tin dustbins and I'd have been living in a black-and-white film, set in the Bronx during the Great Depression. Mind you I *was* in a great depression all of my own. The flat had a brown carpet and I was in a brown study.

Stewart and I phoned each other trying to cheer one another up and when we were both offered roles in *Habeas Corpus* at the Donmar Theatre it seemed like a life-line. We galvanised each other as day one approached, gave support throughout rehearsals and ended up having a much needed laugh. By the end of the show we felt much better.

Then another opportunity came out of the blue. Nigel Planer suggested me for a job he had had to relinquish. I was to take over where he had left off, reading the Terry Pratchett *Discworld* series as talking books. In all there were four books I had to read. I was very grateful to him. Angus was only one-and-a-half, and it was marvellous to get any job at all. The informality of recording talking books meant I could bring Angus up to Oxford with me and, with my sister Katie as his absolutely wonderful nanny, I could record in the studio and then pop out and see Angus during any tea-breaks, and overnight in the hotel. After all, the only thing I had to do was sit down and read a book . . . But what a book!

It was with some trepidation that I arrived in Oxford that brisk morning, armed with my gigantic marked-up copy of *Discworld*. To be perfectly frank, I wasn't all that happy. I had struggled to get through the book at all. To me, it seemed incomprehensible. In fact I barely understood a blithering word of it. I began to suspect Nigel Planer's motives. Had he found the books as indecipherable as I had? Had he palmed the job off on me because he was as lost and panicky as I was? Truthfully I have never been the world's best sight reader. In fact I am quite possibly the world's worst sight reader. Ask Rosalind Knight!

Then came the actual slog of the job. Who knew that recording a talking book entails sitting in a tiny sound studio where there is only just room for you and the script? Who knew that once settled in, sometimes with only a sandwich break at midday, all on your own, you talk solidly into a microphone from 10 in the morning till 6 in the evening? Who knew that your throat aches, your back throbs, your eyes itch, your legs puff up and you want nothing but sleep?

Once the recording day is over, you daren't speak a word all evening in case you wake up feeling even more hoarse the next morning. I spent my evenings playing sign language games with Angus to try and rest the vocal chords.

This was all fine, really, if it hadn't been for the fact that in interpreting this crazy book I also had to find different voices for about 798 various elves, goblins, witches, wizards, werewolves, trolls and zombies. Maybe there were even orks. There might even have been Orkadians!

Think about it. As an actor reading onto a tape, you have nothing but your voice. If you don't have a different sound for each character (or species of extra-terrestrial creature) the listener cannot tell who or what is talking. But *Discworld* had far too many characters for me to get a grip on.

In my desperation to inject a little variety into the myriad of weirdo voices I had to come up with, I ended up resorting to the very cheap trick of holding my nose. One nostril for one character, two for another, a loose hold for a third, a really tight squeeze for a fourth. It was dire.

Discworld truly is another universe. Those who are into it really understand it. The rest of us are suspended in bewildered and dumb-founded disbelief. As far as I could make out it was something about a disc being thrown onto an elephant's head. But what were all those goblins doing on an elephant's head with a disc in the first place?*

After day four, I threw my hands up in defeat and, I am sure to the relief of *Discworld* fans everywhere, got my agent to get me out of the rest of the contract.

I suspect that these books are a man thing. Or maybe even a lonely-men-in-spectacles thing.

The surreal comedy drama *Hospital* opened on Channel 5 and continued my hospital-themed career. I was back in the old nurse's uniform, only this time I played a bossy matron-type who shoved through swing doors in the manner of the late, great, Hattie Jacques and wore an ever-changing sequence of bizarre and ornate white paper origami hats. No one in the film made any reference whatso-ever to the headgear, whether the thing perched on top of my head was the Sydney Opera House, a swan, the Eiffel Tower, a buffalo's head or Battersea Power Station. It was a mad programme to make, much fun was had by all and altogether it left me feeling rather more cheery.

I had a small but interesting part in the thriller *Into the Blue*, starring John Thaw and directed by the great Jack Gold who had directed me in *Return of the Native*. The best thing I remember about the job was my parting scene with John Thaw, standing on a river bank in the rain. He turned to me and said: 'You must buy that mac

---

* While I was telling a friend about my horrors on this job, sitting on the top deck of a 148 bus, a man wearing a mac and horn-rimmed specs sitting in an adjacent seat turned to me and said, 'I'm sorry, I can't help overhearing you. But I must point out there are NO goblins or elves in *Discworld*. They are ALL fascinating characters, many of them multi-faceted vampires and werewolves. The books are all wonderful and anyone but an idiot can understand them.' Blah blah blah . . . I was well and truly told off. But each to his own. Now I have had my warning and I'd better keep an eye open in case I get kidnapped by the Discworldish Society for expressing my opinions in public and now in print.

[my costume] and wear it to the first rehearsal of your next job. It makes you look very swishy.' I thought it was quite refreshing that his conversations were always about extra-curricular things like that, rather than banging on all the time about work.

I obeyed Mr Thaw's orders and wore the coat to the first rehearsal of my next job. Sadly the coat didn't go down awfully well, as the rehearsal was for a rather serious and worthy production of *Dona Rosita and her Daughters* by Lorca, at the Almeida Theatre. Everyone else was wearing the uniform of actors in those extremely earnest theatre shows, faded denims and trainers or long swirling skirts of a rustic nature with fraying mules. And there was me swanning in wearing my very swishy coat.

Unfortunately, two weeks later, while juggling buggy and bags on a train to Southampton, I left it swishing away by itself on a British Rail luggage rack.

That same weekend I scratched my knuckle on the seawall at Cowes. The graze itself, though only the size of a ten pence piece, developed an oddly vivid bright red fringe to it. The whole hand was hot and throbbing. Being a doctor's daughter, I was worried. It simply didn't feel or look right. I soaked it in a bowl of Dettol that evening and when I woke next day to find it was much worse I phoned the theatre and spoke to the director, asking whether I could have permission to be an hour late so that I could pop into the doctor's. She said no. I was told to wait.

At lunchtime a visiting doctor gave it a cursory look but he had no tetanus injections with him. I knew then I had to insist on keeping my four o'clock appointment with my own doctor. I worked all day, feeling increasingly unwell, and then made my way to the surgery. By this time the whole of my arm was swelling in a most unnatural way. I felt quite seriously strange.

The doctor took one look at my hand, realised I was suffering from acute blood poisoning and ordered me to report immediately to St George's Hospital. By the time I got there a red line ran from my hand to my elbow. Had it reached my armpit (the lymph gland) I would have been in serious danger of dying. So, to save one morning's rehearsal, I ended up out of action for ten days, lying in a hospital bed on a drip, with my arm in a contraption which held it pointed up towards the ceiling in a kind of perpetual Nazi salute (even when sleeping!).

Once the play was on, I had a slight run-in with one of the cast. During one of the scenes, which I watched from the wings, there was some important dialogue spoken downstage. However a lot of tripping-over business with a scarf went on upstage behind them. One day it all went too far. I expressed my opinion that pulling focus from the dialogue, for no reason but to draw attention to one's self, was not the best way of playing Lorca (or for that matter, any playwright) and was put down with the remark, 'And what would you know about playing Lorca? You are nothing but a mere TV comedienne.'

Before I knew what had happened I had slapped the offending actor in the face. And to tell the truth I don't regret it. I can call myself a mere TV comedienne if I please, but I will not have it used against me as an insult. In fact whenever I appear at those one-off reading evenings I usually refer to myself as the 'Light Ent'* part of the programme.

After the Almeida, I went back into TV to play the politician's wife, a part loosely based on Christine Hamilton, self-styled battleaxe, in her attempts to help her husband beat 'Martin Bell' to a parliamentary seat. The piece was called *Mr White Goes to Westminster*.

I was thrilled to be playing a 'living person'. But in my determination to pick up a few tips, I chased the poor woman around London, attending every book signing and public appearance she did. I think she must have thought I was a mad stalker. I fear someone must have tipped her off that I was playing her in a TV show, for whenever I moved in to try and get a bit of chat, she'd vanish through the back door. So for all my efforts I never actually cornered her.

It was quite a new and bizarre experience to me, this having to

* Light Ent is a BBC abbreviation of their own subdivision of TV and radio programming – Light Entertainment. Light Ent is most certainly not deemed the equal of the apparently superior Drama Department.

play a real live person thing. It was strange knowing that whatever you did on screen the very person you were representing could actually sit and watch you pretending to be them. It must be said that Christine Hamilton was a tremendous hoot to play.

The greatest thrill for me came early one Sunday morning when I arrived in Parliament Square to see a photo of myself, wearing her carefully styled hair-do complete with Alice-band. The photo was part of a huge poster, plastered along the side of a double-decker London bus parked smack in front of Big Ben.

But the final filming day on *Mr White Goes to Westminster* clashed with one of the rehearsal days for my next job, *The Borrowers*.

Shooting always takes precedence to rehearsing, so I was released from the *Borrowers* rehearsal day, which included lessons in rope climbing. All the other Borrowers attended. My absence seemed inconsequential at the time, but, oh dear, did I regret it later.

When it came to the filming of the first *Borrowers* scenes, we all had to grab ropes and slide down them at speed. They went to lessons for this? I thought. Goodness me, why all the fuss? What could be simpler? Surely you just grab the rope and slide down?

The rope-sliding scene arrived. The director called, 'Action!' The cameras rolled. We leapt out onto our ropes, and shinned down.

OOOOOOOUCH!

I didn't realise that if you didn't apply the hand-change technique which the others had been taught, you get rope burn. I lost most of the skin from my palms, and for days, to protect myself, walked around with my dangling hands held out in front of me. I felt like a puppet out of *Thunderbirds Are Go!*

A few weeks before filming started, Joan Hills, the very fine make-up designer had given us all a tube of sunscreen specially imported from Japan, as it had a higher factor than anything available over here. We had to wear it for a month leading up to the job so that we would have the required pallor of people who live underground. Friends off the set kept looking at me with worried expressions, thinking I was going to faint, or that I was not well. It's amazing how ill you look if you take the sun's effect away from your skin.

We all played tiny people but obviously were really normal

actor-size. The illusion was created by the brilliant designer, Gemma Jackson, through the use of specially-constructed enormous scenery and props. It was fabulous walking around among the gigantic chair and table legs and sitting on huge cotton reels. Our wallpaper frieze was a gigantic tape-measure, constantly reminding you of the scale, and our supper was one green pea each, eaten off a button.

I helped design my own necklace. I had the idea to use the pieces from a bath plug chain, including the little metal triangle. This was replicated in large size and can be seen in all its splendour in the film. However I don't think Christian Lacroix need have any fears yet.

In the film, Jim Broadbent and I played Mr & Mrs Borrower and we had two Borrower kids. In between takes, I kept trying to organise them and came up with ideas for games which they could play to keep them amused. I suppose my Theatre In Education days were still looming large in my head. Repeatedly I would gushingly offer assistance to one of the children and inevitably it ended in disaster, with them getting overexcited when they should have been calm. Standing beside me, Jim would mutter, 'Celia, don't help. Don't help, Celia. Please, don't help.'

It became his mantra. And to this day it echoes in my head always when I go marching in to offer my assistance, or, should I say, to interfere, in things which are of no concern of mine. I always mean it for the best. Somehow it rarely works out that way.

Duck Patrol starred my old friend and a very favourite director Richard Wilson and a young unknown called David Tennant (Who?) and was about the river police. I played a termagant wife who has been deserted by her husband and gets her revenge in the style that was so fashionable in the 1990s, by cutting up her husband's best suits, giving away his precious wine collection, and generally being hysterical. We filmed on the River Thames, and I played an inhabitant of one of those islands once so trendy among the hip arty classes. I believe the actual island we used had once belonged to one of my screen heroines, the fabulous Diana Dors.

My multi-subject education continued, when for this show I had to learn how to perform a difficult canoe manoeuvre in which I had to spin the canoe round till I was underwater then bob up the other side, at night. It was very scary.

I also had to film a scene where, while screaming my head off, I had to throw a whole bag of frightfully expensive golf clubs into the river, club by precious club. I have to say that that bit was enormous fun. My javelin-throwing skills came to the fore as the golf-sticks sailed in an arc, then splashed into the river. Many folk gathered along the riverbank to goggle at me and thought I really was a madwoman.

My extra-curricular education continued for the film *Hilary and Jackie*. This time I was sent off again to learn the piano.

I was playing Iris du Pré, who famously accompanied on piano her two daughters who played flute and cello respectively. I had to try somehow to pretend to play piano concertos. It was my first encounter with the instrument since my humiliation in the Woking Festival.

I was sent to a shy young man in West Hampstead. The very arrival at the tube station gave me instant heebie-jeebies, as an adjacent house had been the site of my hellish rehearsals for my first unhappy foray into 'straight' theatre in *Don't Start Without Me* for the Adeline Genée Theatre, East Grinstead. Even though it was twenty-five years later, as I strode from the tube station, the words of the critic from the *East Sussex Clarion* revolved in my head, '. . . as played by Celia Imrie, the rather wooden Ruth . . .' Let me tell you, you never forget the exact wording of a bad review.

During the lesson, my tutor let it slip that he had, that weekend, played his mother's favourite piano movement at her memorial service. As I plonked my fingers clumsily on the keys I remember thinking how hard that must have been.

Three years later, I tracked him down and asked him if he could find a violinist to accompany him and come and play Kreisler's *Schön Rosmarin*, my own mother's favourite, at her memorial.

In *Hilary and Jackie* I had to wear typical 1950s mid-calf skirts, quite the worst line for a woman like me, with my hockey-player legs. Sometime later I was sitting in a West End theatre audience waiting for curtain up, when a well-known actress came up to me to tell me she had seen the film, and then, just as the lights faded, she whispered into my ear, 'Ankles!'

I don't remember a word of the play or its story, for I spent the whole show rewinding *Hilary and Jackie* in my mind, trying to picture how huge my ankles must have seemed to have provoked her response.

The film was a great hit and as part of the cast I attended the Venice Film Festival. I find Venice rather a spooky and claustrophobic place. It's certainly not for depressives. However I did make the most of my visit, and managed to grab an ice cream and an espresso. I did *not* buy a mask.

I was called up to the hometown of the Bard, the land of ye olde tea-shoppes, Stratford-upon-Avon, to play Mrs Candour in Sheridan's *The School for Scandal* for the Royal Shakespeare Company. In an effort to be rather more modern than the surrounding town, the production had a special feature: all the actors had to stay on stage throughout. It was a jolly device by which the actors were instructed, once their character technically left the scene, to come out of character and simply sit there in full sight of the audience during all the scenes they were not in. On more than one night I was caught onstage, fast asleep. I believe I even snored, which was what woke me up with a jolt. When I opened my eyes and gazed out upon the Stratford audience, then cast a glance round the stage, I hadn't a clue where I was. I am told by others in the company that I had been spark-out for about ten minutes. I was playing Mrs Candour, and I have to say you couldn't be more candid about the show than that.

It's worth adding that on my first night, having so importantly achieved a rather un-Light-Ent status by playing at the Royal Shakespeare Memorial Theatre, I received a brown paper parcel from Dame Judi Dench. Inside was an old grey cardigan.

Victoria Wood had written a new sitcom called *dinnerladies*. Along with Julie Walters and Duncan Preston, from the old gang, the cast included two actresses I really admired, Anne Reid and Thelma Barlow, and two newcomers, Maxine Peake and Shobna Gulati. It was set in a factory canteen in the north of England. I was to play a southern Human Resources Officer called Philippa.

The filming of *dinnerladies* was done the American way, and it was the first time I had ever experienced this. Usually with a sitcom, the actors rehearse from Monday to Thursday, then on Friday they go into studio and play in front of a live studio audience.

For *dinnerladies*, we rehearsed in the week and played to the studio audience on Fridays, as usual. But then, next morning, Victoria would cut and rewrite anything she didn't think worked well enough. On Saturday afternoon, we would come in to rehearse the changes, learning the lines as we went. A few hours later, on Saturday evening, we played the whole thing again, this time with cuts and additions, to another studio audience. The two recordings would then be edited together to make the final show, which was the one aired on TV.

It was a hell of a schedule. The whole cast felt like we were on an ice skating rink.

As we waited in the wings, Julie and I could be seen by nosey members of the audience taking crisis remedies and sniffing assorted pacifying herbal potions to keep us going and to calm us.

At the time, I was living in Colliers Wood. One morning I arrived at the tube station to find the Northern Line had broken down. I stood in the High Street, flapping my arms, trying to find a taxi. Frantic, I marched along to Tooting Bec, looking desperately for any way to get me to the rehearsal room in north London. But there was nothing. All the minicabs were taken, and there were no black cabs to be found anywhere.

In a hysterical and frenzied state, I phoned the rehearsal room, to explain why I wasn't there. I shouted and screamed, using language from which even a trooper might shy away.

The following week the next *dinnerladies* script arrived. It was all in. Skipping some of the expletives which were far too ribald for the BBC, my transport-rage episode became one of my scenes. So if you want to see what I am really like when I cannot get to work on time, take a look at the 'Millennium' episode of *dinnerladies*.

It is what Victoria excels at. Taking real life and using it to great effect. Marvellous writing. And as for playing that episode, well, I knew exactly how.

CHAPTER 20

I first met the writer Hammond Innes through my mother in the late 1980s. Sometime after my father died, my mother became reacquainted with the old boyfriend whose photo had been sitting in the desk alongside my rejection letter from the Royal Ballet School. After she and Douglas Fordham married, they moved to Long Melford, a village in Suffolk.

One of her friends, Mrs Baker-Monkton, threw a summer party in Suffolk and my mother and I were invited. Other guests included two local writers of great fame, Ruth Rendell and Hammond Innes.

I was briefly introduced to Ruth Rendell (this was years before we filmed *A Dark Adapted Eye*) then put into a corner with Hammond Innes and his wife, Dorothy, an ex-actress. Dorothy was elegant, like a thoroughbred racehorse, very sleek, witty and glamorous. Ralph Hammond Innes seemed to me a bit of a crotchety old bugger. I felt quite out of my depth and, while I made the usual small talk, I was wiggling about, looking for an escape route.

'What a shame it's raining,' I said. 'It would have been so lovely sitting out there in the garden on a sunny day.'

'Quite a few more days of rain in store, I'd say,' said Ralph.

'How's that?' I said, imagining he must be expert in matters meteorological.

'Because it rained on Saint Swithin's day.'

'My birthday,' we both said in unison.

'Is it your birthday, too?' we said together.

'Mine too!' we chorused.

Dorothy rolled her eyes, laughed and said, 'It's like standing in a corner with Tweedledum and Tweedledee.'

A year later, as it came up to my birthday, I bought Ralph a card and posted it off. 'Happy Birthday from Saint Swithin to Saint Swithin. Love Celia xx'.

Next morning, on my birthday I received a card from him saying 'Happy Birthday to Saint Swithin from Saint Swithin.' He didn't need to sign his as it came on a card imprinted with his pen name, Hammond Innes.

Shortly after this, while I was doing up my house in Cowes, I read of the sudden death of Dorothy. I realised Ralph must be devastated, because Dorothy, apart from being an extremely glamorous wife, had obviously been his soul-mate. Together they had travelled the world, their work always interlinking. She did research for him and joined him on his many difficult expeditions, writing her own notebooks along the way. Three of her accounts of travels with Ralph were published.

Some months later I received a call from Ralph – would I meet him for drinks in London? After that we met up regularly. He took me to lunch at the prestigious Royal Thames Yacht Club, and invited me to a gathering at a place where, though only a few yards from my front door in Cowes, I had never before managed to get into, the swanky men-only club, the Royal Yacht Squadron. (Membership includes The Duke of Edinburgh, the Aga Khan, King Juan Carlos of Spain, you get the picture?) I let Ralph use my Cowes home as a base whenever he needed it for yachting events, to attend RYS meetings and so that he could spend more time on the project to which he had devoted much energy, the Association of Sea Training Organisations. ASTO is a youth training project with many boats, including a tall ship in the Solent, which encourages children from poorer backgrounds to enjoy the sea, and in particular gives them practical experience on board a real ship, learning to sail every type of vessel from dinghies to huge beautiful square-rigged ships which look like something out of *The Onedin Line* or *Pirates of the Caribbean*.

I went with Ralph to book dos, and when I was working in the theatre he came to see me in plays. He was an old-school gent and very good company. When his new novel *Isvik* was published, I was invited to the launch party. A character in the novel supposedly also had a few of my attributes. However when I arrived at the venue I found that my name was not on the guest list. Ralph had insisted that I must spend the night not wearing a badge which said Celia Imrie, but was to be there as Lady Saint Swithin.

Once when going to join him for a drink in his Notting Hill house we walked past Pizza Express.

'People tell me they're awfully good,' he said. 'But I never fancied going in, not on my own.'

'Come on then.' I said, pushing open the door. 'You're not on your own now.'

The next year we spent our shared birthday together. I invited Ralph to dinner at the Hyde Park Hotel, which at the time housed one of the leading Italian restaurants in London. The food and ambience was so good that it was the regular haunt of Pavarotti and many other famous Italians.

I knew the maitre d', Alberto delle Valle, and had phoned ahead to make sure we got a lovely little table by the window. Some time before, Ralph had told me that his favourite dessert was pavlova, and he frequently lamented the fact that it was now as out of fashion as Black Forest gateau and that no one ever served it anymore. So I arranged with Alberto that a pavlova (not on the hotel's menu) would be specially prepared, then served up for us when dessert came round.

Alberto could not have got a chef to do a better job. The pavlova was delivered to the table on a special trolley. It was so beautifully done, complete with swan-like form, that it almost looked as though it was sailing across the dining room towards us. Ralph's eyes briefly lost the sadness which had been there since Dorothy's death.

Four years later, Ralph invited me up to spend our birthday in Suffolk, where he was having a party, as it was his eightieth. The invitation said, 'Strictly no presents please'. (I hoped a homemade chocolate cake wouldn't count.)

So that I could make the most of the copious champagne, I was invited to stay overnight in his house. In the morning Ralph brought in breakfast on a tray and he sat chatting on the edge of my bed while I ate. His hand rested upon my breast. I left it there. Why not? The old boy was 80 and alone in the world. Despite what various newspapers alleged a few years later, nothing more than that ever happened between us. Ralph was my friend.

When we met again in 1997, I was alarmed to see how badly he seemed to have declined during only a few months. A few weeks later, Ralph was admitted to hospital and I went up to Suffolk to see him

While I was with him, his secretary had the dreadful task of telling Ralph that shortly after he had been admitted into hospital, his beloved dog had died. Ralph's face registered nothing. It was too awful for him.

In the hospital car park, she asked me to help her plan his funeral. It felt all wrong to me, to be making such plans when Ralph was still alive. But she said it was important. He was a world-famous figure and she could not risk leaving the plans to the last minute. I remember sitting there in the car with her and feeling like a false-hearted traitor. It was horrible.

I was alerted soon afterwards that Ralph had come home and would now be looked after by Macmillan nurses in his Suffolk home for his last days. I went up to Suffolk and sat with him. Ralph could no longer swallow solid food. I asked permission from the nurse and then bought him a bottle of Cava, his favourite drink, and sat on the edge of the bed, giving him teaspoons of it, while he held my hand.

In a strangely circular turn of events, that afternoon Mrs Baker-Monkton (at whose party we had first met) arrived at the door. Ralph's secretary and the Macmillan nurse told me to stay in the bedroom. They told her that Ralph could receive no guests. She had brought him a huge chocolate cake.

A few weeks later, in June 1998, Ralph died.

Shortly afterwards, his will was published and I was amazed to find that he had bequeathed me his London house. The press tried to make a big deal of this, implying all kinds of lewd things. They seemed to think it impossible to contemplate the notion of strong friendship between friends of opposite genders. Nor could they see why anyone would leave a valuable gift to a friend unless they'd been having a sordid affair with them. In my opinion the problem is with their own squalid minds. For me, I would have to say that true friendship is the most important thing in my life, and sex often comes quite low in the catalogue.

Ralph had no children, no widow, no family. I recall him once putting his head into his hands and saying, 'I have been very successful. The result is that I have all this stuff.' In some despair he then cried out, 'what am I going to do with it all?'

As it happens he did great good with it. The most part of his estate, something like £5 million, and the future rights to all his books and films went to the sailing trust to which he had always been utterly devoted. That money continues to keep alive the dream of providing practical sailing experience for young people. He left his forests to the Forestry Commission, and the tenants of his farm in Wales were left the homes in which they had lived for years.

As Ralph always said, 'you can't take it with you'. But what he did was leave all his things to the people he believed would most appreciate them.

CHAPTER 21

As many strange things happen in the entertainment world as happen at sea. A casting director came to see *The Hothouse*, saw me doing Pinteresque scenes with Harold Pinter himself, and thought 'that's just the woman we need to play a fighter pilot in *Star Wars*'.

I was summoned to the Athenaeum Hotel to meet George Lucas. As I had never seen two seconds of any *Star Wars* film I decided not to gamble and gush on about things I knew nothing about, so I didn't try. Instead we talked about that evening's beautiful sunset.

I landed the role of Bravo 5, the only female fighter pilot in *Star Wars: Episode I – The Phantom Menace*. My friend the fabulous Trisha Biggar (Vive La Trisha!), who knew my body intimately, having fitted me for so many costumes and corsets up at Glasgow Citz, designed the costumes for the film and gave me a very snazzy outfit indeed, including a gorgeous pair of rust-coloured jodhpurs. I asked the make-up girl to match the lipstick with the trousers, but once we were on set a message came down from the box, 'Miss Imrie, Mr Lucas says remove your lipstick'. So that was that.

We had not been allowed to read the script at all. I had been given only a sheet with my dialogue and the other people's cues, rather like it had been in the days of Elizabethan theatre. I felt a little like Snug the Joiner*, trying to make sense of it. I did my bit and fired my guns, but I haven't a notion what side I was on, who I was firing the guns at, who I was hitting and whether or not we won.

I could not have imagined how devoted and loyal a following the

---

* In Shakespeare's *A Midsummer Night's Dream*.

Star Wars series has. Although my scene was so short and you can barely see me for goggles, I still get stopped a lot by ecstatic men whooping that they never thought they'd have a close encounter with Bravo 5.

Gormenghast was a huge TV project. Apart from starring the likes of Christopher Lee, Ian Richardson and Jonathan Rhys Meyers, it was also one of the first to feature a large amount of amazing computer-generated background scenery and special effects. Based on the book by Mervyn Peake, the job was a mixed pleasure for me. Lady Gertrude was a cracking good part in a strangely wonderful production with an amazing cast.

But while we were filming, darling Mums was seriously ill in hospital. Every time I had a day off, I got myself down to the Isle of Wight to sit in intensive care at her hospital bedside, only a few corridors along from where Angus had been born.

My role in *Gormenghast* necessitated being obese, with skin like clay. I was called to make-up each day at 4am, spent two to three hours in the chair while the brilliant David White fixed various pieces of rubber to my face and neck, and smoothed it all out with something like putty, and then on top of that came tons of foundation and then the usual make-up – mascara, lipstick etcetera. It could have been horrifying but it was surprisingly all right. In fact, photos of the stages of my make-up in *Gormenghast* are now frequently used to demonstrate extreme TV and film prosthetic make-up work.

For me the hardest part of the show was putting on and moving around in the immense and intricate costume, with all its padding. The costume was so elaborate that, in order for it to be ready in time for shooting, they had to start working on it long before I was even cast in the role. Also beneath all this heavy and restrictive clobber I had to strut around on huge platform shoes.

During many scenes, a large white rook perched happily on my shoulder. He was the only one of his kind in the country. When he got bored he started pecking my face off and the make-up department had to stand around with glue ready to fix any loose bits back on.

As my worry about my mother increased, the bird became more

and more edgy until finally, when I came into work one Monday, the trainer came up to me and said, 'He got very upset on Saturday night. What happened?' I told him my mother had died. After that the bird always took a long time to settle in my presence.

You can never be prepared for that moment which you dread. And it is ghastly. In a strange sort of way, having to get back to work helped me stave off the misery.

And when my wonderful agent Belinda phoned me and told me I had been chosen for some new film, but before anything went forward there was to be a script reading for the producers and financiers in a London hotel suite, I was glad to have something to do.

I arrived on the appointed morning at the trendy Metropolitan Hotel, Park Lane, Mayfair. Runners told me that the star of the film, a girl from Texas, wasn't going to be there, but someone was going to read in for her.

We sat round a huge table and we read the script. At the coffee break, I realised I was going to be late for a lunch date I had, so I went out into the corridor and phoned the friend I was going to meet to explain the hold-up.

'It's a reading, for a film,' I whispered into my phone. 'It'll never get made.'

'Why?' asked the friend.

'Nothing happens. It's just some girl's diary.'

'What's her name, this girl?'

'I dunno. The Texan didn't turn up, but the diary person isn't anyone famous and I haven't a clue why anyone wants to make a film of her diary at all. All she does is drink, diet and try to give up smoking.'

'Is this diary person by any chance called Bridget Jones?'

How bizarre! I was astonished. 'How on earth did you know that?' I asked.

'Celia, it's only been a best-selling book for the last two years.'

So there we are. I didn't have a clue. That'll teach me for not reading the newspapers.

The film *Bridget Jones's Diary* was enormous fun and went on to be a worldwide hit. The absent Texan, you will have guessed, was the delightful Renée Zellweger, and I also got to work with one of my heroes, the delectable Colin Firth.

One day we were called up to a stately home between Potters Bar and South Mimms which is frequently used for filming. You'll see it all over the place in everything from *Jeeves and Wooster* to *Lovejoy*. I'd already done about four things there before.

The scene was a party with long speeches. Colin Firth had a great deal to do. Speaking personally, my favourite filming days are the ones where you have no lines, no driving and you just turn up to go into a semi-trance as they apply your make-up and fit your costume. For the rest of the day all you have to do is turn up on set and react. How lovely!

However this day, although I had no lines and no driving, it didn't seem quite as easy as that. I'd had my breakfast in make-up at 7 am. By noon, having stood on set all day listening to Colin (and having drunk rather a few too many espresso coffees) I was crawling up the wall with boredom and yearning for a bit of excitement. It was at this dangerous moment that the spirit of the kindergarten art easels episode rose again and the devil entered my soul. I decided to have a joke with Colin Firth.

When his speeches finally finished being filmed from one angle, and the camera was being set up to reverse the shot, I strolled up to him.

'Have you done much comedy?' I asked straight-faced, an eyebrow raised in incredulity. (How did I dare? Remember he was a total stranger to me!)

'Why?' Momentarily, Colin looked panic-stricken.

'Just wondered,' I said, and turned back to my place on the other side of the room. To this day I don't know why I did it. My heart thundered with devilment. I doubt it had beat as heavily since the episode of the school lavatory plugs.

As I sat down I heard a loud angry male voice, talking with the first assistant. 'Get that woman off the set.' I spun round. Colin Firth was pointing at me. 'I can't concentrate while she's here,' he said. 'Send her away.' My giddy aunt, he'd taken my remark seriously! I stood up, shaken, but quite ready to leave.

'No,' he said, as I took a few steps. 'Get her back in. I can't do the scene at all unless she's standing there.'

His face was set straight. Now it was me who was caught on the back foot. I really had no idea whether he was being serious or that he had clicked on so quickly and was now joshing me back. Afterwards I realised that he had got the joke right away, and was joining in royally. Trouble is, he did it so effectively. Colin Firth really is the master of the poker face.

When the scene was done, I curtseyed in front of him.

'What are you doing now?' he asked.

'Paying due respect,' I said.

Renée Zellweger was the second Hollywood film star I had worked with. The first just sat in his trailer and didn't speak to anyone on or off set, unless it was to moan and grumble, so I was expecting the worst. But Renée was wonderful. She made me feel as though she'd seen everything I'd been in. I'm certain that it wasn't true, but it sure made me feel great. She led the company with charm and generosity.

But I have to tell you that, once every day, everyone on the set did thoroughly hate her. For, as the noon bell struck, at just the moment when all actors are wilting with hunger and they all know that there's at least another hour till lunch, out came Renée's daily compulsory pizza. Then she sat down in front of us and tucked in. You see, in order to keep up the weight for the role, she had to eat these extra meals while we gazed on, dribbling with desire and jealousy.

Renée's English accent was so good that after a while I started to think her actual American accent must be very slight, for, on or off stage I never heard her speak in anything but English RP.

At the wrap party, a few days after filming ended, I came in and was climbing a large circular staircase heading up to the festivities when I heard a female voice yelling down at me.

'Howdy, Celia, come right on up.'

How strange, I thought. They've got someone here from the cast of *Dallas*. For the voice booming down the stairwell was pure

Ewing-Southfork-Ranch-Texas. But of course it was Renée herself, who, having canned the final shot, had allowed herself finally to emerge from the accent she had used for the last few months. It was the first time I had ever heard her speak in her own voice.

CHAPTER 22

I first met Alan Bates when I was at Chichester in 1985. He was there for a one-off evening reading of poems by Philip Larkin. Because Alan was so gorgeous, I bought him a good luck carnation. He found me afterwards to thank me and it was the strangest thing, I adored him on sight, and I felt as though I had known him forever.

Four years later he was playing Marcel Proust in the film *102 Boulevard Haussmann*. The script was by Alan Bennett and together they thought it would be nice to have me in the company, but the only suitable part was very small, and they worried that I would be insulted to be offered it. But how could I be offended to be in such splendid company? On the contrary, I was delighted.

Alan Bates and I sat in the Winnebago together and laughed and laughed. I remember also a taxi ride through Glasgow, where we were filming, as the streets and buildings bear an uncanny resemblance to certain parts of nineteenth-century Paris. I was with both Alans and we laughed so much the taxi driver couldn't understand a word we were trying to tell him. I think the poor man thought we were all drunk.

Another day, Alan Bates turned to me and said, 'You've worked up here in Glasgow before, haven't you? Where's the best place the three of us can go out to dinner?'

So I phoned Rogano, a famous seafood restaurant, which I remembered from my time at the Citz. Rogano is very beautiful, with an original art deco interior, fitted in the 1930s and based on the interiors of Cunard's original *Queen Mary* liner, which was built just up the road in the shipyards on the Clyde.

I phoned to book. 'Hello, could I please reserve a table for three for tonight?'

The waiter laughed at me down the line.

'You are joking?' he sneered. 'You'll get absolutely nothing here at this short notice.'

I put the phone down, seething.

About a quarter of an hour later, I phoned again. I changed my voice ever so slightly and said, 'Hello, it's Celia Imrie here. Might you have a table for me, Alan Bates and Alan Bennett for tonight?'

'Certainly, Ms Imrie. We have a splendid table available.'

It was the first time that I fully realised the positive power of fame. It gets you through doors. But how unfair.

Back in London, I went on seeing Alan. We went to a Montserrat Caballé concert at the R.F.H., and we had many meals and nights out together. When the tragic news of his son's mysterious death came through, he phoned me often to talk about him and the pain of his loss.

We next spent proper time together at a film festival in Dorset, which was holding a retrospective of all his film work. He invited me to be his guest. Alan came back to my B&B and we lay on my bed and talked. Next day when I had to go back to London, he came to the station to see me off. Despite the temperature being well below zero, and a howling wind screeching along the platform, Alan waited with me till the train arrived. But the train was very, very late. He waited one hour and twenty five minutes.

'You don't have to stay, you know.' I kept telling him. 'I'll be OK.'

'You don't understand,' said Alan. 'I like being with you. As long as you are here on this platform, I want to be here on this platform too.'

On Valentine's Day he took me out to the Red Fort, at the time the best Indian restaurant in London. I gave him a lift home. He kissed me and said, 'Whenever our combined schedules allow, we ought to go on holiday, you know.' He wanted us to go to Italy together. I am still so sad that our schedules never did allow for that.

When it came to filming an adaptation of Nancy Mitford's semi-autobiographical novel *Love in a Cold Climate,* Alan and I played husband and wife. As I truly loved the actor, it was easy to play the role. It also gave us a fantastic playing opportunity. As we were so close and comfortable in each other's presence, we could afford not to look at each other, and really give that impression of a familiar married couple, rubbing along.

The Mitford household reminded me in many ways of my own home life. I read up on Nancy Mitford's mother, a version of whom I was playing, and saw there were many similarities with my own Mums. In both families it was assumed that only boys needed a proper education. If the law hadn't forced my sisters and me to the local school I wonder whether my parents would have bothered to educate us at all. There was certainly no question of boarding school or university for any of us. I read that Lady Redesdale, like my mother, had kept chickens. Although it wasn't mentioned in the script, I incorporated it into my scenes. I dressed as my mother did when feeding the chickens, a dirty old coat, men's shoes and a raincoat-type hat. Having had a real-life posh mother, I was under no illusions how posh mothers behave. I was never tempted to follow the cliché, immaculate make-up, pristine hair-do, being well-turned out at all times. Toffs don't have anything to prove and therefore don't care so much about these things as much as do the middle classes. Around the house, my mother was a total rag-bag, but whenever she went out things changed. The clothing, the hair and the jewellery were then impeccable.

(It was on this project that I had my one and only row with a prop master. It was about the laying of the table and in particular the bi-directional laying of the pudding spoon and fork. When the table setting was supposed to be the equal of Lord and Lady Redesdale's I simply couldn't stand back and let it look like something out of *Abigail's Party*. I hear that even to this day the man is vitriolic about me.)

Alan and I saw less of each other when he went to comfort Angharad Rees over the tragic death of her son and they became very close. But a couple of years later he started calling me again.

I bumped into the actor Nickolas Grace at the 2003 BBC radio Christmas party and asked whether he had seen Alan lately. He replied with a sentence which made my knees give way, 'He had a stroke yesterday and was taken into hospital'.

I left the party and flew round the corner to The London Clinic. When I entered Alan's room he smiled. 'So you found me, then,' he said.

He laughed, rolled his eyes and told me that his physiotherapist had just told him he wouldn't last the week. 'Ridiculous,' he said. 'Look at me!' He did look tired, but he still had the famous twinkle, and seemed so full of life.

But the physio was right. A few days later I was in Nice for New Year when I heard the terrible news that Alan had just died.

Some months afterwards, at his memorial, Alan's agent Ros Chatto came up and whispered into my ear. 'He always said to me, Celia, that you were the one.' But knowing Alan (as I know myself) I wonder maybe whether he said this of everyone who ever got close to him.

I realise that Alan was a great flirt and was always falling in love. Like me, he was not the settling-down type. Like me, Alan needed every exit left open, and the moment we both feared anyone was looking for locks for those doors, or started showing signs of clinging, we both made for those openings at breakneck speed.

Thinking about Alan after he died made me reflect a lot on this. And those reflections led me to understand that throughout my life all the people whom I truly adore, the friends and lovers who remain closest to my heart, are always the ones who understand this error in me, who never mistake my fondness for (dreaded word) commitment, my kindness and affectionate words for love, my capability to sympathise for devotion, or my elusiveness for a game of hard-to-get. In many cases I think my greatest friends feel the same way themselves. That was certainly true of Alan.

What he and I had together was a kind of magical romance.

In Alan I met my soul.

CHAPTER 23

There were two good reasons that it was important for me to take the part in *Midsomer Murders* when I was offered it in 2001. One was to play the wife of Alan Howard, an actor I had admired so much since I was a child. (In fact when I was up in the Midlands filming my tiny part in *Death on the Nile,* I used my one and only night off to rush to Stratford-upon-Avon to get myself a front row seat and watch him play *Henry V.*) The other reason was to break the spell of *Bergerac* by working again with John Nettles for the first time since that awful year in Jersey.

Since *Bergerac* was broadcast widely, I had experienced a few funny moment thanks to my spell in the series. Many years afterwards, I was sightseeing in Paris. As I walked around the grand department store, Galeries Lafayette, people kept pointing at me and muttering. It was strange. Then I went to buy a coffee in the bar on top of the Eiffel Tower. I could hear two waiters discussing me. The only word I could make out was 'l'argent' – French for money.

Was I about to be robbed? The two men screwed up their lips and scrutinised me. 'Oui,' said one. 'C'est l'argent.'

'Non,' said the other.

'Oui! Oui! C'est elle!' hissed waiter one, after plopping the coffee down at my table.

The other came up and busied himself about with packets of sugar, all the while surreptitiously squinting at me. He minced away, shaking his head and pursing his lips in that Gallic way. 'Non.' I heard him say as he mimed the crow's feet under my eyes. 'Trop vieille.' ('Too old.')

Afterwards in my hotel I turned on the TV to see that, all those years later, a dubbed version of *Bergerac* was still showing. And there

I was, ten years younger, playing the financial adviser, 'L'argent' ('the money'). I was awfully good in French, I thought, with a lovely deep Simone Signoret voice.

I rushed to the mirror and compared my present self to my previous incarnation. The second waiter was dead right about the crow's feet. *Trop vieille, indeed.*

On my next TV show, *Station Jim,* my enthusiasm got me into trouble.

So that he could be on location with me, my son Angus, now aged five, made his screen debut playing a boy at the school where I played a miserable Scottish headmistress. At the same time as I was working, he was himself busy in make-up, costume, and shooting, and didn't have to hang around the set waiting for me, having yet another boring afternoon.

I stubbornly insisted on doing the first stage of my own stunt, which was falling to the floor while the room around me caught fire. Easy-peasy, I thought.

Wearing a long red wig, and playing tipsy, I went onto the set. 'Action!'

On cue, down I went and the pyrotechnics went up. The only trouble was, so did my hair. That hadn't been part of the plan at all. It all happened so quickly and yet at the same time it felt as though life had suddenly gone into super slow-motion.

I clambered to my feet, dashing through the flames and ran out of the dilapidated building where we were filming, then firemen threw their jackets on my head while others gathered round me and hosed me with foam.

Now I knew how Michael Jackson felt. And that's what comes of insisting on doing your own stunts. A brilliant stuntman with a rather suitable name, Ricky Ash, finished the job.

As Jim Broadbent said, 'Celia, DON'T help!'

And, if only I had had Jim's mantra in my head one day when I was nabbed on the pavement as I walked back to my car after dropping Angus off at primary school, I might have saved myself and many other people a whole lot of trouble.

'Hello,' said this chap to me. 'I'm a fellow parent here, but I am also a screenwriter and I have a script I'd love you to take a look at.'

I smiled and was about to say something like please send it to my agent, everything always works best that way round, when he whipped out the script and plonked it into my hands.

'Please read it,' he said.

I didn't want to be rude, and here we were standing on the pavement, with our children at the same school and I couldn't think of how to say, 'No, thanks, please do not give it to me now, use the official channels.'

So I took his script home and read it, and truthfully didn't think much of it.

Some weeks later the phone rang.

'Do you like the script?'

'Lovely,' I lied, wondering how the man had got my home phone number, and then remembering that he was a fellow parent, and all of our home numbers were on the parents' class list.

'You like your part in the script, Celia? You'll play it?'

Caught on the hop, again (Jim – you are so right) I felt that link of our kids meant that I really was somehow obliged to him.

'Yes,' I said, feeling safe in the knowledge that it always took even the most proficient producer years to get the money together for a feature film, even with huge star names attached and a brilliant script, which this certainly was not.

'That's good,' said the fellow parent. 'Cos it's all stations go. We've raised the money and we're going to start shooting next month.' I think I might at that point have remained silent with shock.

'Sophie Ward is doing it,' he said. 'I know you've enjoyed working together before.' My jaw fell open. I was amazed. Fancy Sophie thinking it was good!

Somehow Sophie's being on the film made it easier for me just to say yes. Maybe I was missing something in the script. Perhaps I had read it with the wrong attitude, having not received it through official channels. I also thought that if Sophie liked it, it must be better than I remembered from my own reading.

What I didn't realise was that the scribbling parent had told Sophie

I was certainly doing it, and she too had had a jaw-dropping moment, having her own worries and concerns. But, like me, she thought that if *I* was doing the film, there must be more to it.

I was told, that the up-and-coming, most sought-after young actress, Sophia Myles, was playing the lead. I couldn't believe it. But when I met her on the first day's filming, I discovered that she had only accepted it because I was doing it, and had had the same misgivings.

We started shooting with this first-time writer's script, only to discover that he was also directing the film. I should point out that he was a first-time director as well.

I think, except in cases of the exceptionally brilliant, those rare creatures like Woody Allen or Quentin Tarantino, screenwriters should let directors get on with it and let their scripts have that additional puff of life and occasional incisiveness which you inevitably get from an outside eye. As a director, he could not see the flaws in his own script, as screenwriter he could not see his own directorial errors.

On top of this I then discovered that the director/screenwriter/fellow parent of a child at Angus's school had raised the finance for the film by mortgaging his own house.

In the great scheme of things, film finance is yet another filter, another outside eye. So I was shocked to realise that now on three different levels of vanity, with no outside force to employ the brakes, scores of professional people (camera crew, lighting people, make-up artists, actors, property masters, hairstylists and the rest) were being employed to fulfil what seemed to me to be the mere fantasy of a man who had never made a film before.

What made it even worse was that whenever I tried to help, by making suggestions, I was told that I should stop wasting time, for, because of *us,* he was in danger of losing his home.

There was no one to turn to. I was in a sinking ship with a novice playing captain, chief engineer and shipping company. The camera crew all got cross, the wardrobe and make-up people all got cross, the actors all got cross, and I got very, very, very cross. It was a daily episode of Living Hell.

I have read many, many scripts in my time. I even went on the brilliant Robert McKee Story Structure course to further my understanding of the mechanics of plot, and I knew that this story was seriously flawed. I pointed out to him that twists must have resolutions, not just lead up to another twist, and that characters' motivation had to come from the most possible and most logical causes from the characters' points of view, and never simply as an expedient to help move the story along. Nothing in this script followed the basic laws of Aristotle, Robert McKee, Syd Field or any screenwriting guru ever to have set pen to paper. Nor did it ever take the simple path of common sense. It was full of misdirected character clues, unresolved twists and not one character in the whole rotten thing could inspire the audience's empathy.

It was the only time in my life that I found myself in daily arguments on a film set. I felt guilty that any of us were there. I knew that I had been one of the first people roped in and that my supposed enthusiasm, which in fact was nothing more than out-of-control politeness, had ignited the project.

Each night the actors and I would all go home and learn our impossible lines, only to find that by morning when we arrived at make-up, that the director-writer-financier had been up all night re-writing and everything had been changed. In a few short minutes we had screeds of new stuff to learn. On more than one occasion, even as the camera rolled, I hadn't a clue what I was supposed to be saying or what came next.

Sometimes in the middle of shooting a scene, a person would ask 'what' or 'why' about some particular line they had to say and be greeted with such an odd and furious reply, that you could see the crew and cast members throwing up their arms in exasperation and walking away, shaking their heads in despair.

As tempers flared around me, I sweated. Everyone was befuddled. Sophie escaped into corners to work on modules from her Open University course, and each evening all the cast members spent hours on the phone with each other trying to think of ways of resolving the situation. But the truth was that nothing could extricate us from the quagmire of the plot.

Oh, Jim Broadbent, Jim Broadbent, Jim Broadbent, I need a tape of you in my head reminding me what happens when I try to help.

What happened in this case is that the film all but vanished but the director/screenwriter/parent made some of his money back. He told a story in the papers about what a monster I was.

It never seemed to occur to him that it might have simply been that the script needed major surgery, if not a total body transplant. Plus he shouldn't have mortgaged his house in the first place. If no one else wanted to finance his script, he should have taken it as a sign. The film ended up being what we in the business call an STD – 'Straight to DVD' – with no cinema release as he couldn't find a Distributor. As I understand, however, I am pleased to say – according to the director's website – the film received good reviews.

Luckily Peter Hewitt, the director of *The Borrowers,* called around this time and invited me to play the role of Miss Rapier in a new kids' film, *Thunderpants.* Phew, some fun at last! The film was about a small boy who dreams of being an astronaut, except that he cannot help farting. It had a fabulous cast including Simon Callow, Stephen Fry and Leslie Phillips.

The *Beano*-esque nature of the script made it a delight for children and adults alike and it went on to become a cult film.

PARP!

CHAPTER 24

A is for Acid was a TV drama about John George Haigh, the real-life murderer. It also came with a real-life script, a real-life director, real-life finance and real-life Martin Clunes in the lead role.

As well as being a serial killer, Haigh was a lady's man, a thief and swindler. During one of his stints in jail, he dreamed up what he saw as the premise for the perfect murder. He would dispose of the body in a vat of sulphuric acid. No body equals no murder, was his theory. But, the gall-stones of Mrs Durand-Deacon, one of the poor ladies who met her fate at his hands, failed to dissolve. This substantial forensic evidence proved the lady's presence at the scene, and after this case the law on the physical presence of a corpse in a murder trial was changed. On the evidence of a few tiny stones, Haigh was charged, tried, found guilty and hanged.

We filmed in Skegness, which passed for 1940s Brighton. During the shoot, the weather was not good. While walking on the beach one day there was a hailstorm so strong it left little bruises up my legs. I looked as though I had caught an exotic strain of purple measles.

I played Mrs Rose Henderson. John Haigh, in the person of Martin Clunes, lures me to his workshop, by telling me that my husband is there, and has fallen ill. Poor Mrs Henderson, it seems, was rather a pretentious person, who boasted of her fluency in French. Again it wasn't in the script, but I tried to use that fact. And as Mrs Henderson also travelled everywhere with her dog, I addressed the dog in French. 'Allons, Prince!' I said. 'Asseyez vous, mon brave. Bon chien!' The dog looked at me as though I was totally mental.

In my final scene, in Haigh's workshop, he shot me and dumped my body in a large vat which he then topped up with acid. Sounds all very well on paper, but when *you* are the person being stuffed inside the vat it becomes something of a terrifying experience.

The vat was prepared from an old oil drum. I was squashed down into it so tightly it was difficult to breathe. While I was compressed in the can I had to hold a little polystyrene cup protecting an Alka-Seltzer type tablet and keep perfectly still while gallons of water were poured on top of me. Then at the appropriate moment I had to release the tablets to make the water fizz, and thereby look like acid. How horrible it was being inside that vat.

From Skegness to Prague. After that a seven-hour train journey into Slovakia to reach the location of the new TV series, *Doctor Zhivago,* starring a new unknown actress . . . Keira Knightley.

The Slovak filming location was pretty grizzly. The shops were almost bare. You walked in, saw rows of empty shelves, with perhaps one shelf displaying two tubes of toothpaste, and somehow it made you feel like walking straight out again without buying anything. The whole town emanated an air of despair.

The weather didn't help. It was terribly grey and dreary the whole time, and the local people seemed exhausted and burdened.

Our first day's filming was a funeral scene. The delicious director, Giacomo Campiotti, had searched out some of those demoralised and downtrodden local people to be extras. It was amazing. The watery eyes, set in work-worn, leathery faces, the bent backs, and gnarled hands, the drips hanging from their noses from standing for hours in the icy cold, the uncomplaining patience – it was a wonderfully evocative use of the crowd and really made the scene work. You'd rarely get anything like that from supporting artists back home.

Having discovered, on a map, the nearness of a Second World War Nazi concentration camp, Bill Paterson and I felt compelled to stop off, en route home, to see it. The place was understandably chilling, but I was most struck by the beautiful drawings done by the prisoners, and the realisation that even in the direst circumstances the human spirit retains this miraculous capability for artistic expression and beauty.

★

The summer of 2002 saw the Queen's Golden Jubilee and I took Angus to join the millions lining the Mall to see Concorde fly over and hear Brian May play *God Save the Queen* from the roof of Buckingham Palace. As we scurried home, making our way through the side-streets of Chelsea, trying to avoid the jam, we were neck-and-neck with an incredibly tiny old lady wearing a beautiful beaded and fringed 1930s' cloche hat. She belted along so fast it was difficult to catch up with her – even though she was 92 years old. I recognised her as the fabulous double-Oscar-winning German actress, Luise Rainer, known in her heyday as the 'Viennese Teardrop'. I hope I have that stamina next year, let alone in when I'm in my nineties!

I was very excited to land a role in *The Gathering Storm,* a film for TV about Winston Churchill in the build-up to the war years. Not only did it star Albert Finney and Vanessa Redgrave but we used Chartwell, Winston Churchill's actual home, as the filming location. Before shooting started I was sent off to Raynes Park for more lessons, this time in shorthand typing and how to use an ancient typewriter, for I was playing Churchill's secretary, Mrs P.

Through Helena Bonham Carter, I got to meet another of Churchill's secretaries, the youngest one, who lived in Eaton Square. She had already read the script. 'He would never have sworn in front of you,' she told me. 'And you certainly would have never touched him.' But these moments were left in the script as part of artistic licence.

I would come onto the set in the morning and barely manage to say 'I've got an i—' before Albert Finney, who played Churchill, shouted 'Oh Christ, not another bloody idea!'

('Don't help, Celia.')

Ronnie Barker had been lured out of fourteen years' retirement to play the butler, and he was nervous, in between the usual filming boredom, with hours sitting around alone in his Winnebago. He gave a sensational performance and proved a marvellous foil for Albert Finney. One day Ronnie popped into my Winnebago and passed me a poem he had just written on the back of a call-sheet about his experience filming *The Gathering Storm*:

Oh, oh, oh what a LONELY war
Shut in the caravan all day
Nothing to do but eat and pray.
My cubicle's semi-detached
You hear every mutter and cough,
And each bounce on the floor
Seems the couple next door
Are continually having it off.

Oh, oh, oh what a crashing bore!
No one to talk to back at base
You just become a mental case
Line up. Checking the gate.
Back to your cell
And just sit and wait
Oh, oh, oh, what a LONELY WAR!

And that really does very succinctly sum up a typical day's filming.

The director of *The Gathering Storm* was Richard Loncraine, one of my favourites. As it happens, the first, second and third assistant directors were also called Richard. One day Ronnie Barker came into my caravan. 'Do you realise that on this set we have Richard the first, Richard the second and Richard the third?'

I laughed. 'So what do we call Richard, the director?'

'That's obvious,' he said. 'Dick Head.'

Rumours had been going round for ages about the possibility of a film being made about the exploits of a group of northern women who had bared all to make a calendar with a difference for their local Women's Institute, and meanwhile raised money for cancer research.

Everyone in the film business heard that the rights to film their story had been acquired by the Disney-owned company, Buena Vista. Then news came in that Helen Mirren and Julie Walters were to lead the cast. So you might imagine how excited I was when a few weeks later I discovered I had won the role of Celia, one of the original Rhylstone WI group, and Miss November.

Inside Out

Outside In

With Mums and Angus. Isle of Wight, Christmas 1994

Ahoy There. Off to The Folly, Isle of Wight. From left: Josie Lawrence, Eve Ferret, Belinda Wright, me, Pam St Clement, Nerys Hughes, Ben Turley, Laura Scott, Marie Claire Turley and Stewart Permutt in the front

Me and 'Jimmy', the rare white crow. On location filming *Gormenghast* in the middle of a lake, 1999

'Don't help' but the Human Beans are hoovering. With Jim Broadbent in *The Borrowers*, 1997

The delicious 'dinnerladies

John Thaw gripping my swishy coat. *Into the Blue*, 1997

Husband and wife. *Love in a Cold Climate* with Alan Bates

Cheers from the Calendar Girls. The night of the premiere in London, 2003

A strict lesson from 'the king of comedy'. *Nanny McPhee* with Colin Firth

Acorn Antiques: The Musical, 2005.
Sir Trevor and his tea girl

Have you met Miss Babs?

Never could help showing off those 'grands battements'. In rehearsal with
Duncan Preston and Julie Walters

The Navy Lark. On board Queen Mary 2

Admiral, Baron West of Spithead, bestows upon
me at the University of Southampton an honorary
degree and a comedy costume, 2009

Larry and me

Angus and I bet a 'monkey' on a pony in *Kingdom*, 2007

M8y and Rupey. *St Trinians (2)*, with Rupert Everett

Another grey cardigan part as Dame Sybil Thorndike and Jack Lemmon playing me in *Plague Over England*, 2009

The lovely portrait of Dorothy Hammond Innes, by Brenda Moore

The reading of *The Cherry Moon*, directed by Sir Richard Eyre, 2009.
Back row: Robin Soans, Jim Broadbent and Hugh Bonneville. Front row: Julia Ford, me and Kathy Rose O'Brien

'Don't you go pinching our butter'. Sally Ann Triplett and me at the London Palladium, 2009

Over the top ... Oh no I'm not. Paul O'Grady's live TV panto, *Sleeping Beauty*, 2009

At home in tartan as Lady Glenmire in *Cranford (2)*, 2009

What a treat of a journey on *The Road to Coronation Street*, written by Daran Little and directed by Charles Sturridge, 2010. Standing, from left: Jessie Wallace as Pat Phoenix, David Dawson as Tony Warren and Jane Horrocks as Margaret Morris. Sitting: Lynda Baron as Violet Carson, and me as Doris Speed

Continuing my adult education plan I was sent off to learn two compulsory new skills, golf and t'ai chi. Now call me old-fashioned, but what is the point of t'ai chi? To me it felt like nothing more than a half-asleep underwater version of Tae Kwon-Do.

For the first bout of location filming we all stayed up north in a hotel owned by the Duchess of Devonshire. It was a beautiful creeper-clad, stone coaching house with a delightful leafy garden. It was marvellous to be working with Julie Walters again, and I struck up an immediate rapport with Penelope Wilton. The pair of us sat and compared our earlier sporting triumphs, me chucking the javelin and she as a fine sprinter.

I spent my time off in Betty's Tea Rooms in Harrogate doing surveillance on the clientele, watching out for tips and costume hints to help me play my role, a lady golfer.

During the first week of filming, my fiftieth birthday came around. I didn't tell anyone the relevance of the day, but bought a cake, lined up 12 bottles of champagne and invited everyone to the garden of the hotel to share them with me. Halfway through the evening Julie guessed. She came up to me and pulled that famous wry face of hers. 'I know what this is all about,' she said enigmatically, then went off and organised a company sing-song of 'Happy Birthday' to me. I have to say this was a great improvement on my lonely thirtieth, sitting alone in Jersey. It was a balmy evening, and we all sat out late in the gentle gloaming, drinking the champagne and getting to know one another.

The Devonshire Arms hotel had a gym. Now the gymnasium is usually the last place you would ever expect to find me. But I was painfully aware that once we got back to London and into the film studios we were all going to have to strip off. Secretly, very, very early one morning, I crept down to the gym, expecting it to be empty. But what did I find? A room crammed with whizzing exercise bikes, clattering rowing machines and those black treading things that make you move like you've pooped your pants while walking through a bog in wellington boots.

And, yes, those machines were all occupied by the other Calendar Girls. Naturally everyone else had the same idea! I climbed onto a treadmill and started to work out. I hated every second of it.

At Shepperton Studios, we got many scenes in the can but there was only one scene on our minds, the one where we all had to take our clothes off. Therefore everything we did was coloured by this awful looming feeling.

A few days beforehand, someone had suggested that we all might like to have a private practice run, going somewhere like a hotel room and all stripping together with no cameras or crew present. No one could have spoken louder than me when I said 'NO WAY!' Honestly, once is enough.

The expert Dame Helen, who was the only one of us who was previously experienced at this stripping off malarkey, led the company with verve and aplomb. She was great, and was very sporting about it all.

The stripping scene was shot one actress at a time. It was my bad luck to be the first one done. On the appointed day I woke in a sweat, with dry mouth, as though I was about to sit an exam. I arrived at the studio feeling quite ill, and made my way to make up and wardrobe. It was as though I was in some horrible dream, walking through treacle.

In my dressing room, I stripped off. Then, with leaden feet and thundering heart, clutching my dressing gown tightly round me, I made my way down to the set.

But even I couldn't put it off forever. The moment had finally come. I tried to imagine that somehow I wasn't really taking my clothes off, it was only a dream, and that, anyway, no one would ever see it. That way I managed to get through the day.

When it was at last all over, I went to get my make-up taken off and I have rarely felt happier. I invited everyone into my dressing room and we celebrated with Twiglets and champagne, while listening to the Beatles and the 1930s dance band led by Carroll Gibbons. After that, following all the nude days, Twiglets and champagne in my dressing room became a regular event.

For all the fright it gave me, that scene has continued to provide me with humorous moments when travelling. Once, in Bolton, walking along the street, I was passed by a woman who exclaimed loudly, 'Oh looook, it's bigger buns.' An even better moment came about while strolling along the Promenade des Anglais in Nice. A French woman passed me, turned to her companion and exclaimed, 'Alors! Les Grands Gateaux!'

The second bit of location filming took place in Los Angeles, where the original calendar girls had gone as their fame shot round the world. It was like a glorious paid holiday. Linda Bassett and I stood in the gorgeous Fairmont Hotel in Santa Monica, gazing out at the Pacific Ocean.

'How beautiful,' I said.

We looked at one another, 'Let's,' we said in unison.

Grabbing our bathing costumes we rushed down to the beach and threw ourselves into the magnificent blue sea. It only took seconds and we were back on the beach, snuggling into our towels, shivering. Let me tell you, it might look wonderful but the Pacific Ocean is freezing and covered in oil. What a disappointment.

One morning I was standing in the hotel lift, when the doors closed and an American man turned to me and excitedly exclaimed, 'Hello! Oh – My – God! I'm standing in a lift with Claudia!'

'Celia,' I corrected.

'No, Claudia . . .,' he said. 'Claudia Bing of Bing, Bing and Bing.' Then the lift went 'bing' and he got out.

Los Angeles is the top spot in the world for star spotting. While waiting for the girls one day, I sat in the lobby and watched a fellow hotel guest, one of my idols, Little Richard, sitting there with his tall bouffant hair, sporting rather a lot of make-up and expressing rather a lot of bad temper.

We went downtown to film a scene in which, as the Calendar Girls, we made an appearance on *The Jay Leno Show*. That was quite an odd experience, being on a chat show, pretending to be someone else on a chat show. Jay Leno was very fast and furious and great at his job, but his eyes gave me the shivers as they reminded me strangely of President Zia.

On one of my days off, the girls all asked me what I was doing. 'Patrick Stewart has invited me over to his gaff,' I said. Thinking I was joking, everybody laughed. Patrick might at that point have been the most famous man in the world, but we went back a long, long way. Of course I had known him since the days when I was an ASM with the RSC (all those initials!)

The girls' laughter turned to astonishment when the car pulled up and there was Patrick waving to me to get in. I was the envy of the whole hotel.

Beam me up, Patrick!

About my next job, one might say I went from the sublime to the ridiculous, as I moved from a Disney-funded Hollywood mega-movie to a tiny cult TV show in Glasgow. The show is called *Still Game*, and, despite its limited geographical release, has a fanatical fan base. I have been stopped all over the world by ex-pat Scots who grab me, squealing, 'Mrs Begg! Mrs Begg!'

While snow lay feet deep in the Byres Road, and on TV southerners panicked about the petrol shortage, I was nude again, though this time I was protected by a shower curtain, behind which I shimmied, all the while imagining myself to be the woman who dances in silhouette at the closing credits of *Tales of the Unexpected*.

Apart from having lots of fun, doing this show meant I was in Glasgow for a week. The news had just been announced that the brilliant triumvirate who ran the Glasgow Citizens Theatre were leaving, and the famous company was to be disbanded forever.

After filming one evening, I made my way back to the Gorbals and walked into the glitzy black, red and gold foyer for the last time. With a lump in my throat, I said goodbye to all the staff who had been so kind to me over the years, saw Philip Prowse's sparkling production of *Chéri*, and spent an evening revelling in the nostalgia of quintessential Citz.

One cold January morning, Selina Cadell and Anna Chancellor called together a lot of actors, including me, for a meeting. A question was put to us.

'How would you feel about putting on a play for no money? We would beg rehearsal space, costumes, and we don't even have a venue. Would you join us?' Their enthusiasm was infectious.

'Oh yes,' I said. 'Come on.'

The chosen play was Congreve's *The Way of the World* and I was to play Lady Wishfort.

I was up in Blackpool, taking Angus to the annual illuminations and to go on the brand new helter-skelter, the Pepsi Max Big One, when I read the play for the first time in my life. The Pepsi Max Big One might have been scary, but not nearly as frightening as reading *The Way of the World*. I almost had a heart attack! I had committed myself to playing a role in a play and I could barely understand a word of it.

In a total funk of panic, I phoned Selina. 'I can't do this. I've got the total heebie-jeebies. No, no, no. Sorry. Not my thing. I'll never manage it. Sorry to let you down, but PLEASE find someone else.'

'Celia,' she said. 'You wouldn't be the actress you are if you didn't have the heebie-jeebies. Sorry, you ARE doing it.' It was an incredible phone call. In one fell swoop I was completely flattered and utterly cajoled.

It was a fantastic company but rehearsals were bittersweet for me, as a few days into the job, my dearest old nanny, Pop, was taken ill and died and I had to rush down to the Isle of Wight for all the wrong reasons, like clearing out her house, and helping to organise her funeral.

Not many days before we opened, the actor playing the role of Fainall dropped out. Remember, we were working for nothing, and he had been offered a lucrative TV job which would clash with the performance dates. No one blamed him for doing what he did, but the whole cast had to spend that evening on the phone ringing round to find a last-minute replacement.

I moved my finger through the pages of my address book. When I came to the letter 'F' I saw a name and thought to myself, 'nothing ventured, nothing gained'. I rang and left a message. I didn't really expect a reply, after all it was eighteen months since our brief time filming together. But a few hours later my mobile phone rang.

'Hello, Celia, is that you?' said a deep male voice. 'King of Comedy here.'

Sadly, Colin Firth was unavailable for those dates, but we did manage to persuade Sam West to join the company. Of course it was now just over ten years since Sam had sent me that Valentine's card, but both our circumstances had drastically changed and I now had an eight-year-old son. So the *Chéri* scenario never played out as I had once slightly hoped it might.

The Way of the World played for a short but sweet three-night run at Wilton's Music Hall, a fabulously atmospheric old theatre near the Tower of London. I loved doing it. It was my first big stage role in a long time, and I had a hoot.

I appeared on the Terry and Gaby TV chat show to publicise the play. I shared the sofa with one of my idols, Robert Palmer. It was Valentine's Day and I was lucky enough to be serenaded and given a red rose by him. Then a funny little Russian band started playing, and Sir Terry Wogan madly suggested it was music made for dancing. Well, try and keep me down! Spontaneously I bounced to my feet and whirled about like a demented dervish. When I flopped back onto the sofa Robert Palmer whispered in my ear, 'When did you rehearse that?' I told him I hadn't rehearsed at all, I just made it up as I went. He laughed and rolled his eyes. 'You're funny,' he said.

After the show, we swapped addresses, hoping to meet up over the next few months. Sadly, only a few weeks later, he suddenly died. He was 54. I was very shocked by his death, and thought it should be a warning to everyone of our age to take care of themselves. Two years later I wished that I had taken more heed of my own warning.

One morning while I was still doing *The Way of the World,* my phone rang. It was Stewart Permutt, my ex-housemate.

'Good morning, non-smoking bit of Ceals,' he said.

This was an old joke going back to the days when we travelled across the Solent together on a late-night ferry which was an old rust-bucket, the like of which you might expect to find only in the third world. There were no internal sitting areas, and the only place I could find a place to stand was under a huge 'non-smoking' sign.

'How would you feel about doing a one-woman show?'

I said, 'I couldn't.'

'Why not?'

'I just couldn't.'

'Well, I've written a play and you would be just perfect for the part.'

'I couldn't.'

Three months later, I was appearing in a public reading of *Exclusive Yarns,* another play by Stewart, at the King's Head Theatre. Dan Crawford, the theatre manager, came up to me afterwards.

'Stewart's plays are so hilarious, aren't they?' I said. 'But at the same time, so sad.' He agreed.

'Have you read his new one?' asked Dan. 'The one-woman show?'

'No,' I said truthfully.

Dan then rushed off upstairs, got a copy of the script, thrust it into my hand and said forcefully, 'Read it'.

The play, *Unsuspecting Susan*, was a one-and-a-half hour monologue following a self-deluding middle-class woman from the Home Counties whose quiet son eventually became an Islamic-fundamentalist terrorist. As it dealt in a personal way about home-grown terrorists it turned out to be rather prophetic. But more important than all that, it was a terrific part for me.

The next morning I rang Stewart. 'It's fabulous,' I said. 'I'll do it. When do we start?'

'Um . . .' Stewart was holding something back.

'Well?'

'The producer and director now have to go into discussions to decide whether you are a commercial enough proposition. Only then do we get the go ahead.'

'Oh heck, Stewart,' I said. 'How nerve-racking.'

'Don't worry,' he replied. 'They promised to let us know on Saturday.' I knew he would be tensely waiting for that call, and so would I.

'Fancy a weekend on the Isle of Wight?' I suggested.

The pair of us went down and waited by the phone. We had the house phone and both our mobile phones, so we felt pretty safe that as soon as the verdict had been given we could be contacted. We waited . . . and waited. We went shopping for food. We checked the phones. We strolled along the beach, clutching our mobiles, just in case. We checked the phones. We came home and cooked, then sat in front of the TV and ate. We checked the phones.

All the while I felt like Diana Dors in that old black-and-white film where she plays an anxious out-of-work actress who keeps picking up the phone to make sure it's working. The whole day long we kept right on checking all three phones.

Nothing. Neither of us dared say a word about it.

We went to sleep, got up on Sunday morning and repeated the whole procedure all over again. Still nothing. It was agony.

When, as we were packing to come home, there was still no call, a gloom fell upon us. Later that Sunday evening, having arrived at our respective London homes, we phoned to tell one another that there were no messages there either. The silence, we knew, could only mean one thing – the financiers had rejected me.

Next morning, as soon as the offices opened, Stewart phoned the producer, Harold Sanditon.

'Oh,' said Harold. 'Didn't Lisa phone you on Friday night? It's a yes. Celia's doing it.'

It turned out that the director, Lisa Forrell, who was in France, had had problems with her mobile phone, which wasn't on European roaming, couldn't work out the dialling codes to the UK, and didn't know how to send a text!

The play runs for about 90 minutes, without an interval, and with no one else on stage. On top of this my character only ever leaves the stage for brief moments, to do costume changes.

I tried to learn a page a day, hoping to have 20 under my belt before rehearsals began. I was very, very daunted by the lines problem. Usually in a normal play the lines that the other actors say frequently lead you to your own next line. The other thing is that, if you waver, other actors can generally pull you back on track. Here, if I dried or faltered, I would have nothing to fall back on but my own resources.

I had to be ultra-sure of the lines. I tried out the John Gielgud method. He wrote out his part by memory, then corrected it with a red biro.

The words were always the greatest worry – that and the fact that at every rehearsal it was you and you alone. There were no mornings when you could catch up while other people were doing a scene. Rehearsals were further complicated by the fact that Lisa had broken her leg and found it frustrating having to direct while in plaster.

Throughout the run I was terrified of forgetting my lines. Nowadays in most theatres there is no such thing as an old-fashioned prompter. In terrible cases of an actor drying, the stage manager, who really has enough on his or her plate, will have to find the missing line and yell it out from their marked up script in the prompt corner. But their thoughts are usually elsewhere. Throughout the show they are busy cuing in lighting changes and sound cues, giving warnings to front of house staff and things like that, and won't have noticed when an actor gets a line wrong.

So I left a script in the wings ready for myself. The plan was that if I really dried I would say a pre-planned sentence, 'Look at the time. I must feed the dogs.' And then rush to the wings, grab the script and find my words. Luckily it never came to that, though a few times I was very close.

When things went wrong onstage, there was simply nothing I could do.

One night was rather charged for me because I knew John Nettles and Bob Banks Stewart, the former star and producer of *Bergerac*, were in. It was just my luck that that was the night of the mobile phone episode.

There is a roof over the stage of The King's Head Theatre. That balmy evening, I was in the middle of the play when, it seems, a woman climbed out of a window to sit upon the roof, and bask in the evening sun. Which would have been fine . . . if only she hadn't taken that moment to make a phone call. Her voice bellowed in from the roof above the stage.

'Oh yes, Maureen, it was a lovely party. Lovely . . . No she *was* rather tight on the food, I agree. And that dress! Gawd, the tits hangin' out. Two white blancmanges . . . Trouble is, she thinks she looks good!' (Raucous laughter.)

I pressed on with the script.

The woman on the roof pressed on with her call.

'She never? She shagged Bob? I thought he was gay? Well he will be now!' (Screams of laughter.)

I tried to carry on, but my words were all over the place as I attempted to drown out this wretched woman and her frankly hilarious party tales.

On she went, 'No! I said to her, I said . . . I said "Mo, if you *do* do that, you're a f★★★ing prat." But did she listen? . . . What, Roger? She never. With Roger the lodger? Gordon F★★★ing Bennett, she keeps herself busy, don't she?'

I was totally thrown. I stepped forward. I was going to say 'Ladies and gentlemen, perhaps we ought to take a short break until this fascinating phone call is finished.'

Then I saw Stewart sidling briskly out of the auditorium. A few minutes more scandalous tittle-tattle ensued, until I heard Stewart's footsteps land on the roof, then a short interchange between Stewart and the woman. And all the while I continued with my monologue.

Another day a more sinister event threw me. In the second half of the play I had to down the best part of a decanter of whisky – or rather the stage version, apple juice.

One night, as the second act started, I took my first swig. Ugh! I thought, as I continued the play. Someone should change this juice, it's gone off. It tasted disgusting. It had a fiery tang to it and was very bitter. I was scared that if I drank the lot I was going to be very sick. But I had to go on drinking it. What else could I have done?

After about the third glass I started feeling quite hot. But I knew there was much more drinking and a lot more speaking to come and there was nothing I could do about it. After a few more glasses I was decidedly dizzy. I thought now that I might faint *and* puke. It was difficult to stand straight. I gripped onto furniture and rattled away at the lines, trying to be as true as I could be to the play, but feeling really quite rough.

I discovered later that the fresh apple juice had been spiked with real whisky. Someone had thought it would be an amusing prank to see how I coped, and what I would look like trying to play such a sad and moving role while actually being pissed out of my mind.

I was not in the slightest bit amused and ever after that I took care to sample the apple juice seconds before curtain up.

Some weeks later, just before the end of the run, I was intrigued to hear that there were talent scouts in, from a theatre in New York. I waited afterwards to see if there was any news. But at the time no one said a thing.

For most of the show I wore a cardigan that I had been given by Hammond Innes. I'm sure Judi would have been thrilled.

So, after a few weeks, I went on to my next adventure, filming an episode of *Marple,* with a spring in my step – literally. In a kind of proxy way my dream had come true, for I was playing a French ballet-dancer-turned-tutor. I had a thrilling time being taught the choreography by Tom Sangster's mother, Tasha Bertram, and I bowled onto the set, really looking forward to working again with my darling friend, Geraldine McEwan.

First thing in the morning, we all lined up for the master shot. The director looked very pale to me, and I mentioned it to some other people on the set. They just shrunk up their shoulders and carried on. We did the first line-up then went off to our dressing rooms while the lighting was rigged. When I got back, the poor man looked even whiter. His whole complexion had a glistening sheen and putty-like quality. I went to the first assistant director, pointed it out and he shrugged a reply.

'Get a doctor.' I insisted. 'Please, please get a doctor, *now.*'

People got pretty fed-up of me banging on. Unbelievably nothing had been done when everyone broke for lunch. The director still believed he had indigestion. But as work began again after the break I would not give in and a doctor duly arrived, took one look at the off-colour director, called an ambulance and had him blue-lighted to the nearest hospital. That afternoon that director had a massive heart attack. But at least, by then, he was in a place where professionals could deal with it.

We continued filming with a new director. One day, on location in a beautiful Regency theatre in Henley-on-Thames, Geraldine and I sat in the dark at the back while the crew were setting up.

'This is where I feel completely at home,' she said.

It's funny but her saying that made me realise that I didn't find the inside of a theatre so comforting at all. After all these years, I understood that the magic for me is not in the theatre but working on location, filming.

Richard Loncraine, the director of *The Gathering Storm,* phoned me and said 'How would you like to do me a favour?' He asked me to play a tiny role in his new film which was called *Wimbledon*. As you might have figured it is about tennis. (Well, it could *only* be that or, I suppose, at a pinch, *The Wombles*.)

Here is everything I know about tennis:

1. In the score people talk about love and deuce, words better encountered elsewhere.

2. The onlookers eat strawberries.

3. Women players wear very short skirts and consequently have to choose their knickers with care.

4. The net is one-and-a-half racquets high.

5. They have people called ball boys who are in fact girls.

6. There is an umpire who sits at the top of a ladder and drinks lemon barley water.

7. The stars are McEnroe (who shouts at the man drinking lemon barley water), Virginia Wade and two sisters called Venus and something else, and a boy called Henman at whom for some reason women scream and throw their underwear. There is also a Russian one called something like Navatalia Barishnova (actually I think I'm getting confused with a pair of ballet dancers).

I thank the gods I didn't have to spend days filming at the Lawn Tennis Club. I'd have gone out of my mind swivelling my face back and forth while the balls ponged into the bats. Instead my scenes were filmed over a day or two spent in a hoity-toity country club in Golders Green.

The experience did remind me, though, of my summer all those years before at Regent's Park in 1977, where I was the lone tennis-hater in a company of Wimbledon fanatics. We had many matinée performances which clashed with important games. I had devilish fun finding out the names of the players of the day and in particular the most fancied one, then rushed from dressing room, where we had a radio, and into the leafy wings, whispering urgently: 'McEnroe's crashed out!' I waited to hear the groans of despair. The other actors really thought I knew what I was talking about. Hopefully they would have all been so very happy later on, when they got back to the dressing room, to discover their favourite seed, or whatever they're called, had in fact won.

I was in the first ever episode of *Doc Martin* so we really had no idea what it would be like, but it was quite a novelty having a lead character who was a really grumpy doctor. The director was Ben Bolt, who had directed me twenty years before in an episode of *Shoestring*. *Doc Martin* was filmed in Port Isaac, where I had shot *The Nightmare Man* all those years before. It was nice to see Martin Clunes again, this time without a vat of acid and an Alka-Seltzer. But while I filmed my scenes, we fought against a terrible gale. My skirt kept blowing up over my head.

I played Susan Brading, the TV wife of the actor Richard Johnson, a man brimming over with old-time glamour. I had heard how, at the RSC many years before, the whole company referred to him as 'Golden Balls', on account of his glittering accomplishments. He certainly has the twinkliest eyes I have ever seen.

As it was the Easter holidays, I brought Angus down with me. One afternoon during filming, I left him in the hotel room, and told him that if I wasn't back and he got hungry, he must phone down and order room service. I was thinking along the lines of a plate of sandwiches. I came back to discover my seven-year-old son tucking into a plate of venison.

To Wiltshire next to film *Mr Harvey Lights a Candle* with Tim Spall. The plot concerned a school trip. Most of the filming was done on a coach travelling up and down, over and over again, along the M3. We did also spend a few days filming in and around the Cathedral

Close, in Salisbury, a town which has always given me the shivers. It's all a bit twee for me, the ye olde tea shoppes and ye olde English fonts on signs outside everything from ye olde cinema to ye olde chip shop. I was very uncomfortable the whole time as many years before I had appeared in a platform performance one Sunday at a small theatre within the sanctified hallows of the Close. During my pre-show warm up, I had gone off for a stroll and came back, humming a jolly tune (one of Sybil Thorndike's recommended ways of limbering up for a show) and a man (N.B. a total stranger) had come up to me, finger on lips and sprayed my face with spittle as he said:

'SSSSSSSSSSSSSSSHHHHHHHHHHHHHHHHHH!'

Singing in public areas, he told me in a high-pitched weasly voice, was strictly forbidden under the bye-laws of the Close.

And that just about sums it up, Salisbury, 'No singing in the streets'. Just like Pakistan.

CHAPTER 25

Nanny McPhee, the brainchild of Emma Thompson, was another of my favourite jobs. Emma not only played the name role, but had adapted the story from the *Nurse Matilda* books, with which I had been familiar as a child. But the job also gave me the opportunity to work with the legendary Angela Lansbury, and reunited me with Colin Firth, and the pair of us even had love scenes – of a sort.

As we rolled passionately on the floor during one scene, our arms somehow missed and Colin managed to get his elbow in my face, giving me a black eye. Who cares?

Within the film I also had two spectacular encounters with wildlife. In one scene a gigantic tarantula had to alight on top of my head. I was surprised at how heavy the darned thing was, and, even through the wig, I could feel its plump body, together with all eight hairy legs, pulsating and vibrating. It was horrible. However, I managed it. (Though I tell you if it had been a snake I'd have had to say no to the role. I could not have handled having a pulsating snake on my bonce. No, sirree, Bob.)

The cameras rolled. Once the spider was lowered into position on my blonde wig and merrily bouncing there, I decided to tease away at a curl on my forehead, using a finger and laughing gaily, as though oblivious of the giant spider's presence.

Ho. Hum. So far so good. But at the exact moment I raised the finger to twiddle the curl, the spider reached out a hairy leg and stroked the tip of my finger. I froze momentarily, and then continued acting. At the moment the spider and I made contact, however, the focus puller screamed loudly, leapt back, and fell to the floor, jolting the camera and ruining the shot.

Cut! So we had to reset and do the whole thing again.

In another scene I had to eat a live worm in a sandwich. I was asked before whether I would be willing to try the real thing or would I prefer to take the coward's way and chicken out by using a plastic replica.

Well, what a question. I had to be brave, didn't I? So the real worm went into my mouth. I have to tell you that it wriggled violently around the inside of my soft palate for what seemed to me a very, very long time. I even managed to lick my lips with the worm still in situ. Unlike in the tarantula scene, rarely has the word 'Cut!' been such a welcome sound. Once the camera was off, I carefully spat out the worm and we continued with the bit where I appear to chew it. So folks, don't worry – no live animals, albeit worms, were hurt in the making of that scene.

Nanny McPhee was the first film I had done after the new laws about paedophiles had come into place. I had to have a police check to assure the world that a child would be safe in my presence, while standing in front of a movie camera and being filmed by a crew of 50 or so people. Sad days.

This kind of over-protection echoed in my head some time later, just before the film was released in the UK. Neil Morrissey, star of *Men Behaving Badly* and voice of *Bob the Builder*, told me he had spent the day doing voice-overs in one of those London studios dedicated to post-filming technical effects. He told me the studio was full of people working on *Nanny McPhee*. Apparently the film had been shown to a sample audience of American children and they had run out of the film screaming and crying. They were terrified. And what had scared them so badly? Was it Nanny McPhee's horrid moles? The worm, maybe? Could it have been the tarantula?

Not at all. It turns out that terror had been struck into their souls by the sight of my non-surgically-enhanced bosoms, framed by an eighteenth-century style corset (nothing particularly risqué about that – no Janet Jackson wardrobe malfunctions or stray nipples). The sight of my bazookas had so petrified the little Yank children that the studio had decided that there was nothing else for it but to airbrush out a large percentage of my cleavage. And I am reliably told that, for this episode of modern-day prudery, the production company had to stump up the grand figure of a quarter of a million dollars. Who said we weren't going into a new age of Puritanism?

The rumour that there was going to be a full-length musical theatre version of *Acorn Antiques* was going round. When I heard about it, I wasn't sure it was a good idea. After all, the original sketches only ran for six minutes per programme and there had only been two series. That was where Victoria had been so clever. *Acorn Antiques* had had a total TV air time of around 40 minutes. Also there had been a ten-year gap since anyone had even seen *Acorn Antiques*. I had loved playing Miss Babs, and felt worried that reprising the role so much later and in a two-hour version might spoil it. After all, it was such a glorious memory for so many people (myself included). I told Victoria my anxieties and she replied, 'Well, we'll look elsewhere then.'

I thought nothing about it again till Julie Walters phoned me and said, 'Look Ceals, come on. I'll do it if you do it.' So we both agreed to be in it.

The next week we both flew out to Swaziland to start filming Richard E. Grant's film, *Wah-Wah*. Richard was an old friend, and this film was a kind of quest for him. He was directing a script he had written about his childhood and I was to play Lady Riva Hardwick, a character based on one of his parents' friends.

The plane took us to Johannesburg airport, which I found quite a scary place. I was biffed so hard by so many people that next day I was covered in bruises. From there we were taken on a four-hour drive into Swaziland, which was a place with a totally different atmosphere. It reminded me of the Isle of Wight in that visiting it felt rather as though I was going back in time. The people were calm, gracious and smiled a lot, which left you feeling good and full of energy for work.

Believe it or not, this was the first film ever shot in Swaziland.

We were put up in a hotel on the edge of the Songimvelo Game Reserve. My room reminded me of Ingrid Bergman films, and came complete with wooden veranda overlooking what I imagine someone talking with Meryl Streep's accent in *Out of Afreeca* might describe as the veldt.

The hotel porter advised me to keep all the windows shut at night. I asked him if this was against intruders and he shrugged and said, 'kind of'. So that night I left the window ever so slightly ajar, but in a way that no one could get in or possibly open it any further.

I was awoken by the sound of rustling paper somewhere within the room. Barely breathing, I looked round and made out a small figure perching on the end of my bed. I slid myself to a sitting position and turned on the light.

A monkey stared back at me. On his lap he had the brown paper bag of fruit which I had bought that afternoon and he was busily searching through it. As I hissed, 'Shoo! Shoo!', he calmly took out a pear and, impudently staring me out, he chomped away at it. When he got to the core he dropped it onto the bed, then he casually flung a few things he didn't fancy out of the bag. Next, with some gusto, my little simian friend tackled a peach, all the while keeping his eye on me as though challenging me to stop him. After a short time, he peered into the empty bag, tossed it away and stalked off, bottom in the air. He then leapt up to the window and swung out of it, leaving me bewildered and keen never again to disobey the porter's instructions by so much as an inch.

In the film there were a few scenes about an amateur dramatic production of *Camelot*. The character I played choreographed the dance in these scenes, and Richard was kind enough to let me *actually* do the choreography, which as you can imagine, I revelled in.

Angus had a small walk-on part in the film. I always tried to take him with me, whenever his school holidays coincided with my location work. And this time, thanks to Richard's characteristic understanding, Angus could also feel he was actually part of the work rather than just a hanger-on. But naturally he had free time, and he used it well, along with Zac Fox, who played the mini-version of Richard. The two boys went on a safari with Zac's mum, staying overnight in a game park. When Angus got back he told me it had been very exciting and that the scariest part was when he had been bitten by the crocodile. Of course I almost had a heart attack on the spot, but then realised I was looking at a complete boy, with every limb intact and not a scratch on him. God only knows what had really happened.

I had less time off than Angus did, and certainly did not have enough time to go camping (even if I ever actually found myself so inclined). However, I did manage to arrange myself a mini-safari.

On the appointed morning, the guide called for me and I was led off on horseback. I saw one hippopotamus and one zebra. That took almost a day and I have to confess that the minute we set off I already wanted to come home. Safaris are such a lovely idea, and look so gorgeous on TV, but the reality is too hot, too long and too smelly. Do I need to mention flies? Photographs make it look all very glamorous, but truly I'd prefer to sit comfortably in my living room and look at the photos any time.

As though to prove my point about foreign wildlife, during the last couple of weeks we spent out in Swaziland I developed a smallish itchy spot which I took for some little midge bite. A few days later it was about five inches across and had taken on strange circular markings rather like an archery target. My midge bite turned out in fact to be the bite of a particularly nasty local spider.

Aaaaaaaaaaaaaaaaaaaaaaaaaaaaaaaaaaggh!

Angus and I both went down with high fevers, and were confined to our room. I was convinced it had to be related to that spider bite, but who can tell? After two days lying in the dark, tossing and turning, we both felt very weedy but much better.

On the way home to England, I was on my own, except that I was accompanying Angus and a couple of kids from the production team. My hand luggage was jammed with things to entertain the boys on a ten-hour flight. I was stopped at the gate and told that having one piece of hand luggage was all right, but if I had the one with toys for the children then I could not also take my laptop on board. That must go into my suitcase in the hold. So, under the instruction of British Airways staff, I shoved the thing inside my huge suitcase.

It was only when I arrived home in London and opened the case that I discovered that everything was just as it had been when I last opened it at the airport, except that the laptop was missing.

I phoned British Airways who told me the laptop should have been with me in the cabin. At Johannesburg things frequently go missing from cases, they told me. It was not a problem for British Airways to sort out, it was an insurance claim.

I phoned the insurance company who explained that as I had lost the laptop after my case was checked in with BA then it was entirely BA's responsibility. Your insurance doesn't cover you at all from the minute you check your baggage in until you pick it up from the carousel at your destination. Who knew?

I went back to British Airways but they told me 'hard luck'. I was particularly miffed by their refusal to help me, as the newspapers of the time were full of stories of how they had paid compensation to the Duchess of York and Posh Spice for exactly the same kind of thing, only they were zillionaires and their losses were jewellery worth thousands of pounds.

The man at American Express told me a few terrible tales of pilots confronting gangs of men in the transit areas of Johannesburg airport. The men were smashing suitcases to the ground, trying to make the locks break open. When the pilots stepped forward and ordered them to stop, the men had rushed at them with knives.

Thus it is that my journal of the stay in Swaziland and all the photos Angus and I took of our adventures and safaris were lost. So for all that suffering, all those flies, and that hellish day on safari, I will never have the pleasure of sitting on my sofa and boring my friends with the photographs of it all.

CHAPTER 26

Rehearsals for *Acorn Antiques: The Musical* started just before Christmas. It was great to be back with the old gang, plus a few new faces. Not only were Victoria, Julie and Duncan and me there, Neil Morrissey and Sally Ann Triplett were joining the cast, as was my old friend Josie Lawrence. It was also the first time I had worked with Trevor Nunn since I was tea girl at the RSC.

On top of it all, I couldn't wait to put on my Mary-Janes, and sing and dance my heart out.

We sat around for the first read-through and when it finished, I was surprised and distraught to find that Miss Babs didn't have a song. Nor a solo dance. In fact I had nothing at all in the way of a point number. This was the musical version. Surely Miss Babs should have a song? I felt very unhappy, particularly when everyone else in the cast gathered round the piano to start work on their solo moments and there was nothing for me.

I finally plucked up courage to ask Victoria if there was any possibility that Miss Babs could have her own song. She turned to me and said that it had never occurred to her, and that the problem now was there was no room for one.

But when I took the job, my own song had been the moment I was really looking forward to. It had never occurred to *me* that Miss Babs would not have a song of her own.

We came back from our two-day Christmas break to a company meeting to double-check no one had had any friends or relatives in the Boxing Day tsunami. Not having a song seemed pretty unimportant after that, but then some other members of the cast were given second solos.

I approached the director, Trevor Nunn. Last time I had worked with Trevor I had been an assistant stage manager on the world tour of *Hedda Gabler*. So I introduced myself first, 'Do you remember I was once your ASM and tea-g—?'

Before I could finish my sentence he laughed and said of course he did. He promised me that he would look into the song situation.

Rehearsals banged on. We had choreographers and répétiteurs to knock the ensemble dance routines and choral songs into our heads, while we pressed on blocking and rehearsing the actual play. Meanwhile in side rooms, the others thrashed about with their solos and I felt increasingly vexed and miserable.

Christmas came and went, and the first night loomed. But I still had no song. I was now told that putting in an extra song at this late stage might mean that someone else, possibly one of my friends, Duncan Preston or Josie Lawrence, would have to lose one of their songs, which they had spent a long time rehearsing. I agreed that that did seem rather unfair. I bit my lip and tried not to show my disappointment.

Run-throughs started. We moved into the theatre. The excitement of the first band rehearsal came and went.

Finally the day of the technical rehearsal arrived. The tec, as it is known, is a day-long ordeal during which the actors wear their costumes and make-up for the first time, and have to go over and over little bits of the play ad nauseam while around them electricians fiddle with lights, music cues get re-rehearsed and cued in, the wardrobe department dash about, quick changes are timed and repeated until they are just right, while the set exposes all its electronic and mechanical problems, driving the carpenters and electricians to the limits of their sanity.

It was at this moment, to my surprise and thrill, the glorious Victoria handed me the sheet music for my solo, a torch song.

The timing was frantic. During tea-breaks, I grabbed the musical director to make up a tape which I could rehearse with at home that night. Next day was the dress rehearsal and, while the rest of the cast were confidently getting used to running the show, my song was slipped in for the first time.

The following night, when we first played before an audience, I had only sung the song twice before. It was utterly nerve-racking.

As for the show itself, none of us expected the deluge of applause which greeted the first performance. The laughter and cheers raised the roof. We should have realised. All those people who know all the words of the original sketches were there in droves and, what's more, they were having the time of their lives.

Miss Berta, owner of Acorn Antiques, played on TV by Victoria herself, was played on stage by Sally Ann Triplett. I had seen Sally Ann some years before in Cole Porter's *Anything Goes*. She caught my eye not only for her excellent performance but because she had Happy Xmas written in red lipstick on her bare back, between the straps of her evening dress. She had a hard job following in Victoria's footsteps, but we were instant friends.

I am not a great fan of make-up and in particular false eyelashes. I think I have the wrong shape eyes or something, as they inevitably go wonky on me. I suspect these days false eyelashes are only of major interest to transvestites. The minute the eyelashes were in place I certainly felt as though I looked like one!

One evening during a scene, Sally Ann started piercing me with a particularly intense glare, while surreptitiously nodding like a dog in the back window of a car. Thinking she was on the verge of having a fit, I looked worriedly at her, but carried on regardless.

What had happened was that my left lash – the upstage one – had come free of its moorings and was flapping around on my cheek. It felt no different to me. I always felt uncomfortable in the horrid things.

The harder and more seriously I carried on, trying to ignore her, the more intense she became in her stares, until she stopped staring and burst into giggles. That was it. She giggled, I giggled back, though it was true I didn't even know what the joke was. We must have looked quite unhinged, although the only thing that was actually unhinged was the lash.

Eventually I realised what had happened, ripped it off, and flung it onto the sofa. For the rest of the show people were wary of sitting there and they all perched at the other end, mistaking it for a gigantic spider!

★

Later on I was asked to appear at a charity bash for the Air Force at the London Palladium. It was to be held in the semi-regal presence of the Duke of Kent.

Having been brought up on *Sunday Night at the London Palladium* and *The Royal Variety Performance* I wasn't going to pass on this one. It had always been my ambition to do a special curtsey to the royal box and to stand in that line-up afterwards where the royal personage strolls down the line shaking hands and chatting.

As luck would have it, Desmond Carrington played a wonderful comedy song from the wartime that Sunday on his radio show, so I phoned him asking for the details. The song was 'Everyone Keeps Pinching My Butter', as performed by the wonderful Gert and Daisy (aka Elsie and Doris Waters, sisters of *Dixon of Dock Green*'s Jack Warner). It was a hilarious little ditty, full of double entendres and quite racy jokes. I believe that at some point it had been banned by the BBC. But it was perfect for an evening with a Second World War theme.

It was a two-hander, so I asked Sally Ann to join me. We had enormous fun, and we made a little comedy routine, trying to out-do each other at the royal curtsey (as I had seen comedy acts do in my childhood). After the show, the Duke raced up the line to get to us and I feel sure it was because of our curtsey, although someone had the nerve to point out that he seemed quite interested in our cleavages too! Perhaps it's a royal thing.

I loved playing in *Acorn Antiques*, and meeting the fans afterwards.

Despite the bouts of coughs and colds which went around I am proud to say that I was the only member of the company not to take a show off. While actors around me were felled by flu, colds and bronchitis I soldiered on.

One day between matinée and evening shows, the choreographer made me keep the promise I'd made her to go and have a massage. The masseur told me that my circulation was very sluggish. It didn't mean much at the time, but within six months it proved to have been a very portentous and ominous remark.

My non-matinée days and Sundays during the four-month run of

Acorn Antiques were spent re-rehearsing *Unsuspecting Susan*. Those New York talent scouts had come good and I was booked in to play it at the 59E59 Theatre as part of its 'Brits on Broadway' season.

There wasn't much time. I was due to be leaving for New York as soon as the *Acorn Antiques* run ended at the end of May.

CHAPTER 27

Stewart Permutt and I flew out to the United States of America together in early May 2005.

The 59E59 Theatre kindly arranged a typical Upper East Side apartment for me to stay in during the run. I had loaded hundreds of songs onto the laptop, so once my suitcase was open and Stewart was in the kitchen making a cup of tea, I set it up, complete with speakers, ready to flood the place with music. I was very impressed with my own technical prowess for I had never done such a thing before.

First song up was Bette Midler singing *Old Cape Cod* – wonderful. Stewart and I danced round the flat, singing along at the top of our voices. Then *Old Cape Cod* came on again. And then again. Unfortunately during the whole stay I never quite mastered the computer's music programme and, despite the fact I had loaded about 3000 songs onto the computer before I left the UK, the only song I *ever* got it to play during the entire six weeks was *Old Cape Cod*.

It used to be one of my favourite songs, now not so much. However fond I might actually be of sand dunes and salty air, enough is enough. But whenever I have heard it since it means only one thing to me – New York!

Unsuspecting Susan opened on a steamy hot day in June. Everything went to plan. As I have said, Stewart and I make a point of never reading the show reviews until the run is over. But everyone in the theatre was going on and on about the importance of reviews all day long and then again at the after-show party. In New York they told us the critics can break a show, and in particular the critic of *The New York Times*. If the NYT likes you, they told us, then you have a hit, but if they damn you the show closes in a week or less. We went back to the apartment and sat up drinking and talking into the early hours. At about 3am we caved in and went out onto the streets to find a paper stall. With some trepidation we bought a copy of the dreaded *New York Times*. Although when I read it now I can see that it's a very good review (especially considering it was the NYT), the only thing which leapt out at us that night was this phrase, 'the funny, engaging (mostly) and tragic' play.

'Mostly?' said Stewart.

'Mostly!' I repeated.

And that was it for the rest of the run.

'How's your pizza, Stewart?'

'Delicious – mostly.'

'Has the kettle boiled yet?'

'Mostly.'

We were off on a jag. Mostly.

We both adored New York. I don't think Stewart and I slept for the whole six weeks. In between rehearsals we went for walks and to concerts in Central Park, we sat in delis sipping coffee, we did our shopping late at night and carried groceries home in brown paper bags like they did in *Cagney and Lacey*, we went to Broadway shows and met Kathleen Turner after a performance of *Who's Afraid of Virginia Woolf*, and John Lithgow after a matinée of *Dirty Rotten Scoundrels*. After a hectic week of rehearsals I also saw the Pulitzer prize-winning play *Doubt*. (I *doubt*ed I'd stay awake. I didn't.) One night I even met Charles Strouse, genius composer of *Annie* and hundreds of famed standards like 'Put on a Happy Face' and 'A Lot of Livin' to Do', when he came to the 59E59 theatre.

One blistering hot day, I got blissfully soaked on the wet water ride called the Beast, a fast speedboat whizzing round the Hudson River. I ate pizzas at John's and drank cocktails at the Waldorf Astoria. I had waited all these years to get back onto that electric carpet which is New York, and wasn't going to miss a moment of it.

The show came to the end of its allotted run the night before the big 4 July holiday. Therefore on the Independence night, I was able to stand on the FDR Driveway, which was shut to traffic for the evening (mostly), and watch the best firework display I have ever seen, outside Versailles.

Stewart had flown back home before the end of the run, but I had been asked to give a few talks on the *Queen Mary 2* and so sailed home in considerable style.

I boarded the beautiful ship with tremendous excitement. As I stood on deck, in the evening sun, watching the brass band play us out of New York Harbour, while all around me streamers flew, I thought to myself, 'there is no other way to travel'. No wonder it was the favourite transport of all those chic old movie stars and musicians. There's truly nothing else like it. I adored knowing I was following in the steps of Mae West, Marlena Dietrich, Noel Coward, Ella Fitzgerald, Duke Ellington, Liz Taylor and the rest.

While other passengers had stampeded down to the restaurants to start the week-long eat-in, I went up on deck and said farewell to wonderful New York City. I blew a kiss to Lady Liberty and watched the ship scrape through the gap beneath the Verrazano-Narrows Bridge by a whisker.

Then I thought 'enough sightseeing', and, as it was well past cocktail hour, I wandered down to the Sir Samuel's bar for a glass of champers.

A gaggle of crewmen, including the captain, was gathered. If ever there was an opportunity to say, 'Hello Sailor!', this was it. I went up to them, and told them how handsome they all looked in their gorgeous costumes. To a man, they gave me an old-fashioned look.

Apparently I should have said 'uniforms'.

Anyhow, I thought their costumes were heavenly. The usual naval style, very chic black or white, with an elegant gold line down the pants, and bits of coloured braid signifying their departments - white for hospitality, red for medicine, black for sailing etcetera - on the sleeves and epaulettes. I told them all I was green with envy and would kill to have the opportunity to ponce around the ship dressed in the Cunard uniform. As I left the bar, Jamie Mansfield, then the *Queen Mary*'s executive housekeeper, gave me a knowing wink. I had no idea why until the next morning after breakfast when I returned to my cabin to find, hanging on the back of the door, a full set of *QM2* costume. The only trouble was he'd given me a skirt. I was in no mood to have some passing actress whisper 'ankles!' at me again, so I phoned him and asked whether it would be enormous trouble if I could possibly have a pair of trews instead. Jamie not only obliged but sent a tailor in to nip and tuck the suit and make sure it was a perfect fit. He then told me I was to muster, wearing this costume for the 'formal night' in the Winter Garden Lounge at 6pm. Naturally I obeyed orders.

The charming and debonair Captain Bernard Warner welcomed me and placed me in the line-up with the rest of the officers. Some members of the crew I had never met before arrived and kept glancing anxiously at the number of rings on my sleeves, clearly an indication of rank, so that they could correctly place themselves above or below me in the line. I had such fun shaking hands with the passengers, just as though I was a real sailor.

My place in the dining room was just down from Sir Harold Evans, Tina Brown and family. At my own table sat the Heinz family (57 varieties, but only two on mine) and two gentlemen in white tuxedos who came from Illinois and had the largest cranberry farm in the known universe (or so it appeared). They talked cranberries solidly for hours, interspersed only with the recurrent joke about how they'd left their wives at home to do all the work while they took a vacation.

The eye-rolling waiters, it turned out, were great fans of *Still Game*, and we shared a few winks.

I gave a little introductory talk about *Calendar Girls*, and it really *was* a little talk, as the person who was lecturing before me, a religious speaker from Oxford University, seemed uninfluenced by the fact that it had only taken God seven days to create the whole universe, and overran their allotted one-hour slot by at least ten minutes. This meant that I had to start talking while the outgoing audience was heading up the aisles, battling against the downward flood of the incoming one. It was something very like the Armageddon which the religious lecturer had just been referring to in her talk.

If I had waited for everyone to settle, I was told, the ensuing film itself would overrun into dinner time which could not happen, for then the whole routine of the ship would be running late. It was horrible, shouting above the mêlée while all the Holy Joes stampeded for the exit, and the film fans battled to grab a good seat.

Next day, I gave a Q&A session which was altogether more relaxed. The questions from the audience were far more diverse than usual. I was even asked which was my favourite flavour of Green & Black's chocolate. Answer: Espresso Coffee. But I was persuaded to try Cherry, which I did the moment we got back to Blighty. It is now my new favourite.

I raced about that vast ship with much the same energy I had devoted to New York. I got a hoot from the rallying boys when I accidentally walked through a room which was hosting a meeting of an onboard club called 'Friends of Dorothy', and not such a friendly welcome when I attempted to sit down in a nice quiet room in a corner of which a meeting was going on of something with a mysterious name which I later discovered was the code word for a club of People Against Alcohol. I joined a team in the Golden Lion for the nightly pub quiz, and our team won quite a few tokens towards Cunard caps and badges to give to Angus. My greatest contribution to the team was knowing the meaning of the word Thallasaphobia*
– something I certainly do NOT suffer from.

I only remember half-an-hour of waking time where I was totally free and not rushing off to do something. During that brief period of repose, I grabbed my swimming costume and made my way to the pool. However I hadn't even got my toe into the water when a man appeared from nowhere and handed me a large buff envelope. 'Hi there, Celia,' he said. 'I have a film script I'd love you to take a look at.'

Well, now, I'd learned my lesson about accepting unsolicited scripts, and so had to spend my half hour swim-time explaining how the best way was to send any script to any actor is via the agent. And, no, I never did have that relaxing swim.

On the final night, after dinner, I was escorted by the captain up to a little private room where a party had been laid out by all the

* Fear of sea water.

247

members of the costume-wearing crew I had befriended during the voyage. They'd ordered champagne and a whole tray of iced buns with cherries on top. A photographer came in to take pictures of the merry line-up. God, those ship boys are a hoot!

When they were all summoned off again to perform their on-board duties, I headed back to my cabin, exhausted but happy, knowing I had a completely free time between now and the morning and when we docked in Southampton. Although I was looking forward to arriving, as I would be reunited with Angus after two months away, I hoped finally to let my hair down, maybe visit the casino or go dancing for a few hours. But first I would need to brush up a bit.

It was almost midnight. I had barely got into the cabin when the phone rang. It was my sister with some terrible news. My brother had died.

I was shattered by the news. I could not sleep, and next morning got off the boat in an awful daze. I met Angus at the Southampton quay and we went up to London. Within a few days I started feeling very ill. At around this time, the spate of attempted London tube bombings took place. The whole of London was in state of high alarm. The following day, while all the local tube stations were closed following the shooting of Jean Charles de Menezes, and confusion reigned throughout London, I felt dreadful, but put it down to stress. My dear friend Lally suggested I was very over-tired, after all I had not actually had a day off now for more than six months, and I was distraught, drained by my brother's sudden death. She advised me to go to an acupuncturist she knew in Wimbledon. With heavy heart I made my way there, and lay still on the treatment table while this man stuck needles into me.

When I left his practice, my head was swimming. I walked slowly, feeling more and more dizzy and nauseous. I was finding it hard to breath. I lurched along, grabbing onto the walls of houses to steady me.

I was staggering along a narrow alleyway when I fell to the ground. My head was reeling and I felt terribly, terribly tired. All I wanted to do was lie down on the ground, and go to sleep, curled up like an animal. I don't know how long I lay there. A road sweeper found me in a huddle and asked me if I was all right.

'Yes thank you,' I replied, like a fool.

A little later on, a man walked past who luckily recognised me. This time, when he asked me if I was all right and I again replied, 'Yes, thank you.' He said 'I don't think you are.' He took me into his house and suggested calling for an ambulance immediately, but I told him I would be all right, I was just a bit tired.

I'm not sure what happened next but when I came to, the ambulance was there. The paramedics worked on me as I drifted in and out of consciousness. When we reached the hospital, I was admitted to the high dependency area of intensive care.

I had suffered a pulmonary embolism, and, it turns out, was very lucky to be alive. Blood clots on the lung are one of the most frequent causes of sudden death in the western world. As I lay there in my bed, hooked up to so many machines, with nurses coming every few minutes to take my blood pressure and read my vital signs, I could not think clearly at all. I was finding it hard to grasp the seriousness of what had happened to me, and kept asking everyone how soon I would be released.

I was in hospital for about two weeks, at the end of which I went home and spent less than a month resting.

Against all advice I went back to work as soon as possible, accepting a small role in *Poirot*. I ached for things to be back to normal. And the most normal feeling for me is when I am at work. But once the cameras started rolling I knew I had made a mistake. I had no energy and wanted to do nothing more than lie down and sleep. It was unfair on everyone else. The cast and crew didn't know I had been ill. I hadn't told them. To them I must just have seemed exceedingly listless, possibly bored and utterly unenthusiastic. But the truth was, I simply should not have been back at work so soon. I should have been at home recuperating.

But by the time *Poirot* finished, I still had not learned my lesson, and went right on working, this time on location up in Yorkshire for an episode of the sentimental ITV series *Where the Heart Is*. Again I was weary and lethargic and, despite the name of the programme, my heart really wasn't there at all. It is very hard to work up energy and enthusiasm when your body is under tremendous pressure.

On top of the physical weakness, I had lost all inner joy and my usual sense of cheekiness. I felt burdened and exhausted. These feelings seemed to me to be self-perpetuating – the more burdened I felt, the more burdened I became, the more exhausted I felt, the more exhausted I became. I yearned to relax, to feel easy and sit again among friends and laugh till I cried.

I took a few weeks off but started feeling that my house and life in Abbeville Village among all the 'yummie mummies' was claustrophobic in the extreme. Strictly against medical orders, a neighbour even smuggled me into her house to smoke cigarettes so that Angus would not see. But by accepting this 'kindness' I was actually being cruel both to myself and to him. The doctors had shown me pictures of what the embolism had already done to my lungs. I was mad to think that somehow it didn't matter if I disobeyed the rules. It was idiotic and stupid of me.

But I received a major boost early in the new year of 2006 when I was nominated for an Olivier Award for Miss Babs in *Acorn Antiques: The Musical*. Rupert Farley, my great friend from the old Citizens' days, escorted me to the ceremony – he is just about the perfect escort. He's funny, always dresses perfectly for the occasion, knows when to step forward and when to take a step back (believe me, getting this right is quite an art) and for an actor he is refreshingly un-showbizzy. You'd certainly recognise Rupert's cheeky voice as he is the man whose jolly tones frequently cajole you to buy everything from cakes to cars both on radio and TV ads. Rupert comes from a family of suppliers of film furniture whose motto is 'Farley isn't just a business, it's a destination, a source of inspiration and a repository of knowledge'. The same can be said of Rupert himself. We share a mutual passion for Southern Indian snack food.

I was not expecting to win the Olivier Award. And when my name was called it was such a thrill and an honour beyond my dreams. I picked up the prize from Piers Morgan, and was wearing one of my favourite dresses, which the exquisite Jenny Packham had made me. It was designed to look like a mermaid. I still treasure the lovely little statuette, a bust of that gloriously handsome and charismatic actor, Laurence Olivier. It sits proudly in my bedroom where I can remind myself that even when things look utterly bleak, surprises can come along to cheer you.

Lynda La Plante phoned. She wanted me to be in an episode of one of her many terrific series, *The Commander*. I still felt exhausted but said yes anyway. Since I had first seen *Widows*, back in the 1980s, I had always wanted to be in a show written by Lynda. I had admired her as an actress (she really was so marvellous and terribly underused) and her TV writing is beyond compare.

The role would also reunite me with Simon Williams, who is such a sweet man. Years before I had nursed him in the trenches of *Upstairs, Downstairs*, while still a young novice in the acting business, but now I was to play his wife.

The role was gruelling, not only because we had a tight schedule and were working in extreme winter cold, but I had some particularly nasty scenes to film. In one, my character was stabbed to death by her own son. Then, once that was done, I had to spend a whole day covered in blood, lying in a blood-sodden bed, pretending to be dead. It was quite unnerving. I hadn't felt so weird about acting in a scene since the hanging in *A Dark Adapted Eye*.

My agent managed to land me the co-starring role in the new Nicholas Lyndhurst sit-com, *After You've Gone*. Sitcom was something I had never really tried, and it seemed a good idea to make a new start, although I was worried by having to sign a long contract of three years. Like marriage, signing up to such a long commitment made me desperate to find an escape route. The worry about that, and the fact that I had not taken proper time off to recuperate, left me still feeling tired and, though I went round telling everyone not to worry, I was fine and 'strong as an ox', I still felt strangely weak, and was unusually nervous about the job.

I attended a read-through and first rehearsal. That night when I went to bed quite early as the following morning location filming began, I was feeling a little wheezy.

I got up very early next morning, as my car was due to pick me up at 6.30am. I lay in the bath feeling very unwell. By the time I got out, I already knew things were very wrong.

Luckily Fidelis had arrived the previous evening so that she could get Angus off to school for me in the morning after I'd gone to work, and then make his tea that afternoon when he came home. I climbed up the steep stairs to her attic room to ask what I should do.

'I'm not feeling very well,' I said, shaking her awake.

Before she had a chance to open her eyes, I crashed to the floor. She immediately called an ambulance. While she waited for it to arrive she repeatedly hauled me back from unconsciousness, shouting at me to breathe and stay awake, while also haring up and down four flights of steep stairs to open the front door. By the time paramedics arrived and applied an oxygen mask I was unconscious.

The bustle of men rushing up and down the stairs, carrying bags, oxygen canisters, and a chair to carry me in, had woken Angus, who emerged from his room rubbing his eyes and asking what was going on. By the time I was stretchered into the ambulance my whole body had gone a uniform waxen yellow.

Once I was conscious and in the ambulance, I asked the paramedics if Angus could come with me to hospital. They said no. I now realise that they were worried I might die in front of him.

As I sped away, Angus turned to Fidelis and said, 'Why is my mother that terrible colour?' I wish he had not seen it. I was the colour of a dead person.

Within half-an-hour I was back in intensive care. Despite being on a daily dose of warfarin, I had had a second huge embolism.

The paramedic told me I had been very lucky that it had happened to me so early in the morning when there is little traffic on the roads. If the ambulance had reached me two minutes later, he said, it would have been too late. I would not have stood a chance, and would no doubt have died.

My agent, Michael Foster, was brilliant. From an airport departure lounge, he swung into action, getting things organised. He phoned the producers of *After You've Gone* and persuaded them, rather than recast the part, to wait for me to get better, however long it took. The rest of the cast was given time off and this time at last I stopped trying to be brave, and dedicated myself fully to my recovery. This second brush with death within a year had taught me a lesson which for some reason the first one had not. I realised that if I had not survived this last embolism, Angus would have been left in an intolerable position. Losing your mother is horrible enough at any stage of your life, but at 12 years old is unthinkable.

And besides that, I wanted to live. I wanted to share Angus's life and watch him grow into a man. I also had so much still to achieve for myself. I knew I needed to change things, to jump-start my life again.

I went down to the Isle of Wight and at last took my recovery seriously.

Once I was fit and well, we started rehearsing *After You've Gone*.

For three years I spent half the year working and the other half off. During the working half I did work very hard, alternating between playing Diana in *After You've Gone* to live studio audiences, and playing Gloria, Stephen Fry's secretary in *Kingdom*. I was chauffeured between locations in Norfolk and the BBC studios in west London.

Kingdom proved a joy because Angus landed the role of my son, and therefore, even though I was working, we could be together. He was excellent in the role and I was very proud. We took a small cottage in Swaffham, the village where we filmed, and on the very rare days I was off from both programmes we went to the seaside together and had picnics on the beach.

Both series were filmed during the summer. The winters I tried to keep for myself and my continuing recovery.

I moved out of the Abbeville house and into the one which Ralph Hammond Innes had left me. Now that Angus was a teenager and no longer needed a live-in au pair, the Abbeville house seemed like an aircraft hangar in the middle of nanny-land, and a small house in a bustling cosmopolitan area was just the ticket.

I first started using the new house on my (and Ralph's) birthday when I threw a moving-in party there. It was a different kind of party for me because the house was utterly empty and therefore very tidy. Possibly it was the only time I have ever spent the night in a tidy place of my own.

Perhaps it is something to do with having been brought up by a nanny. I don't know. But I have to confess I am famously disorganised and messy. Poor Angus. He must be the only teenager who always has an impeccably clean and tidy room. It's his own form of rebellion against my chaos which litters the rest of the house.

Once, when I still shared in Clapham, police were called to the house when, on entering late one night after a show, a few of the other inhabitants heard creaking noises from the upstairs rooms.

The police duly arrived and, flashing their torches, they stalked tentatively up the stairs. They inspected everyone's room, then crept along the corridor to my bedroom at the back of the house. Fidelis, Stewart and Jo Cameron Brown waited anxiously downstairs. They heard a groan from above.

'Miss Morgan, Miss Morgan,' said a constable, leaning over the banister and shouting down. 'There might not be anyone here now, but you'd better come up and take a look at the back room. It's been ransacked.'

The three of them then had to explain to the policeman that nothing was in fact wrong, and that this was how my bedroom always looked.

Sometimes people have looked into my bedroom and asked 'But *where* do you sleep?' Well, the answer is that at night I throw all the stuff piled high on the bed onto the mess covering the floor, then in the morning I toss it all back again. It bothers other people far more than it does me. I don't mind not being able to see table tops, or the patterns on carpets for piled up stacks of old envelopes and plastic bags full of this and that. And the thing that mystifies most people is that in spite of it all looking so chaotic I can usually lay my hands on anything I want pretty quickly.

So on my birthday, my guests gathered in the immaculately clean Hammond Innes house and during the party every one of them begged me to try and keep it nice and clear.

Nearly all of my great friends were present, including Harold Pinter and Lady Antonia Fraser, Penelope Wilton, Stewart Permutt, Fidelis Morgan, Rosalind Knight, Lally Percy, David Schofield, Eve Ferret, Rina Gill, and Rupert Farley. Michèle Wade, actress and patissière, arrived with a gorgeous Maison Bertaux cake. It was a balmy July evening and we all sat in the small paved garden and had a lovely time, with champagne and much laughter.

Moving into my new house proved to be just the kind of fresh start I needed. In the six months between the summer filming of both series I took more time out to see my friends, and learned again how to live properly.

When Angus was on school holidays we went on trips, travelling always by train and boat now, as I was no longer permitted to fly. We went down to Nice, probably the city in the prettiest situation on earth, to Monte Carlo, San Remo, Paris and Rome. We travelled on the mountain railway up the Jungfraujoch, but sadly on a foggy day, so the view we had from the top of a mountain 11,300 feet above sea level was much like looking into a white sock. We went to Zurich, where I finally got to visit a Kunstmuseum (it was wonderful), and to Milan, where, despite being told tickets were booked out for the next three years, managed to see Leonardo's wonderful fresco, *Il Cenacolo* or *The Last Supper*. (If you were wondering how, the trick is to arrive at 7am – or whenever the doors first open. Many people who have booked that early simply don't turn up.) I visited Ireland, seeing Dublin and Achill Island, where I made the shortest possible crossing of the Atlantic (a bridge spanning the Achill Sound) and spent New Year's Eve witnessing the last European sunset of the year and seeing in the New Year with the three mysterious sisters of the Minaun Bar.

CHAPTER 28

My travels with Angus took us as far north as Kiruna in Lapland within the Arctic Circle. It was quite a trip. We set off on a train from Brussels to Cologne and had been sitting at our places for only a few moments when a terrifying dark-haired German woman advanced up the aisle with a trolley.

'Food? Yes?' She wore a smile which said 'We have vays of making you eat'.

When I saw that the only option on the menu she thrust at me was wild boar, I asked if there might be a vegetarian dish. 'You vant snack, yes?' She plonked a packet of Sticklettis (which are in fact long straight pretzels) and a small bottle of wine on my place and thundered away. I stashed the wine for later. I had been hoping for the bread and cheese which I could see poking out of the trolley but it appeared that was only possible as a second course for those who took up the offer of boar. When Heidi with the long black hair reappeared, I told her I had changed my mind and please could I have the boar. 'So vy you didn't say so!' She slammed down the cardboard platter.

Scared stiff, I waited while she disappeared along the carriage then dared open it, discarded the wild boar and took out the bread and cheese. She passed again, 'More drinks, please?' It was not a question. So I got another bottle and stashed it too.

Before we arrived at Cologne, Heidi returned. 'You did not eat your meal. Yes?'

'I had the cheese,' I stammered.

She glared at me with her frosted Germanic smile and repeated, 'More drinks. Please?' Shaking my head, I clanked to my feet.

I was relieved to arrive in Cologne, or Köln, as it is known locally.

Our next stop, Copenhagen, also had a new name, Kopenhavn, and the train left from platform 5. Unfortunately the sign on that platform indicated a train to Münster. Angus and I huddled at the bottom of the windy passage leading up to the platform, being biffed by crowds of cheery Germans in Santa hats, waving sausages wrapped in paper while singing merry verses of something which sounded suspiciously like the Horst Wessel Song.

Eventually the train with our departure time was announced. The sign said Prag, Kopenhavn, Gdansk, Moscva and Minsk. How could one train go in all those directions? It was obviously going to be very important to get into the right carriage or at dawn we might find ourselves mistakenly changing onto the Trans-Siberian Express.

Angus worked out the Kopenhavn carriage, 201, was fourth from the front. So we dragged our luggage along through a throng of gypsies and arrived just as the train pulled in. We only had a few minutes to get aboard, but the carriages passing us were numbered 187, 184, 188, 180, 193 and were labelled Minsk and Moskva. We shouted Copenhagen at the guards leaning from the doors. They gave us an 'It's not my problem' look.

Fighting against the oncoming tide of bedrolls and plastic bags thudding towards the Minsk carriages, the departure time was upon us. We screeched back along the platform with no sight of either Koepnhavn or 201. We passed 200, 203, 204, then it suddenly switched back to 199, 198, 197. The clock was past departure time and so I yelled, 'Just get on!' but Angus was running forward, screaming, '189, 194, 205'. The last carriage on the train was 201. We threw our luggage up the steep metal stairs and flung ourselves after it. The train pulled out before we got to our feet.

We slept like logs. During the night, the cabin door opened and a huge black dog rushed in.

'English?' asked a female guard wearing combat uniform, and holding up a police warrant. 'Sniffer dog for drugs.' The dog got very excited around my case and the woman's eyes lit up. But Rover happily lapped at an open carton of milk left over from our late night picnic.

Next morning, we pulled into Wonderful, Wonderful Copenhagen, while Angus told me his school research on how very clean and efficient Denmark was, and how it was possibly the best place in the world to live, both environmentally and sociologically.

We wheeled our luggage down to the left luggage department. The entrance was flooded with a dark red liquid seeping from a discarded plastic bag. 'That's all we need,' I thought. 'Body parts.' Luckily a young man decided to investigate. Tremulously he peeked inside then let it drop, with a clank. I have never seen wine that thick or dark but, thank God, wine it was.

Luggage-free, Angus and I hit the streets of Koepnhavn. We spied one pile of vomit, two piles of vomit, three piles of vomit, four . . . so we took to looking skywards, two Johnnie-Heads-in-Air, strolling along a narrow alley trying to avoid that vile sight so early in the day.

And it was because we were looking up that we noticed the young man in grey frock coat and black mittens who stood balancing on top of a fence a few feet in front of us. As we approached, he jumped down and performed a robot dance, while his thick-set Bill Sykes of a friend clambered over the wall behind him. The Artful Dodger said, 'Somebody doesn't say good morning. I wonder why?' We tried to pass him, attempting to look unfazed by the fact we were being sussed for a mugging. Jack Dawkins danced on.

I gripped Angus's hand and exclaiming, 'Good morning', we marched on with such determination and speed that we had reached the open street before the Dodger's bull-necked accomplice hit the ground.

We ran across the main road, out of danger, sidestepping more vomit, and hit the town centre. McDonald's, Accessorize, The Body Shop, H&M, United Colours of Benetton . . . Where are we exactly? Was this Denmark or Derby?

In a small square, we saw a lovely fountain, with verdigris cranes and frogs. The trouble was, there was no water and yet more vomit. Angus shook his head, saying, 'I am so disappointed.'

After this, we took in Tivoli Gardens, a mini Chessington crammed with little huts selling wooden dolls, dried-up spicy bread and other Danish Christmas wares. While Angus took a few rides on whizzy things which went backwards and upside down, I got more and more freaked out by the aggressive Christmas spirit.

Finally, we caught an earlier than planned train heading for Stockholm. The temperature there was very, very cold, about minus 6 degrees, although there was no snow but a heavy frost. Next morning we made straight for the historic centre – all windy quaint little streets leading up to the Royal Palace. We arrived in time for the Changing of the Guard.

To begin, there was a trumpet call, then a sound like someone beating out time on a tin tray and the palace doors burst open, revealing a troupe of male and female soldiers in beige uniforms with blue berets and black boots with spats. Upon what passed for a drum roll on the tin tray and a shout from the captain, the ceremony started. The soldiers didn't so much march as prance into position, then did a little moonwalk to get the spacing right. More shouting, then a fellow at the side told us in Swedish, then English, that this was the Royal Helicopter Corps, founded in 1967.

The soldiers shuffled about a bit, kicked their feet up, while waving a blue-and-yellow flag with a helicopter blade on it and went inside again. After this edifying display we visited the Royal Shop.

Inside were racks upon racks of postcards featuring Jeffrey Archer. No, it couldn't be! Ah, no. I realised, it was King Carl Gustav. Hard to tell, though.

In Sweden the word for Hello is Hey! (spoken very brightly and with a slightly upward inflection, like 'Hey, where do you think you're going?' or 'Hey, get your hands off that'). So when the girl in the glögg stall or a man in the paper-shop goes 'Hey!' you instantly think you've done something wrong. But I enjoyed saying both Hey and Tak (thank you). In fact I said little else for days.

As evening fell, we climbed aboard the sleeper heading for a small town 200 miles inside the Arctic Circle. This was a delight, a replica of the Swedish Royal train from about 1870, with plush seats and velvet curtains with tassels, and wooden tables lit by quaint lamps with fringed shades. In England it would be in a museum. Our fellow passengers were all male and looked like ancient escapees from a heavy metal band, long hair, long beards, t-shirts with skulls and daggers on them, smelling vaguely of dirty hair. But the illusion was shattered by their talking in voices like the chef from *The Muppet Show*.

We spent a dark cosy night looking out at the magical landscape, copses of white fir trees and rows of little red wooden houses lit by a candle in each window, snug beneath heavy hats of snow. Next morning, we awoke to what I imagined was tundra, a kind of grey nothing with little black bushes and skeletal trees. To be frank, it was a bit depressing, but onwards and upwards.

The sun was just below the horizon, and would not rise above it for our stay. I had imagined a dark twilight, but it seemed just like England in November, a normal day only a bit dull. Looking about as we waited for the taxi, all we could see was a gigantic slag heap, and two chimneys belching black smoke. The taxi took us along a depressing dual carriageway, skirting a town which reminded me of Cumbernauld.

When we got out at the Ice Hotel, the ground was like a piece of bathroom window – hard, shiny, slightly bumpy, frosted glass. We slid into reception where a grim woman gave us our number, 313, and told us to go to the Dressing Room, a 'chalet' fifty yards away.

When I say chalet, do not imagine anything like those cheery little gabled wooden houses in Pinocchio or Heidi. Think more in terms of internment camp. To bolster this illusion, we had also been given neck ribbons displaying our number which we were told we must wear at all times. We were handed gigantic snow boots and a zip-up waterproof, cold-proof suit which, in red and beige, made Angus look like someone out of *Star Trek*, while I, in my turquoise one, looked like a twit.

'You must assemble at 3 or 5,' a girl announced, 'for instructions on how to behave while at the Ice Hotel.'

'We're supposed to be going cross country skiing now,' I said.

'So you must go to the assembly point when you return,' snapped the girl. She pointed to a pole in between two Nissan huts.

Gingerly we slid along, wearing so much clothing it felt like being in an iron lung. At the meeting point, five people were already assembled.

'Oh look', said a cheery woman, as we staggered along, clinging to one another and slipping four foot backwards with every step we took. 'It's that Celia Immery off the telly.'

I put on my best smile. A squat man with a Hitler moustache told us to get inside what looked like a cattle truck attached to a small tank. He drove for about ten minutes then in some deserted bit of the forest he told us all to get out.

'It's all right,' whispered the cheery woman. 'We all know who you are, but we won't say anything.'

'Who is she?' murmured a man under his breath. I tried to put on a smile like the Queen's.

Our guide showed us how to put on the skis. While we were all fiddling about with these, he climbed back into the tank and drove off, waving from the window. 'Now you ski back to the Ice Hotel.'

'But we've never done it before,' cried cheery woman.

'Don't worry,' said Hitler-moustache. 'You'll pick it up.'

The ground seemed even harder out here. The ice was deep and hard, and had bushes sprouting through it. It was also full of pot holes and dips.

'Help,' said Angus clambering to his feet.

I lurched forward and swaying from side to side, grabbed out for twigs and bushes to steady me. Angus was by now shuffling ahead like a Chinaman in a 1930s film, bent down, head bowed, both hands stabbing poles into the thick ice to try and get a grip. I decided that being bold was probably better than being tentative, so took a step forward and shot onwards about 14 feet, then crashed into a tree and landed in the middle of a gorse bush. Angus was now yards ahead with the rest of the party, who were all managing rather well. So I put my best foot forward and thought if I trusted I would be all right.

At last, that 'session' ended and we rolled up for the assembly meeting, where a woman with a grating voice, who spoke so slowly that by the end of each sentence you'd forgotten how it began, made us dread everything about the night to come.

'Why are we doing this to ourselves?' said Angus as we marched behind the Swedish corncrake.

We went back to our 'warm quarters', literally a wooden changing room, not unlike the ones at swimming pools, and sat glumly staring at our clothes hanging three feet ahead of us, our feet up on our suitcases.

'It's exactly like *The Prisoner*,' I replied. 'Complete with the fact that we are number 313. Can't we escape?'

So we sat in the sauna changing room, with piped musak, a loop of an Eskimo wailing *Amazing Grace* accompanied by a theremin, maracas and someone smacking a dinner plate with a soup spoon. But at least it was warm, and gave us somewhere to sit for the half hour before we were due to leave for 'Northern Lights Deluxe'.

We were greeted at the assembly pole by a tall handsome young chap who looked just like a blonde Elvis, circa *GI Blues*.

'You're the only two,' he said, leading us towards a minibus.

He drove us along the dark ice-packed roads for about 40 minutes till we reached a few metal sheds, and then said, 'This is the European Space Centre'.

Inside the shadowy deserted building, we were shown a film about the centre and then shown platforms where, seemingly, Europe launches its feeble contribution to the space race. Elvis then sat us at a table which seemed like a film set of the launch pad control board, where we were photographed. Finally we were taken outside. I looked up to see a big grey s-shaped serpent in the sky, like an odd green cloud.

'The Northern Lights,' cried Elvis. 'You are very, very lucky.'

I was very, very disappointed.

'Can you see them more clearly without all these lights?' I asked. We were, after all, standing in a car park lit like a night football pitch.

'In the wilderness camp, yes,' said Elvis.

Elvis drove us into the forest. This is when he said, 'My friend is meeting us there.'

My heart started thumping and I thought, here we are in the middle of nowhere, a woman and a child, with two strange men, and no one in the universe knows we are here. He pulled up the van on a deserted road in the middle of nowhere and said, 'Get out now, please, and follow me.'

Like lambs to the slaughter, we trotted behind him into the dark forest. We walked for about five minutes then another shadowy figure loomed out from behind a tree. The two men talked in Swedish and then, pointing to a little hut, said, 'Come inside please'. My heart beat so fast I'm surprised I didn't have a seizure.

But the cabin, lit by candles and a log stove, was delightful. The new man served up a hot meal, our first in days, some kind of potato and onion creamy cheesy stew which was delicious.

Then we went back to the hotel for the terrible ordeal. The ice bedroom.

It was now that we had to walk across a courtyard in nothing but our thermals and snowboots, clutching an insulated sleeping bag and a sewn up sheet.

'Why are we doing this?' said Angus.

'Why indeed?' I replied.

We arrived at our icy cell. There, like gigantic caterpillars, we slithered onto the slab of ice and lay there.

'Now what?' I asked.

'I suppose we pretend to sleep,' said Angus.

We turned off the light and lay there, with only our faces peeking out of the body bags, a silver hood over the top of our heads. We lay awake most of the night and were wide awake before the official wake-up call at 7.30am. When permitted, we leapt off the bed, into our boots and thermals to make the dash back into the changing room. We were up so fast we were sure we would be the first, but the place was humming. Obviously no one wanted to relish their ice bedrooms for a nanosecond longer than they had to.

I asked at reception what time we could move into our chalet.

'3pm,' said the manageress curtly.

'You have got to be kidding.'

'I hope you have moved your things out of your warm accommodation?' (By which she meant the locker.)

'No,' I said.

'It is compulsory to vacate the warm accommodation by 10am.'

'So where do we put our stuff?'

'The locker room cupboard.'

It has long been a dream of mine to sit astride a snowmobile and drive through the virgin snow, powdery white spraying from the machine's giant skis. It still is. About a mile out of town our guide powered up the snowmobiles.

'This is the throttle,' he said, 'and this is the brake. Let's go.'

'Don't we wear helmets?' I asked.

'If you want,' said the organiser pointing towards a garage lined with shelves full of black helmets with visors. They seemed to have some kind of earplugs too, because when you put them on, you were suddenly deaf.

Angus was taken on board with the organiser and the rest of us followed the leader round a field of ice and over a main road. These machines were very powerful, and, with ice rather than snow under us, there really wasn't much we could do to steer, and using the brakes only sent us whirling out of control.

Then one of my snowmobile's skis dipped into a massive hole in the track and, narrowly missing a tree, went right over, landing on top of me. The man behind came running up and helped pull it off. When we caught up with the organiser, I asked if I could please go back.

'No,' he said, 'you have paid for four hours. We are going onto frozen lakes and through the forest and . . .'

'I don't want it,' I said. 'I want to go back.' Reluctantly he agreed.

Back in prison they told us our accommodation was unexpectedly ready. We moved in. The chalet was not unlike the ones at Maplin's except that there was no bath and no tannoy announcing fun activities about to start in the Beachcomber Bar. (If only there had been a Beachcomber Bar!)

We set off on another frozen adventure. As we neared the kennels we could hear very excited dogs barking. They were ready for us, to take us on a dog sled ride.

I will never forget the sight. The full moon was high in a black velvet sky, the white wilderness shimmered all around us, the fur-coated driver strode along, pulling on his long brown beard as he tightened the leashes, and, before us, at eye level, contracting and dilating, were ten pink dogs' bottoms. For the next 40 minutes as we whizzed along through the icy night, these were my only view.

Every corner we turned, the dogs went skittering all over the place. At the end of our ride, when the dogs were put back into the kennels, we noticed that their mouths were bleeding quite badly. Used to taking mouthfuls of snow to whet their whistles at the roadside, they tried to bite at the ice but it had cut their gums.

'It's what's happens when there is no snow,' said Eric, our dog man.

I felt ill and realised he should not have taken us out at all on such a night.

We got up very early, packed and left the chalet ready to be picked up for the 'Wilderness Moose Safari'. The same minibus that was to take us to see the mooses (meese? What on earth is the plural of moose?) would drop us at the railway station that evening.

'My name is Bjorn,' announced the bearded safari driver with a laugh, as we threw our luggage into the back. 'Which is odd as I have never seen a bear.' We laughed politely at his Swedish joke and gave each other cross-eyed looks.

Bjorn turned out of town and into the wilderness. By the way, this 'wilderness' everyone talked about was simply what we in Britain would call 'open countryside'. The only difference is that it's got ice on top. A hill here, a field there, a farm or a couple of houses dotted about, a river, another farm, a few fields, a little copse. It was like driving twenty minutes out of Glasgow and calling it 'the wilderness'. But the one thing which never went out of view was the gigantic slag heap with two belching chimneys on top.

'I couldn't live in the town,' growled Bjorn, when we said we lived in London. 'I like to live where you can't see the air, or smell it.'

'What do those two chimneys do?' I asked, in all innocence.

'It's some kind of evaporation, I believe,' said Bjorn, putting his foot down and hurtling further into the other word they all kept using – the 'hinterland'.

'There!' shouted Bjorn, slamming his foot on the brakes, causing the van to career across the highway into the path of oncoming traffic. 'A moose!' A greyish creature, a bit like a cow with Mickey

Mouse ears, stood about fifty yards away from the road, staring at us, slowly chewing the cud. 'Isn't it marvellous? This is the winter grazing area for the moose.' I noted that Bjorn carefully chose never to use the plural.

We drove on. Bjorn didn't look at the road much. He leaned this way and that, peering into the grey countryside for Mickey Mouse ears.

'What is the plural of moose?' I asked.

'I think British people usually refer to them as elks,' said Bjorn, cutely avoiding the answer.

Every mile or so Bjorn slammed on the brakes again and we'd go hurtling forward.

'Our train goes at two o'clock,' I said. 'We don't mind arriving at the station a bit early.'

My hope was that he'd turn back, but now he was on the mobile phone – no hands-free – stabbing out numbers, and chattering away in Swedish. We'd been in the minibus for the best part of two hours and had seen our fill of mooses, which was about eight. See one moose, you've seen the lot.

'Perhaps we might head back to Kiruna,' I said.

'No, no,' said Bjorn. 'You see that farm there – that's owned by a Sami chap. He's fighting the authorities about his slaughterhouse because they want to bring it up to European standards.'

I crossed my fingers and toes, praying he was not going to take us for a visit.

'I am taking you for a visit,' he said, as my heart sank, 'to see another Sami friend, who runs the Sami Culture Centre.' Phew!

On either side of the road lay huge, flattened fir trees, their roots in the air. The wind, which had kept me awake in the night, had hit this area really badly. We passed about 200 felled trees, one of which lay across an electricity sub-station. Broken cables dangled from the gantries like spaghetti.

Eventually we came to (literally) the end of the road, a monstrous wooden house designed by some lunatic architect to get attention.

'The Sami Centre,' announced Bjorn opening the minibus door for us. 'Watch out. It could be slippers (sic).'

Inside the wooden house, a squat woman who looked like a half-breed Eskimo greeted us with a miserably tired look.

'No electricity,' she grumped. 'So no coffee.'

We both pretended to be frightfully impressed by the wooden house and the primitive drawings all over the wall. While I was paying a candlelit visit to the loo, I was mercifully spared the sight of a painting which is apparently some great Sami treasure. While it was displayed, Angus had to bite his lip to stop himself laughing out loud.

'I can't deal with visitors right now,' cried Mrs Sami, cultural ambassador for the primitive Sami people who clearly cannot cope during a power cut. We were given a couple of biscuits and sent on our way. Thank God.

So, it was back into the hinterland with Bjorn. Now, to test me further, Bjorn pulled out his mobile phone and, looking down into his lap, started texting.

'Shall I do the texting for you?' I yelled. We swerved, narrowly missing another car and sliding right over the carriageway.

'I'm all right thanks,' said Bjorn. 'Ooops. There's another slipper.'

After an endless hour, we sighted buildings.

'Now I can show you the town,' said Bjorn, driving us up the side of the slagheap. Up and up and up we went. Darkness was falling fast and it had started to snow. As we headed up the slope, the minibus's wheels began spinning on the spot and we started sliding backwards down the hill at a 45 degree angle. I started recalling my terrifying bus ride over ravines in Italy.

'I think we'd prefer to go straight to the station,' I gulped. 'If that's all right with you, Bjorn. It would be awful for you if your van got stuck.' We turned back and had the equally hideous journey sliding forwards down the monstrous icy hill.

After a two-minute whiz through a Swedish branch of the Co-op to buy a picnic for the journey (including some Swedish chocolate bars called Plopp), Bjorn left us at the station, a deserted place covered in graffiti.

Overnight, Angus and I sailed down the coast of Sweden, heading again for the light. Angus made a great linguistic analysis. 'Isn't it interesting how languages let you know that pulling is harder than pushing?'

I looked at him, bemused. 'In Italy they put "Tirare" on the doors, cos it's so tiring to pull, but "Spingare" on ones you have to push cos they just spring forward, and here in Scandinavia it's just the same, it's "Tryk" to push but it's a "Drag" to pull. You see?'

CHAPTER 29

After two years with this six months off/six months on schedule, I felt quite well again. It was as though a great black curtain had been lifted, and the weights which seemed to have been pressing down on my shoulders evaporated.

When up in Norfolk for the third season of *Kingdom,* I really enjoyed the summer filming. My first ever scene with Stephen Fry had been many years ago in Simon Gray's *Old Flames,* when I had had to stand in the street screaming at him. My last shot in *Kingdom,* was kissing him and asking him to marry me.

And as I started work on the third season of *After You've Gone,* I felt better than I had done in years. On the first day, my make-up girl bent down and whispered in my ear. 'Welcome back,' she said. But it was the conspiratorial tone which made me think there was more to it than that I was simply back at the studios, ready for season three. I asked her what she meant.

'You've got your mojo back, Celia,' she said. 'You're yourself again.'

She was right, thank the Lord.

People often ask me how long it took to recover fully from my illness, and the answer still can be divided into two: my *physical* recovery took a few months, but the genuine revitalisation, the return to how I felt before I fell ill, took years and came about suddenly.

Some people call this period between the technical and full recovery a period of post-traumatic shock, a time in which people (particularly the spirited ones, I have been told) once physically safe, take an abrupt psychological dip. The explanation doctors give is that spirited people use up a great deal of psychic and mental energy fighting to get better from the moment they are physically struck down. Then as soon as their body has recovered, the emotional fright of the situation kicks in.

Most people deal with the whole thing at the same time.

I think that this second dip, when you are physically fit again, is so much scarier because it feels as though there is no excuse or reason for it. It frequently manifests itself in alternating panic attacks and feelings of total and utter exhaustion. In fact, you seem to feel tired and scared all the time. That was certainly what happened to me and it lasted way too long for my liking.

During the first two seasons of *After You've Gone*, while I was going through this post-traumatic period, everything seemed so daunting. I tried not to let it show to the rest of the very clever and comic cast but now at the start of season three, I felt as though I was back in my own element again.

For the first two seasons, I still had that inner tiredness. But now playing to the live studio audience was no longer something which terrified me — it had done for the previous two years.

In fact I was so relaxed that I must confess that frequently Ryan Sampson, who played my grandson, and I got the giggles so badly we had to restart scenes many times.

That kind of thing can only happen when you are calm within yourself. When you are tense and frightened it is almost impossible to laugh on set. There are some directors who think a tight acting ship consists of people milling about seriously, always on topic, with never a smile, a joke or moment out of character, but I have found that this always leads to the dullest kind of prose-lytising work. All the most interesting actors are gigglers — Lord Olivier, Sir John Gielgud and Dame Judi Dench, Ken Branagh, Rupert Everett and Helena Bonham Carter. When you are relaxed enough to laugh, you are relaxed enough to be creative too. And there is nothing worse than those days when you are so fearful, insecure or nervous that merely feeling able to laugh is out of the question.

So I was laughing again, I had got my mojo back, my health was tip-top again. But the best thing was that, for the first time since I was in New York, every morning I really looked forward to getting up and going to work.

Another thing which I suppose was marvellous for me was that I got to talk to Nicholas Lyndhurst's wife, Lucy. Like me, as a child, Lucy had wanted to be a ballerina. But she had *not* been too large, and therefore *had* achieved her dream. Lucy had done the whole ballet thing. She had trained and become a professional ballet dancer. She had even danced with the Royal Ballet.

'A lot of it was hell,' she told me. 'Not at all what I had thought it would be. It often made me very unhappy.' She described the strife and tension of the work, the painful muscles, the bleeding toes, the rivalry and the starvation diet.

For the first time in my life I wondered if I had been fortunate and had a better chance by *not* getting what I had set my heart on, by being forced out of dance and into the world of acting.

Thanks to our conversation, I appreciated I had been very lucky in never having realised my lifelong dream of being a ballet dancer. I felt a tremendous surge of relief. I started to wonder what had impelled me into the desire to be a ballerina anyhow. I thought back to the little Royal Worcester 'Tuesday's child is full of grace' statuette my mother had been given when I was born, and which now sat on my own mantelpiece. Could it be that this tiny pretty dancer, which supposedly represented *me* within the family, had been the thing which had spun me off in pursuit of a dream which was never to be, and to chase a desire which would almost lead me to the grave at 14 years of age?

After speaking to Lucy Lyndhurst, I finally knew then that in fact my life had really gone the right way, and that I had taken the best possible career path.

Penelope Wilton discovered I had moved in a few streets from where she lived. In fact she walked past my house once a week on the way back from a regular walk in the park. We talked about her popping in for a coffee whenever she passed, but she worried about ringing the bell unannounced at the wrong moment, if I had friends or family staying or had been on a night shoot and therefore might have only just gone to bed. So we arranged a secret code. My at-home-and-open-to-impromptu-Wednesday-visits would be indicated by the front door looking normal, but when a pink ribbon hung from my door handle it told Penelope, 'no coffee today'.

The first time we tried it, I waited excitedly. At around 10am, the doorbell rang, and there was Penelope. It was perfect.

I had to go away for a few weeks on a job, and then she was away, but once we knew we were both in town again, we phoned one another to announce the continuation of the ribbon code.

Next morning I got the ribbon out. But I had forgotten whether a pink ribbon meant I was receiving or not. I thought it must be no ribbon for 'in' so left the door bare.

As she passed, Penelope hovered at my door. She too had forgotten which sign meant in and which out. She decided no ribbon equalled not available and marched on, while a few feet away, inside my kitchen, I waited and waited.

We spoke later. 'I thought no ribbon meant in . . .'

'But I thought no ribbon meant out . . .'

The following week, at the time I knew Penelope would pass, I had covered the door with hundreds of multi-coloured ribbons, and strung up my Christmas fairy lights too. There was no mistaking that this was a welcome sign. Penelope duly arrived and rang the bell for a catch-up coffee, but after that day we ditched the code.

When Rupert Everett called offering me some fun playing Matron in *St Trinian's,* I leapt at the opportunity. Rupert is a real tonic. He really can make me laugh till I cry. *St Trinian's* always amused me as a child, and the full-throttle cast would also include Colin Firth and gorgeous Russell Brand. I couldn't wait.

Rupert and I go back a long way. Not only did I witness his embryonic steps onto the stage as an over-painted extra, I also did some early cloak and dagger work on his behalf. Not long after the Glasgow Citz marathon Proust adaptation, Rupert started an affair with petite blonde TV presenter, Paula Yates. Paula and her husband Bob Geldof (at that time only a Boomtown Rat, not yet the Live Aid hero) lived a few doors up from us in Clapham. Rupert would come over to see Paula, but not dare to knock on her door in case her husband was in. Instead he would lounge around in our living room, sending me out at regular intervals to see if I could see Bob Geldof leaving his house.

'Go and put something in the bin,' he'd insist.

'But I only put something in the bin three minutes ago, Rupert.'

'So put something else in the bin. I don't know . . . Clean the bin. That'll keep you out there for a while.'

'Rupert, I am not going to be seen in the street cleaning my dustbin. I'll look like some waste fetishist.'

Years later, when Rupert was appearing in the West End production of Noel Coward's play, *The Vortex*, which had transferred down from Glasgow Citz, I accompanied him on a birthday outing to Lennon's, Cynthia Lennon's short-lived nightclub. After only an hour there, we moved next door for a few drinks at Stringfellows, an interesting experience which I am unlikely ever to repeat.

Rupert was at the time trying to embark on a career in music. He got a record deal and wrote a song called *In the Vortex*. In it there were various background snatches of dialogue from the Coward play. As I have a posh voice, he brought me in to read Maria Aitken's lines for the record. Somewhat later he came over all superstitious and thought that by not having Maria he would somehow curse himself. So Maria was brought in and re-did the lines. He then thought it was bad karma to have dropped me, so in the end the record was released with both Maria and I doing little alternating bits, but essentially playing the same role.

And now Rupert and I were to work together professionally for the first time since *A Waste of Time* at Glasgow all those years ago.

As I was playing Matron, I phoned my sister, Rosa, who had worked as a matron at a school in Sussex. Perhaps she might be able to come up with a few quirky things for my role which I could put forward to the director and add to my characterisation in the film.

'What are the principal things I should know about being a matron?' I asked my sister gaily.

She replied, 'The first thing is that you spend most of your time cleaning up vomit.'

End of conversation.

I was certainly never going to put *that* in as a suggestion to the film team. Even if they used tins of soup for me to clear up the very thought would make me vomit myself, and though it might be wildly funny for everyone else, not so much for me.

The first film went like a dream and we had great fun making it. The numerous young girls playing the St Trinian's schoolgirls seemed quite alike to me, all except one, that is.

One morning I got in and sat in the make-up chair while around me there was a great buzz of excitement. Despite the early call, the night before many of the cast had gone out to a nightclub to see the rather memorable St Trinian's girl give a concert, one of her first.

The girl's name was Paloma Faith. I so wish I had thrown caution to the wind and risked feeling shattered all day on set so I might have gone along with them. But who was to know that she would be so good? What a performer! I'm mad about her and her 'zhuzhy' outfits.

On the first day filming St Trinian's, part two, Rupert and I had to shoot a scene where I (or Matey as Rupert called me – short for matron, you know) had to hang out of the window smoking a fag while chatting to him, or should I say her, for Rupert was playing the role of the formidable St Trinian's headmistress, Camilla Fritton. Once the cameras were rolling, Rupert suddenly had the idea to notice halfway through the scene that I was smoking in front of the girls, and had to stop me. I had not been warned about this, nor had anyone else for that matter. He stepped towards me, registered the cigarette then gave me the most amazingly hard wallop across the chops. I almost fell out of the window. The crew let out a choral gasp and the director yelled 'Cut!'

But by this time Rupert and I were helpless with laughter, anyhow. To tell the truth we were both disappointed when the scene didn't make it into the final cut of the movie.

Neither did another memorable day's work. I must admit that Rupert and I, whether to the front or the rear of the shot, are never knowingly underacting. Like in the best newspaper cartoons or programmes like *Police Squad* and *Creature Comforts,* with us two there is always something fascinating going on in the background. In one scene we decided that while the other action was going on I would take his blood pressure, the old fashioned way with a puff-up sleeve and a stethoscope. When Colin Firth (or Frothy, as Rupert dubbed him) playing Geoffrey Thwaites, the Minister for Education, appeared on the screen of a laptop we were watching, Rupert suddenly got another impromptu idea.

Camilla, the headmistress of St Trinian's, always dreaded school inspectors and in particular the Minister for Education, so, once she caught sight of him, decided she would bolt. Once again, with no warning, Rupert surprised us all when he got up and ran like hell out of the shot.

But he had forgotten that I was attached to him via the blood pressure kit by arm and ear, and so where he went, I duly had no choice but to follow. Only, having had no warning, I was not quite ready to go anywhere, and being yanked out of my original position at 90 miles an hour, I dragged along behind him, entwined in the BP kit.

It was marvellous. But it didn't make the final cut either. Which is where the wonder of DVD starts. Both scenes can be seen in the Special Features section.

Every day during filming, Colin and I would load our trays at the catering wagon then make our way to Rupert's Winnebago, or, as he dubbed it, Fritton's Club. We had a merry time over our lunch, Rupes, Frothy and Matey, dishing the dirt and chewing the fat. (Though I really mustn't be rude about the caterers, they were marvellous.)

One day we sat in the caravan talking fondly about Alan Bates. Suddenly Rupert turned to me and said, quite casually, 'But then of course, you and Alan are the same person.' I understood.

Months later, when the film was about to be released, Rupert asked me to join him to do the press junket.

I had never been on one before. The most I knew was from watching those little TV interviews that appear on breakfast and morning TV and then occasionally in evening shows. It goes like this: a celebrity, usually of major status like a Hollywood star, can be seen sitting in an elegant hotel room, while an interviewer throws fairly standard questions at them, occasionally trying to inject it with a kind of ingratiating but cheeky banter.

What most of the public do not realise when they watch George Clooney, Julia Roberts or Johnny Depp casually chattering about their latest film is the exhausting day those stars put in.

You arrive at a (usually) wonderful and lavish hotel. You are taken to a bedroom where you are made up and your clothes checked for camera flaring, clashing with the curtains and such visual problems. A beautiful and lavish breakfast is brought to you. Trays arrive brimming over with everything you could care to eat. So far so good.

But, just when you really start to enjoy yourself, you are yanked out of the comfort and taken to another hotel bedroom, where, for the camera and lighting's sake, the curtains are drawn and strong studio lights are pointed at you. Windows cannot be opened for sound reasons, or should I say for reasons concerning sound. The rest of the room is crowded with PR people from the companies interviewing you, as well as those PR people working on your own project. There are cameramen too, and so much equipment that you can barely move.

Then, without so much as a coffee break, for three solid hours, the interviewers come in. Each has an allotted time span of about 10 to 15 minutes. In they come, one after another, asking the same questions over and over, in Groundhog Day fashion, until you have forgotten what planet you are on let alone which film you are promoting.

Rupert and I were squashed together so closely it was very easy to tread on each other's toes, or press down on each other's feet, when a tiresome or funny moment came up which we wanted secretly to share. Next day my feet were black and blue.

When either one of us went off track or became pompous and highfalutin in our reply to a question, we would receive or give a nudge to the other, privately pressing our elbow into the other's ribcage. On a few occasions I do remember myself saying aloud, 'Rupert what on earth are you talking about?' Once he turned to me and said with that winning smile, 'Oh do shut up!'

A short break for lunch was spent back in the comfy room, then the onslaught recommenced for another four hours. To break the monotony you would find yourself nodding and looking sage, as though you were engaged in a serious debate about nuclear warfare or famine on *Newsnight*, when in reality you'd be suppressing a yawn as another person asked whether, as a child, you had enjoyed Ronald Searle, or were you yourself naughty at school. Maybe a hundred or so interviews later (one bubbly effervescent person after another querying whether we had fun working together, and inquiring what we were both doing next) the interviewers from TV, radio, magazines, local radio, internet fan-sites and newspapers national and regional dwindle out, till there is only the crew, packing up their equipment, and the PR people, ticking off their checklists, left in the room.

Exhausted, Rupert and I staggered out into the real world for air and light.

Hats off to all those Hollywood stars who keep looking fresh and bright throughout. And they probably have ten times as many interviews as we had.

Before we started the interviews, Rupert and I had decided that when all was finished we would go out to supper together and spoil ourselves with a bottle of champagne. The truth is that when it came to it we were too tired to do anything but pile into a pair of taxis and each head home to bed, our heads still repeating the old mantras 'We had enormous fun . . .' 'Oh, Rupert and I go back years . . .' 'Yes, we love working together . . .' 'St Trinian's has been a favourite since we were ourselves naughty children . . .' 'No I didn't go to boarding school but always wanted to . . .' till we reached the Land of Nod.

CHAPTER 30

I was browsing round the gourmet food shops at Nice's Cap 3000 shopping centre in the autumn of 2008 when I received a call from my agent.

'Do you want to play Sybil Thorndike?' he asked.

I mentally ran through what I knew about her: she was the original George Bernard Shaw *St Joan* in the 1920s, she did shows for miners, she was a dame, she had white hair, a wobbly voice and was 94 years old.

'No,' I replied.

'Read the script,' he commanded.

Well, of course Dame Sybil wasn't always 94. In this script it turns out she was only 71.

Plague Over England seemed jolly and I thought it might be fun, so I said yes.

I did my usual preliminary research, reading about her in books, watching her films (she was marvellous with Marilyn Monroe in *The Prince and the Showgirl*). In this case I also sought out people who had worked with, or known Sybil personally. I also found a copy of a TV interview she had done on *The Russell Harty Show*. I met her grand-daughter in a coffee bar in Islington where she gave me Sybil's gloriously spirited holiday snaps, which I displayed in my dressing room and was nightly inspired by her sparkling eyes.

By the end, I was thoroughly energised. My word, this old bird had been a hoot of a woman, and not at all what I had expected. She was obviously enormous fun with a great sense of devilment.

My favourite story was utterly relevant to our show, which concerned the arrest of John Gielgud for cottaging in a known gay public lavatory in Chelsea.

The day after Gielgud had been charged with soliciting and his story splashed across the newspapers, he was due to arrive, at any minute, in the rehearsal room.

The producer, Binkie Beaumont, himself a gay man, called everyone to a corner, Dame Sybil included. 'Now it's a dreadful thing that has happened to John. He must be feeling pretty grim. I would like us to give him a bit of room. No one should mention anything about what you have read in the papers this morning, you understand? We must all just carry on as though nothing out of the ordinary has happened. Here he comes . . .'

As John Gielgud entered the room, the company dispersed and tried to look normal. For a couple of moments, an embarrassed silence reigned. Then Sybil stepped forward, looking up through her eyebrows, wagging a finger, a smile across her face.

'So . . . *Who's* been a naughty boy then?'

I was disappointed that, although the scene of Gielgud's arrival in the rehearsal room the morning after the night before was a scene in the play, Sybil's well-intentioned atmosphere-breaking gaffe was not. Apparently it was too late to put it in. But I think it was a pity, as it would have also showed the humorous side of the situation, both on Sybil's and John Gielgud's side (he was famously hilarious about the most serious of things). It also might have got one of the best laughs of the evening, but there we are.

I always think rehearsal room creativity is better encouraged by a kind of (strict) freedom. Our rehearsals were pretty strange, as the playwright, Nicholas de Jongh, came to almost every one, and stayed all day. Usually playwrights don't attend that many rehearsals, some come to the read-through and don't reappear till the dress rehearsal. But Nicholas de Jongh was a critic, and a nervous critic at that. After all, he'd doled it out for long enough and now he feared it might be his turn to receive it.

An author's presence at rehearsal is always rather off-putting. In fact one reason many actors love working in the classics is because then you're pretty certain the author won't turn up at all, having been dead for a couple of hundred years. Playwright presence makes an entire company rather tense. The writer often gets pernickety about exact words at a stage when you're still trying to learn the basic sense of the whole piece. Occasionally they won't let go of an idea which has actually already gone out of the window due to casting, shape of the stage, scenery limitation or some other post-writing theatre feature. Great screenwriters and playwrights leave enormous gaps for the actors, set designers, lighting designers, costumes, directors (and Uncle Tom Cobley and all) to fill. And those gaps are what allows a play to breathe. Throwing a lasso round the actors during rehearsal rarely works.

I would go so far as to advise any writer who wants his or her writing to come out *exactly* as they imagined it while sitting at the typewriter, to write a novel instead. You'd be better satisfied with the end product.

Once the tec came and I was put into my costume, I got a Polaroid photo taken and mailed it straight off to Judi Dench. Of course my costume did include an old grey cardigan.

The company was great fun and we enjoyed playing the show in the West End, despite the atrocious conditions backstage. On the first day of rehearsal we had been assured that the dressing room and stage area of the theatre had been totally refurbished. However the leading man, Michael Feast, had Niagara Falls running down one of his dressing room walls. The stairs and fire exits were often blocked by piles of rubbish. I myself had many encounters with rats. One ran across my path as I made my way under the stage, from one set of wings to the other, and I frequently came back to my dressing room to find small mouse faeces around my shoes and little rat teeth marks in my lipstick.

Anyhow, in *Plague Over England,* apart from a rat-infested Sybil, I also played a tough, but fun, nightclub manager. For this role I was decked out in an orange flapper costume, complete with silk bandana.

The photos outside the theatre were supposedly pretty good. I had great trouble seeing them, as I was trying to shield my eyes from reading the reviews which were splayed everywhere around them. As you know I try not to read reviews and that means even when people tell you they are very good.

Paul Scofield described it best when he said that whenever you read a good review in which the critic singles out a bit of business, or the way you deliver a speech, during the performance the next night, and forever afterwards, you go on to the stage and somehow play the review rather than the piece of business or the speech. If you're clever enough not to play the review you spend all your time *fighting* playing the review. Either way your performance has been hijacked, and what you play is not the same as what you played before you read the review.

So please, if any among you saw me in front of the Duchess Theatre walking along slowly, with my hands stretched out before me, as though doing t'ai chi – I wasn't. I was just trying to see the photos without reading any of the words around them.

One night during the show, well on into the run, the extremely handsome Simon Dutton, who played Binkie Beaumont, was standing beside me in the wings while we waited for our cue. I was wearing my flapper nightclub hostess costume, complete with burnt orange bob wig, and bandana.

I felt that Simon was intermittently staring at me, then anxiously biting his lip. I wondered if I had a coffee-froth moustache or something.

Without any warning (and please remember we were standing in the wings and the show was going on only a few feet away) he exclaimed in a very loud voice, 'Oh my God! I've got it!'

I ssshhhed him. He had spoken so loudly that the actors on stage were turning round to see what was happening in the darkness beside them. Simon, unable to subdue his excitement, now reduced his voice to an exceedingly loud stage whisper.

'I know who you remind me of in that costume,' he said, grinning like the Cheshire Cat.

I experienced a moment of coy delight. Who would it be? Norma Shearer, Clara Bow, Mary Tyler Moore in *Thoroughly Modern Millie*?

He beamed at me and said, 'You're exactly like Jack Lemmon in *Some Like It Hot*'.

CHAPTER 31

In the middle of the run of *Plague Over England,* I organised a reading of *The Cherry Moon*, one of Dorothy Hammond Innes' plays.

How the whole thing came about is quite a strange tale.

When I was having Ralph's house decorated just before I moved in, I had the auctioneers come to take away some of the heavy old furniture so that I had some space to fit in my own stuff. The auction-eers' van had arrived late, I had had to go out, and the decorators who were in the house believed that the auction-house's delivery men knew exactly what they were doing.

Because I was decorating, all the pictures had been taken from the walls. One of those paintings was a beautiful oil portrait of Dorothy Hammond Innes by Brenda Moore. It had hung on the wall in such a position that my little photo of Ralph on the windowsill seemed to look up at her.

Some weeks later when the decorating was finished and I started putting pictures back on the walls, I couldn't find the portrait of Dorothy. I imagined that, as it was not among the chaotic mound of mess which had been shunted from room to room during the work, it must have been put away safely in a cupboard under the stairs which at the time was crammed with more inaccessible stuff waiting to be put back into place, so I wasn't unduly perturbed. But a few months later when I finally got round to clearing out every cupboard in the house in my search and there was still no trace, I phoned the auctioneers to check whether they might have acciden-tally taken the painting with the furniture.

At first they said they had not, but after I pressed a bit they became rather cagey with me. They then admitted that though it had not been on their list, they had possibly taken it, because it appeared that an oil portrait of an unknown woman had been among my things and it had been successfully sold for £60!

I was absolutely furious. But small print on the contract seems to allow their mistakes to go unpunished. I was told there was nothing I could do. To add insult to injury they would not tell me the name of the purchaser. But I did not give in.

Eventually I wrote a 'To whom it might concern'-style letter to the unknown buyer, explaining what had happened and asked the auctioneer to pass it on to them for me. They agreed to do this. Again weeks passed.

Then, one evening I got a mysterious call like something straight out of *The Spy Who Came in from the Cold*.

'Hello,' said a posh and learned voice. 'To whom am I speaking?'

Well, as you might imagine, I wasn't about to announce myself to an unknown caller, so I asked him to whom *I* was speaking. But he was no more inclined to tell me his identity than I had been to tell him mine. We circled each other like alley cats.

My cold-caller changed tack. 'Did you know the author Hammond Innes?' inquired the mystery-voice phone challenge.

A journalist, I decided. I had already been pestered by them after Ralph's will had first been published and my name appeared on it. I clammed up further and suggested to the stranger on the line that he should call my agent.

After some further to-ing and fro-ing, the anonymous voice identified himself as Professor Christopher Cairns, the owner of my portrait of Dorothy. He eventually believed that I was also who he thought I was – the person who had written him the letter.

He had originally suspected my letter was from a scammer intending to burgle his house. However when he googled my name he saw that in fact my claiming ownership of the portrait was utterly logical: I had known Hammond Innes and I could prove to him that the portrait was in fact not an unknown woman, but Dorothy. This was easy enough as Dorothy had professionally used the portrait. It was printed in black-and-white on the back jacket flap of one of her published books.

The professor then told me how he had attended the auction,

been entranced by Dorothy's face and had bought the painting, not knowing either its provenance or who the sitter had been. He insisted however that he had bought the painting in good faith and did not want to part with it. He did offer me the chance to come up and see it whenever I was nearby.

By the time I had the opportunity to get up to his south London home, Professor Cairns had followed his trained professional instinct and done some research on Dorothy's life and career, and was now determined to write a scholarly account of her life and work.

Over coffee I told him as much as I could remember of her. Our first meeting also coincided with my emptying the loft cupboards of my Abbeville house, and discovering box upon box of Dorothy's plays and unsorted correspondence.

These had been bequeathed to me with Ralph's house, along with the request that I should try and get one of the plays professionally produced. It was his dearest wish. A few years earlier I had presented a couple of the plays to a few people in the business, but with no luck.

But Professor Cairns, an internationally respected theatre historian, had now got the bit between his teeth. He was fascinated by the subject of his painting, and really wanted to go through and annotate everything in all the boxes. He read each play meticulously and compiled a detailed report about each one, together with his estimation of the viability of getting one of them done in today's theatrical climate. He picked out the two which, in his opinion, were the most likely to succeed.

I sent these to Sir Richard Eyre. He decided on *The Cherry Moon*.

I wanted to use the reading as an opportunity to raise money for Alzheimer's Research. In her last months, Dorothy had suffered from something like it, caused by oxygen deprivation to the brain.

Jim Broadbent and Hugh Bonneville agreed to take part. Coincidentally, all the leading participants, including Sir Richard Eyre, had personal links to Alzheimer's, having lost parents to the disease and/or been involved in the film about Iris Murdoch, another famous Alzheimer's sufferer and fellow St Swithinite. (Incidentally Ralph always said she was the most perfect example of a Blue Stocking.)

While we rehearsed, purple clouds hung heavy in the sky. Next day we would continue rehearsals and in the evening do the public reading. But overnight the heavens opened and laid a thick blanket of snow across the UK, crippling transport and bringing London to a total standstill.

Christopher, concerned that members of Dorothy's family might not be able to make it to the reading, phoned telling me we must postpone the performance. I had to explain that it was by mere chance and the most wonderful luck that we had managed to assemble such a brilliant team for this *one day* and that the likelihood of them all being available for another day was nil. The show must go on today, I declared, or it would never go on.

We held the reading at the University of London. Dorothy's family did manage to get there, as did many other people, despite the atrocious weather conditions, and we raised a couple of thousand pounds for the cause. I believe we did Dorothy proud.

I had been phoning Sue Birtwistle at regular intervals for years. She had been my director in the old Edinburgh Theatre in Education days, and was now Sir Richard Eyre's wife. She was also the producer of *Cranford*.

'I don't suppose there might be a parlour maid I could play?'

The answer was always hesitant and inconclusive.

Then one day, shortly after *Plague Over England* closed, she phoned me. I almost burst with anticipation.

'You know your parlour maid?' she said.

My heart thundered.

'Well, I'm not going to offer you one.' Total deflation. 'However, I do want you to come and be a Scottish widow.' And she wasn't talking insurance.

My role in *Return to Cranford* was the sociable and aristocratic Lady Glenmire, a loud and jolly woman who alienated the Cranford locals with her flamboyant ways.

Although the book *Cranford* is set in the town of Knutsford, Cheshire, now best known for its motorway service station, the actual filming takes place in Lacock, Wiltshire. The cast was put up in nearby Bath.

I arrived on the set and, after swooning at the brilliant art direction which had successfully transformed a modern street into an idyllic piece of nineteenth-century rustic England, I was taken to wardrobe and decked out in my costume, a bright tartan swathe of colour, complete with feathered hat. Immediately I rushed to Dame Judi Dench's Winnebago and flaunted myself.

Judi sat inside wearing her costume, a mélange of various shades of grey and beige (or, these days, should I call it ecru?).

'Good morning, Dame Jude,' I said, giving her a twirl. 'Who's wearing the grey cardigan now?'

Cranford was a delight. I was not only working with so many of my friends who were part of the regular cast, I was also reunited with the wonderful Tim Curry, an ex-Citz actor who I had last seen when I was out in Los Angeles, filming *Calendar Girls*. During the *Cranford* shoot, I also discovered that Barbara Flynn makes the most delicious marmalade. I was very lucky to be given a jar.

For me there was only one slight blip. Before filming started, I had been sent a few times to Gypsy Hill, a good two hours' worth of traffic jam in each direction. The reason for this journey was so that I could take piano lessons. I was to seem to play a delightful jaunty and happy piano accompaniment to a pretty little song written by the brilliant Carl Davis. His arrangement was very flamboyant and funny and gave a beautiful contrast to the previous more muted scenes in the episode, which was exactly its purpose. Within the plot, after playing the song, my character became accepted into the village, having brought a brief moment of gaiety to that little world.

At home I practised on my own piano, but I also bought myself a roll-up keyboard to use during the time when I was travelling. I played merrily (and silently) away on it at every moment I could find. Over those few weeks you might have sat in a train carriage with me, my roll-up piano on the table before me, as my fingers danced silently up and down the keys, trying to make sure I got it perfect.

The night before we were due to shoot the scene, I was sent a message that Julia McKenzie was going to be singing the song practically à capella, with only simple church-like chords from me. I was both furious and utterly disappointed. I had done all that work, and loved Carl's very amusing accompaniment. (He too must have been frustrated, as he had written the piano part so brilliantly, and now no one would ever hear it.)

The piano-playing was meant to be the turning point for my character, in that it was the moment she made the locals all smile and, despite her differences, she was finally accepted.

Towards the end of shooting, Sue Birtwistle instigated a 'Ladies of Cranford Bake-Off'. On the appointed morning, before my car arrived for the 5.30am pick-up, in the darkness of my London kitchen, I whipped up one of my chocolate cakes (see page 164 for the recipe). I recall that Judi produced a Victoria sponge and Claudie Blakely some chocolate brownies.

Unfortunately I had to rush off early that day, so, miserably, missed out on the tasting session. Nor did I witness the final judgment. Hmmm. Anyhow, sad to say, I didn't win the prize. The baking laurels went to Deborah Findlay for her mouth-watering brandy snaps.

I was rather pleased, for Deborah has great taste. Ten years before, we were next-door neighbours in the riverside dressing rooms at Stratford-upon-Avon and, while wearing our eighteenth-century *School for Scandal* costumes and bright white make-up, together we sang out our shared love of Bonnie Raitt's *Too Soon to Tell,* at the tops of our voices. It must have been an interesting sight for strollers along the opposite riverbank.

I was called to read for one of two potential roles in a film to be shot in London over the summer of 2009. The film was to star Sir Anthony Hopkins and the director was Woody Allen.

With some excitement, I went to the interview held in a small room off Fenchurch Street. Mr Allen himself was not present. I was handed a couple of sides of script, and plonked in front of a camera to play my part, while the casting director threw me my cues.

A few days later I was thrilled to hear I had got one of the parts.

Every day I waited expectantly for the script to arrive. But the only thing which popped through my letterbox was an envelope containing exactly the same pages that I had already read at the interview. Along with the script sides there was a letter directing me not to show or tell anyone what was on those pages.

About a week later, I went away to France for a few days and forgot to pack them. I phoned the production company and asked if I could have a replacement emailed to me. No, I was told. Nothing could be transmitted electronically. Another page was sent through the post. Secrecy was supreme.

Since I was a child I have had a crush on Sir Anthony Hopkins, so I was thrilled to be working with him. It became even more exciting when he knock, knock, knocked on my caravan door, on my first day of filming to introduce himself (just in case I might not recognise him). He was, as you would expect, utterly charming.

Mr Allen kept to himself, as movie directors usually do, only a bit more so. We were given various instructions. We must not touch Mr Allen, we must not attempt to shake hands with or kiss Mr Allen. I have a few friends who are the same way about physical contact, so all that was fine with me!

One day I saw him pacing around the Kensington garden location and could hear that his headphones were playing jazz. When he took the headphones off, I asked him if he'd ever been to the Nice Jazz Festival, held in Henri Matisse's garden. He looked at me with new eyes, as though he felt refreshed. I suppose he was expecting me to ask for notes, or something related to the film. He asked me to tell him more, so I told him about B.B. King and all the other fabulous musicians I had seen performing there. I tried to describe how gorgeous it was lying in an olive grove on a balmy Riviera night, sipping champagne and nibbling socca, a local delicacy, while listening to great musicians chilling and jamming. He seemed very interested. I hope he was.★

He is a magnificent enigma.

Woody Allen's film was similar to *Star Wars: The Phantom Menace,* in that I only knew about my own pages in the script, and had no

★ Sadly, since then the Mayor of Nice has decided to change the venue to the noisy Promenade.

idea how they slotted into the whole piece. I didn't have a clue what the story was about and what impact my character made to the rest of the plot.

There was an additional mystery. When people asked me what I was doing I could only say 'a film' as we were not allowed to know the title either. When filming ended, Mr Allen sent the whole cast a gift. The gifts had been embroidered with the acronym WASP.

It took me a little while to work it out. It was the working title of the film: Woody Allen Summer Project. We know now, a year later, that the title of Mr Allen's film actually is *You Will Meet a Tall Dark Stranger*.

YWMATDS would not have had nearly the same ring to it, and would have cost a fortune in extra embroidery.

CHAPTER 32

A few weeks before Christmas 2009, *The Paul O'Grady Show* called to ask me if I would like to play the wicked fairy in Paul's TV panto. There was not a nanosecond's hesitation.

Yes! I adore Paul and I adore panto. What could be finer? The researcher told me that I would be sent a script but not to worry, we wouldn't have to learn it as the whole thing would be rolled out on an autocue.

But what would be the point of that? The fun in playing something like panto is being able to muck about a bit, and you can only really do that when you know what you are doing and saying. So I learned it anyway, and turned up to the rehearsal that morning to discover that only three of the cast, Paul, Mrs Krankie and I were off the book.

Some of the others were treating it a bit like a Christmas party, slopping out glasses of booze and hoping for the best. I could see a slight tremor of panic in Paul's eye. It was easy to see that he really wanted it to be great. Plus, it was going to be going out live on TV, for God's sake.

To compound matters, one member of the cast, Larry Lamb, who I don't think had learnt any of it (and he is one of my greatest friends) turned to me and said 'So who's the little swot, then?'

I felt horrible. But it's hard to explain to someone who hadn't come from my theatrical beginnings. I had started out in pantomime, playing tiny miserable chorus parts. I had played pantomime to the exacting standards expected by a Glasgow audience (they actually boo people off up there) and adored the precision of it. And here at last was the opportunity to do a real part in another professional panto, this time live on TV. I also think that as we were going to

293

perform the panto for a studio audience, not to mention the unseen but massive audience at home watching their TV sets, it was only fair that those people watching should get the best we could offer. To many actors who think of themselves as 'serious', panto is thought a joke and an easy option. Anyone who has actually done it knows that it's quite the opposite. To pull it off successfully, playing panto takes energy, determination, meticulous timing and the superhuman strength of the Incredible Hulk on crack.

As it happens, just one year later after New Year 2011, Larry phoned to tell me he had just finished a run of playing Captain Hook in the panto *Peter Pan* at St. Albans. I asked if he'd enjoyed it.

'It was fucking brilliant,' he told me. 'But you know what, Ceal, you were right, you can only really have fun with it if you're absolutely on top of your lines.' I smiled to myself.

But back with Paul O'Grady, I was led off to the wardrobe department. Luckily enough the wardrobe mistress, the wonderful Amanda Monk, had worked with me on *After You've Gone*, so knew both my figure and my foibles. She knew, for instance, about the ankles thing.

My costume was simply gorgeous and to top it all (literally) I was given the most fabulous head-dress to wear, all feathers and chic. The producer later let slip that it had cost half the budget for the whole show. On my feet I wore thigh high black patent leather boots with towering stiletto heels, the type which might once have been called kinky boots. Only this time they really *were* kinky boots, having been bought in a Soho shop which catered exclusively for drag queens.

Paul took me aside while I was being made up and told me that the two of us were going to do a little duet together. How terrifying and thrilling all at once!

After a few hours, with minimal rehearsal, really barely more than blocking, we sailed forth to perform the piece. I was in awe of little Jimmy Krankie, who managed to fill the screen with a ladder routine. Then it was my turn to sing and dance with Paul.

Some people might say I was over the top, and maybe I was. But what does that mean anyhow, which top, where, how far over? Personally I think there is no point even attempting to go over the top unless you are prepared to head for the stratosphere.

Panto is a real art and I love it. The great panto performers, Stanley Baxter, Jack Tripp, Les Dawson, Angus Lennie have famously given performances which were mammoth in size, but which all resonate with truth, otherwise they wouldn't have worked. Panto is an interesting form. In it you manage to play a part with no side, and there is a Brechtian thing going on there too, for you play the part and somewhere you also display yourself at the same time. To my mind there is little more embarrassing and dull than panto done on the cheap or in a lazy way. But when done properly there is nothing in the world of entertainment that can beat it.

A few weeks after doing Paul's TV show, I went to Wimbledon to see him in action on stage as the genie in *Aladdin*. I was not surprised to find that he was pure magic.

A letter arrived from Charles Sturridge, esteemed director of *Brideshead Revisited*, *Longitude* and *Where Angels Fear to Tread*. 'Dear Celia, would you like to play Doris Speed?' Would I! I have been a fan of *Coronation Street* since its black-and-white days. I watched Elsie Tanner slug it out with Ena Sharples. I was transfixed as Deirdre sorted through the rubble yelling 'Tracy!' (How she must since regret having found her.) I sat gripped through Mike and Deirdre's affair. I adored them all: Raquel, Rita, Audrey, Hilda and the rest, and now he wanted me to play 'the Queen' of Corrie women for the fiftieth birthday celebrations.

The nearest I had got to those famous cobbles had been working with the fabulous Thelma Barlow (Mavis) in *dinnerladies*. Also, in 1997, I had volunteered myself as chaperone to 15-year-old Emily Aston, while she played Becky Palmer in the *Street*. We had appeared together in *Oranges Are Not the Only Fruit*, and in real life Emily is the sister of Sam Aston who plays Chesney. While I was on set, as a special favour, the very fine director, Noreen Kershaw, had let me sit on a bus going past in the background of one scene. I had also played in *Particular Friendships*, a stage play written by Martin Allen, who regularly writes gripping episodes of the *Street*.

My research for the role was heaven. I sat at home on the sofa and watched old episodes of my favourite soap. I also spoke to people who knew Doris, and was appalled to hear of her demise. Most actresses (and actors come to that) have lied about their ages at some point in their careers. Doris always kept her true date of birth carefully hidden. She had to appear slightly younger than her actual age to get the role, so it was not just vanity, there was a pressing practical reason. Then some newspaper took it upon itself to expose her real age by publishing her birth certificate and letting the whole world know she was a lot older than she claimed. It destroyed her. She left the *Street* and never came back.

The TV film, *The Road to Coronation Street,* was written by the fabulous Daran Little, and concerned the massive efforts made by Tony Warren back in 1960 to get the show on. In the course of the Manchester-based rehearsals we filmed inside the Granada Studios, but never on the cobbles of the *Street* set, for the show was made by the BBC!

Early one morning I was sitting in a hairdresser's chair in Los Angeles, mid-cut, when my phone rang.

When Fidelis Morgan had told me she was going to the States over the summer of 2010 to promote her historical crime series, the Countess Ashby de la Zouche books (mine and Paul O'Grady's favourite read) I leapt at the chance of chumming her round the American mystery book stores and playing the glorious Countess in a mini-show.

It also gave me the chance to enjoy the round-trip, seeing America by train – a means of transport which no Americans advise. They see travelling by train as a social disease to be undertaken by only the lowest of all members of the underclass and escapees from lunatic asylums.

But I was really enjoying it. You get to see parts of the country that no American even knows are there. I'd travelled on trains with names like the Lake Shore Limited, the California Zephyr and the Coast Starlight. I'd seen low flying storks and high flying eagles. I'd seen some of the bridges of Madison County. I'd seen kayakers standing in their little boats on the Roaring Fork River, baring their bottoms at the train. I'd passed through tiny towns which claimed to be 'the Garlic Capital of the World', 'the Artichoke Capital of the Word' and 'the Sweet-corn Capital of the World' (I don't think anyone ever told the rest of the world about this). I'd seen mountains and prairies and lakes and deserts. I'd even seen 'the most metropolitan cow town in the west', whatever that means. But it was certainly civilised compared to the atrocious and inhumane cattle stockyards we passed further along – miles and miles of land filled with bare bleak pens, in which thousands upon thousands of bewildered cows huddled, sliding around in puddles of their own shit. I'd seen any number of state penitentiaries, and ghost towns, I'd witnessed wild weather, during which the train was actually struck by lightning, I'd tasted grits (think wallpaper paste), and I'd met at least two thousand people who opened every encounter with the phrase, 'And where do you hail from?' (Their second sentence was generally, 'And how are you enjoying our *wonderful* country?')

We'd already been to New York, Chicago and San Francisco on our bookshop travels and I was now seeing Los Angeles for the third time in my life. Los Angeles is rather like lots of very different towns linked together by freeways. I'd been here first with the *Hedda Gabler* world tour, when the hotel and work was all based round the Hollywood area, which was quite seedy and run down, but very exciting. On my second visit, doing *Calendar Girls*, we'd been put up and filmed at Santa Monica, glamorous and glitzy. This time round I thought I'd sample Beverly Hills to see what that quarter of LA was like . . .

Well! Yes. It's not just another town. It's another world.

Every other door is smothered in signs for plastic surgeons. You stroll past shops in Rodeo Drive, where to buy even a hairgrip you'd have to take out a second mortgage, and most of the other people on the pavement are wearing surgical scrubs, obviously having popped out of some complex operation to scurry to the ATM or pick up a packet of Oreos. Women older than Methuselah teeter around on zimmers, with Disney-fish-style plumped-up lips, and that wrinkle-free, wind-tunnel look. In fact almost every woman I saw in Beverly Hills seemed to be in a perpetual state of utter astonishment. It was very disconcerting.

So, anyhow, there I was, at 9.30am sitting amid rows of elderly women under driers looking perpetually surprised, in the hairdresser's salon on Wilshire Boulevard, when I answered my phone.

It was my agent in London telling me to be at Fox Studios in twenty minutes. Twenty minutes? In Los Angeles, without a car? Plus all my stuff was at the hotel and I had to check out that morning and do a show miles away in South Pasadena at 2 o'clock that afternoon.

I asked the stylist please to cease cutting, leapt from the seat, my hair in a lopsided bob, cut short one side, dangling rats tails the other, and summoned a taxi, pronto. I glanced around me. Had I made a gaffe? All the women in the hairdressers looked utterly astonished. Then I remembered that that was how they always looked.

The taxi arrived in minutes, and dashed me to the hotel to pick up my bags, the script for the afternoon's show, and my onward tickets, then raced me straight to the studio.

It was so wonderful driving into the Fox Studios lot. I had to present my passport at the gate, as though entering another country. I was driven to the appropriate block, then walked to the correct building, passing actors in costume being driven around in golf buggies, glimpsing wonderful sets for historical New York Streets, and, through open scenery doors, modern day TV sets from shows you'd all know, like *Bones* and *Glee*. Meanwhile I realised that I was stepping through the streets where once Bette Davis, Marilyn Monroe, Cary Grant, Liz Taylor and all those 20th Century Fox stars had once walked.

I had a rather self-conscious meeting with a casting director and five producers for a film which was to shoot in October and November. Remember, one half of my hair was shoulder length and the other half cropped short.

I then sped to Los Angeles Union Station (what a beautiful place that is) to take the little train out to South Pasadena. Miraculously I wasn't late for anything all day. Once again Fidelis and I did our bookshop show to great success. But I was very hungry as I hadn't had time or opportunity to eat between 7am and 6pm when I climbed onto the train for the two-and-a-half day journey to Chicago. Fidelis whipped out a little packet of Shropshire Cakes, seventeenth-century biscuits (not literally – only the recipe was historical!) which the ladies from the bookstore had made to celebrate our presentation. How do you say 'Yum!' in Restoration English?

It was while I was sitting on the South West Chief (not a Native American in a feathered war bonnet, but the name of the train), and rattling through the Painted Desert, that I discovered that I was short-listed, and when I arrived at the Drake Hotel in Chicago I was told I had got the part which I had interviewed for at Fox Studios, and was now going to play Madge in the John Madden film, *The Best Exotic Marigold Hotel*.

CHAPTER 33

There was only one cloud on the horizon. Before I had left for the States, I had said yes to an offer to play Judith Bliss in Noel Coward's *Hay Fever* at Kingston Rep and, while I rode the American railroad, the film dates were slightly changed and the two jobs overlapped by a fortnight.

I hadn't signed the *Hay Fever* contract, and there was still more than a month during which the company could easily recast from the famous glut of actresses of my age sitting at home waiting for just such an opportunity.

This kind of thing happens all the time in our business. I myself have frequently been offered jobs which started rehearsal only a few days afterwards (let alone a few weeks) because at the last minute someone else had had to pull out. In America, Alan Rickman tells me, it is the norm for regional theatres to expect actors suddenly to withdraw when a film or TV role comes up.

But Kingston is in England, and this director would not budge. He refused to release me and insisted I did the role. But I knew if that happened, it would mean losing the film role, the opportunity to go to India with Dames Judi and Maggie and the chance of being directed by the great John Madden.

My agent put up a fight. A stand-off ensued.

Eventually the management agreed that they would let me out of doing the last two weeks of the performance, but added the rider that if I decided to go ahead with that choice, I would have to pay the theatre a compensatory fine of £20,000 and would receive no pay at all during the time I rehearsed or played the role (during the run this was changed to a nominal £1 a week, which I suppose was some legal technicality). No one I know had ever heard anything like it, but I was damned if I was going to let the wonderful opportunity of making that film slip away because of a short rep theatre run.

All of these financial and calendarial negotiations were going on while I steamed around the States. It was nerve-racking. Meanwhile, my darling mother's voice played in my ear. It came from her love of gambling on the horses, 'You have to lay out to pick up Ceek,' she would say. Frequently on the railways, I had no phone signal for ten hours at a time, then would pull into a station at 4am and get a glut of conflicting messages, to which I didn't have time to reply before we pulled out again into the telephonic wilderness. The final points to the contract were drawn up when I was totally out of communication, sailing home across the Atlantic. I only knew the ultimate details of the job when I disembarked at Southampton, the day before rehearsals began.

Luckily the cast of *Hay Fever* were delightful and I had great fun playing the part. Noel Coward is always a hoot to play (as long as you aren't playing one of his victim characters, in which case, I am told, it is hell!).

Two sets of posters were produced: one with a photo of me; the other with a photo of the very sporting Nichola McAuliffe who gamely was going to take over the role for the final two weeks. Both were posted all over Kingston, including the sides of buses, I was told and, naturally, all over the theatre. But with two quite different actresses advertised in the role of Judith Bliss, each of us taking the part for two weeks, there was much confusion for the ticket-buying audience.

The other inconvenience concerned the poor cast who, after we opened, had to re-rehearse the play all over again.

During the Thursday matinée performance of my final week, the posters with my photo on were taken down from the foyer (even though I had four more performances to play) and the audience was left totally confused.

Truthfully I think that the theatre would have saved itself a lot of bother if it had let the extremely accomplished Nichola play the whole run.

I played my last two shows on Saturday 9 October. During the flurry of packing up my dressing room at 11pm, the charming chairman of the theatre board summoned us all down for a farewell drink in the foyer, which was a lovely way to go and, though I was sad to leave the heavenly cast who had supported me unstintingly all the way, I was excited as I made my way home to pack my suitcase, for next day I would leave for the film location in India.

I wanted to have a bon voyage treat before I flew out and discovered that the very next morning, the Savoy Hotel was re-opening after a massive refit. It seemed like a great symbol for new beginnings, so a couple of friends joined me there before I set off for Heathrow. It was serendipitous that, at the same moment on the auspicious date 10/10/10, as we sat in the Thames Foyer bar, raising our champagne glasses, over in Udaipur, India, *The Best Exotic Marigold Hotel* clapped its first slate.

Next morning I arrived in Delhi where, before heading for the railway station, I had a sit down in the famous Taj Hotel. I ordered a vegetarian meal from them to take on my 17-hour overnight train journey. They provided me an enormous elaborate box, the very sight of which filled me with drooling expectation.

The station was packed. The heat, the smells, the crowds – I was plunged immediately into that strange land of extremes, India. It has to be the hottest, brightest, smelliest, filthiest, spiciest, most vibrant country on earth.

As the train, after a very long wait, pulled into the station, 70-year-old men were running along and flinging themselves onto the train before it had stopped in order to grab any seat that might be possibly vacated by a disembarking passenger. Mayhem.

I found my sleeper. I was sharing with an electrical engineer named Raj, who got into his pyjamas rather too quickly for my liking. Within three minutes of pulling out of Delhi station he was sitting there in his jammies.

Needless to say I did not sleep. However I did have my lovely meal box to comfort me. With some excitement I opened the delicious looking parcel only to find that my dinner was an exquisitely packed lettuce sandwich made with soggy sliced white bread spread with margarine, and a few stale crisps. And there was me believing all day that I was carrying a precious cargo of dal and sag, pakoras, bhajis, parathas, jalfrezis and all kinds of Indian delights for dessert.

It was great to catch up with old friends Judi Dench, Penelope Wilton and Maggie Smith at the hotel in Udaipur. Though utterly luxurious, a palace in fact, the hotel slightly gave me the creeps especially at 3am. Everywhere you went there were silent pairs of padding servants, bowing at you and saying 'Have a pleasant stay, good morning'. I took to calling the place the Convent, as it had exactly that feel. We were advised not to step outside the hotel alone for our own safety. I wasn't surprised by this as it seems to me quite wrong to plonk so very extravagant a place so near to absolute poverty and squalor. The ravishing beauty of the building and its furnishing sometimes was hard to swallow when you knew that just outside the gates young girls and cows were rummaging for waste cabbage leaves.

I swam each morning before work. On my first morning as I lay drying I was approached by what seemed to me the hugest weasel I had ever seen. It was as big as a dachshund. I was later told that this creature was in fact a mongoose, an animal which hunts cobras. I only hope he was on a wasted errand that morning and that I didn't have a hissing, rearing snake under my sun-bed.

Many actors go for the familiar continental breakfast. But who could resist starting the day with a masala dosa? Not me! For a curry-loving vegetarian it was food paradise, of course. I worked my way through the breakfast menu: bhel puri, rava uttapam, vada sambar, hari mirch pakora. Yum, yum. And my only slight blip was the day I ignored the rules and had an ice-cream which led to a tiny stomach upset. But so what?

One delight I missed out on came when I was offered a fizzy drink, just after I had glugged my way through a whole bottle of Kingfisher.

'Very good, new drink,' I was told. 'Gau-Jal. Refreshing, non-alcoholic. Very healthy, very tasty and devoid of all toxins.' As I was full to the gills, I declined. I later discovered that the exotic beverage was in fact a soft drink made from distilled cow's urine. There's a wee novelty for you.

Every day we were driven the one-and-a-half hour trip from the hotel to the location. The drivers in India never look from side to side, even at junctions, they just keep on driving forward, all the while honking their horns.

Thus, the drive to location, usually a reflective time where you can peacefully go through your lines and get yourself psyched up for the day's scenes, was a nightmare spent willing the car safely forward and mentally driving.

One day I saw an elephant walking past. I asked the driver to stop and wound down the window to get a better look. Then his big hairy trunk came in through the window.

'Drive on!' I cried quickly.

Despite the horror of traffic, in our free time, Penelope and I used many tuk-tuks. Tuk-tuks, officially described as motorised rickshaw taxis, are in fact exactly like dodgem cars let loose off their usual fairground circuit and into a town in which there are not only no traffic restrictions, but where freewheeling cows, donkeys, goats, pigs and bicycles hurtle towards you in streets only wide enough for one.

One evening after our thrilling ride into town, we walked back to the hotel through the back streets, where we spied the pretty Diwali art, intricate and colourful works lay on each doorstep, and for extra good luck some had a huge pile of cow pat slapped on top. In some of the cow pats the children had fashioned little dolls probably to multiply their good fortune. I yearned to move out of the convent, and onto Jaipur.

The dashing director, John Madden, took us aside and warned us what to expect about our move. 'Udaipur is Harrogate,' he said. 'Be prepared. Jaipur is more like Birmingham.'

Not being a fan of flying, while the others flew on, I took the night train. When I rolled up at the hotel next morning, I found my fellow cast members already in the hotel, but also in despair. Although it was another palace, the hotel was rather like the shopping mall in the old Birmingham Bull Ring. We were all in rooms along something like Oxford Street. At the same time, security was so tight that friends from other hotels were frowned on.

The bustling, stinking city outside the gates, though, was altogether more of a frenzy than even I had expected. I bumped into John Madden.

'You said Birmingham,' I said. 'No, no, no. This is Catford.'

Dame Maggie stopped me in the bar. 'Glad we left the Convent now?'

On set we sweated and sweltered through days during which the thermometer frequently hit 34 degrees. Even at night the temperature rarely fell below 2 degrees. Meanwhile friends in London emailed us whining about November snow and minus 6 degree nights, where even the central heating seemed to have no effect. It was bizarre.

The thunder and lightning storms were the most vivid I have ever witnessed, and came upon us very suddenly. During an early morning one about 7.15am, the cast huddled in their Winnebagos, quaking with fear. Well, I speak for myself. Meanwhile, braving the elements, out on set, one of the Indian crew, our props master, heroically holding an umbrella, was struck by lightning. Though his arm went a bit numb, he was shaken but otherwise unharmed. The storm seemed to abate for a while, then another angry rumble of thunder and bang. The same crew member fell to the ground. Who said lightning never strikes twice? Miraculously, he came up smiling. According to local folklore the man is now considered a god.

Then, just when the schedule was looking good, down came the rain. It was still hot, but the streets were huge rank rivers of mud, with puddles the size of small lakes, while tons of water were dumped from the glowering slate grey sky.

We were due to film the scenes travelling along in our tuk-tuks.

'No point shooting,' said John Madden. 'Or people will think we filmed it all driving along the North Circular.'

We sat and waited for the rain to stop. On those rather unwelcome days off I tried to take in some of the sights. I phoned Dame Maggie's room.

'I'm off to see the Monkey Palace. I don't expect you want to come?'

She replied, 'I've been there.'

And in those three words I knew what to expect. Dank, smelly, run-down. And it was all those things. That's great acting, ain't it?

While filming *The Best Exotic Marigold Hotel,* John Madden taught me one great lesson. When the camera stays on you at the end of a scene reaction, you don't have to go through every expression on a wrapper of a bar of Five Boys chocolate. You just look. From now on I'm going to call it my 'Madden ending'.

I am mad on Madden!

I don't think Dame Mags was so mad about India to start with, Dame Jude on the other hand seemed intoxicated. Second time around, the country had an odd effect on me in spite of its ravishing sights, this time the mess, the filth, the smell, the rows of men pissing unashamedly in the streets, the shit underfoot, all rather got to me.

I am going home to tidy my house!

THE END

To sum up my thoughts on my life, both past and to come, I could refer you to the lyrics of my three favourite songs: *I Hope You Dance*, by Lee Ann Womack, *Is That All There Is?* by Peggy Lee, and *Que Sera Sera* by Doris Day (and recently wonderfully covered by Corinne Bailey Rae). They're all united by a common theme. They ask you always to celebrate the art of stepping into the unknown, and living forever in hope. Peggy Lee and Lee Ann Womack want you to dance at the same time!

But I had an encounter the other day which gave me a line which says it with even more clarity.

An elderly foreign lady standing in the queue at Waitrose let me in before her so I could join a pal who was already at the checkout.

I said, 'Thank you so much.'

She replied, 'Don't think about it. It's my good deed for the day.'

'You'll go to heaven,' I said.

There was a slight pause and then she said firmly, 'I don't want to go to heaven. I want to go to hell . . . and dance a bit.'

Me too!

Let's all go to hell and dance a lot.

The end

Ps. I hate ends.

It's only ever au revoir isn't it? I feel as if I've only just begun.

CURTAIN CALL

Thank you to:

August Paul Alesky 'Augy' at Centuries and Sleuths, Chicago

Catherine Ashmore

Alan Baker

Michael Foster

John Giddings

Rina 'Basil' Gill

Angus Imrie

Ed and Jeannie Kaufman at 'M' is for Mystery, San Mateo

Diane Kudisch at San Francisco Mystery Bookstore, San Francisco

Rowan Lawton

Kiaran W. MacDonald at The Savoy

Kate and Don and Stephen Miller of New York City

Fidelis Morgan

Lord North, Admiral Baron West of Spithead

Gilbert, Raymond and Richard at Le Safari

Mary Riley at Book 'Em, South Pasadena

Nicole Rubi at La Petite Maison

Laurie Rudic

Giacomo Sain

Laura Scott

Peter Tear at 59E59 Theatre, NYC

Maggie Topkis at Partners and Crime, Greenwich Village, NYC

Simon Ward

Belinda Wright

Jamie Mansfield, Queen Mary 2
Paul O'Loughlin, Queen Mary 2
David Stephenson, Queen Mary 2
Captain Bernard Warner, Queen Mary 2

The Staff of the Newspaper Library, Colindale

PICTURE ACKNOWLEDGEMENTS

Author's collection: 1, 2 above, 4, 5, 8 above and centre, 9, 10 above, 11 above left, 14 above right, 15 below. Courtesy of Alzheimer's Research UK/photo Bob Alfrey: 15 above left. © ArenaPAL/Nigel Norrington: 14 below left. © Catherine Ashmore: 12. © BBC/ITV Studios: 16 below left. © BBC Motion Gallery: 6 below right. © BBC Photo Library: 7 below right, 16 centre. © BBC/Ronald Grant Archive: 7 above. © John Vere Brown: 6 above and below left. Courtesy of Cunard: 13 above. © Getty Images: 13 below right. © John Gill: 2 below. © Kobal Collection/Polygram/Working Title: 10 centre. © Ivan Kyncl: 8 below. © London Weekend Televison Ltd: 3 below. © The Brenda Moore Estate/Bridgeman, reproduced courtesy of Professor Christopher Cairns: 15 above right. © PA Photos: 10 below. © Rex Features: 7 below left, 11 above right and centre, 14 above left and below right, 16 above left. © Kenneth Rimell: 2 centre. © Donald Silverstein: 3 above right. © D. Straughan: 3 centre. Courtesy of University of Southampton: 13 below left. © Working Title/Ronald Grant Archive: 11 below left.

Every reasonable effort has been made to trace copyright holders, but if there are any errors or omissions, Hodder & Stoughton will be pleased to insert the appropriate acknowledgement in any subsequent printing of this book.